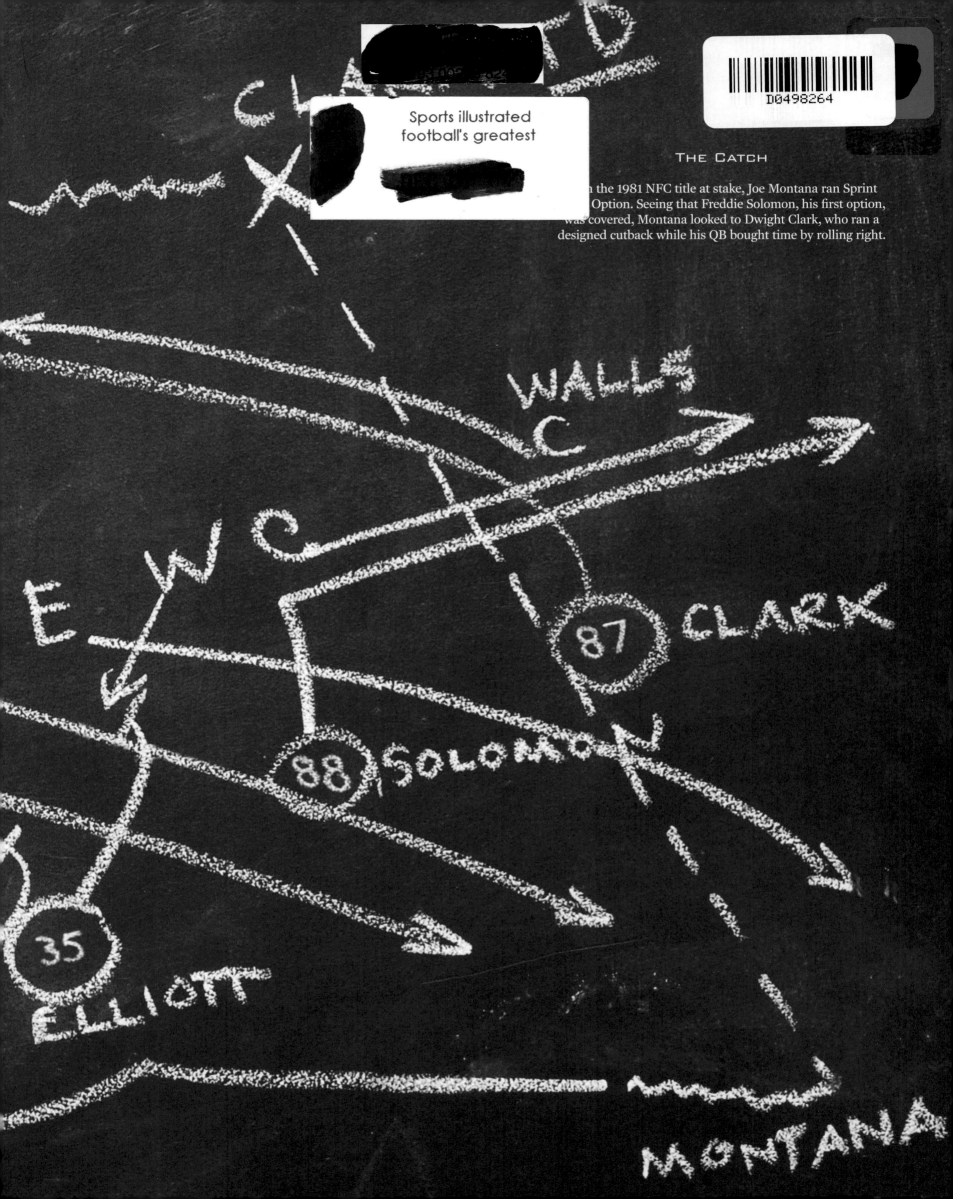

THE CATCH

With the 1981 NFC title at stake, Joe Montana ran Sprint
Right Option. Seeing that Freddie Solomon, his first option,
was covered, Montana looked to Dwight Clark, who ran a
designed cutback while his QB bought time by rolling right.

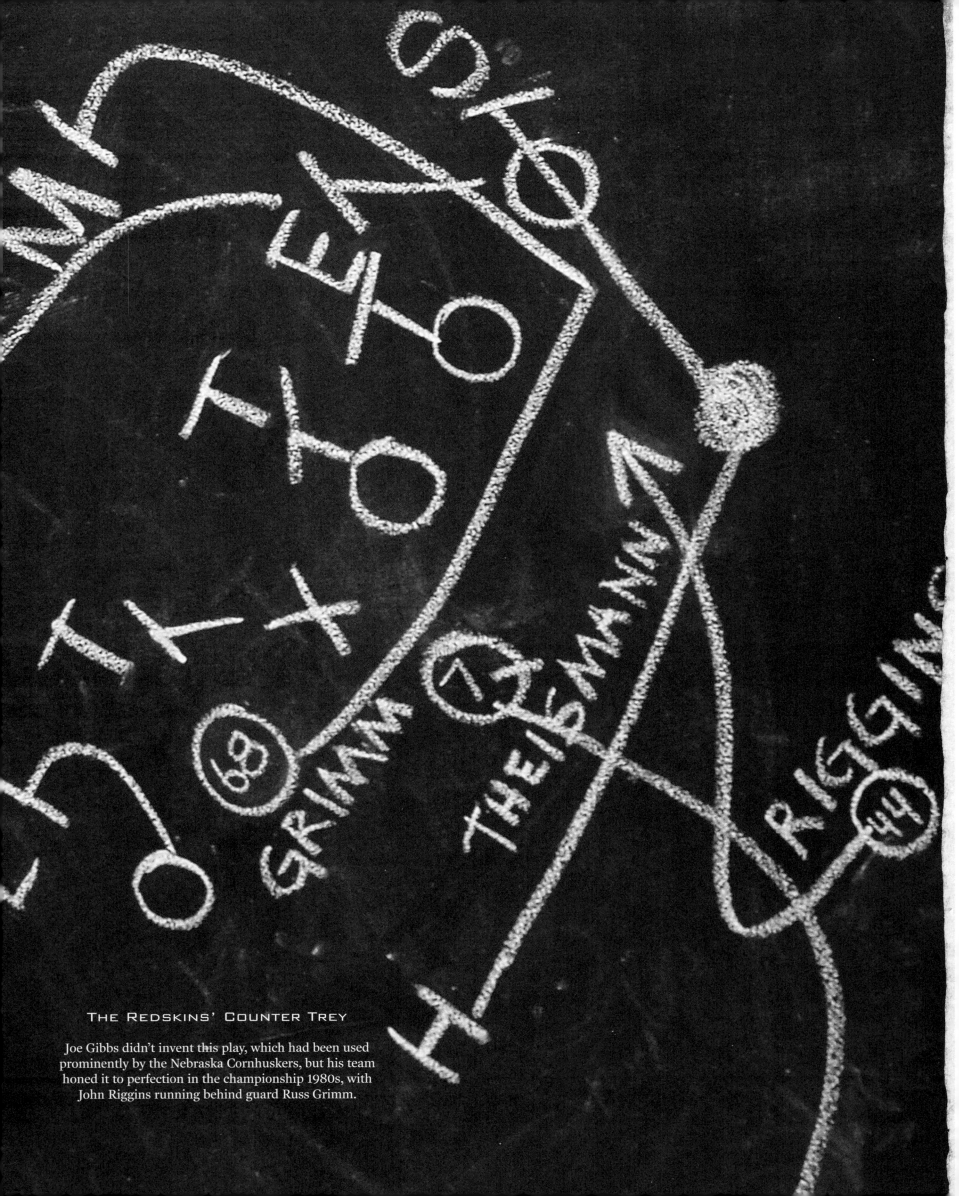

THE REDSKINS' COUNTER TREY

Joe Gibbs didn't invent this play, which had been used prominently by the Nebraska Cornhuskers, but his team honed it to perfection in the championship 1980s, with John Riggins running behind guard Russ Grimm.

Sports Illustrated

FOOTBALL'S GREATEST

FOOT
GREA

A muddy Jim Brown prepares for a handoff in December 1962.

PHOTOGRAPH BY NEIL LEIFER

DICK BUTKUS

NO. 2

LINEBACKER

PHOTOGRAPH BY NEIL LEIFER

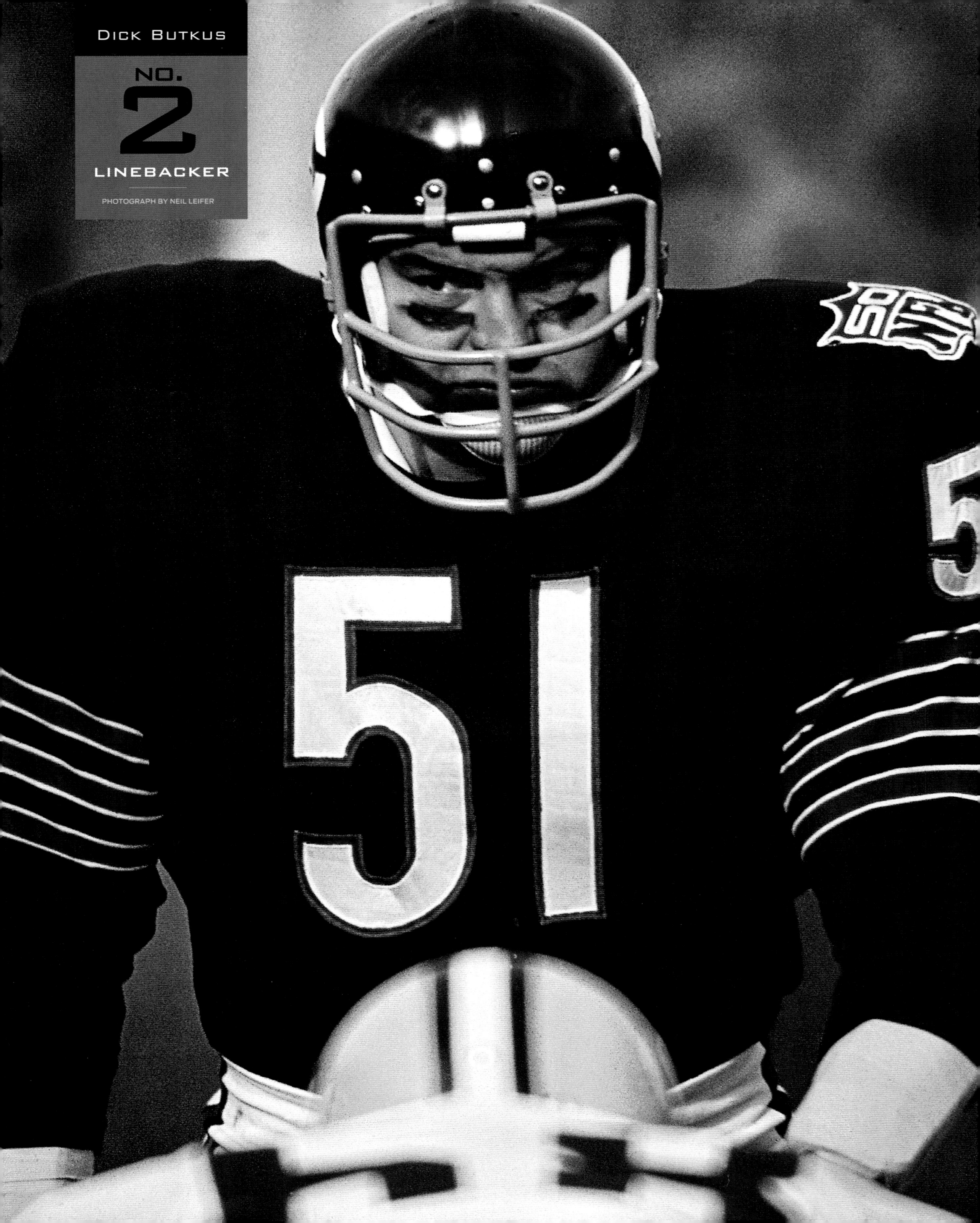

CONTENTS

BILL SYKEN *Editor* / STEVEN HOFFMAN *Art Director*

CRISTINA SCALET *Photo Editor* / KEVIN KERR *Copy Editor* / JOSH DENKIN *Designer*

STEFANIE KAUFMAN *Project Manager*

WE'RE NO.1 (THROUGH 10)

THE URGE TO RANK AND ORDER ANYTHING AND EVERYTHING IS EASILY AMONG THE TOP 10 MOST IRRESISTIBLE HUMAN IMPULSES

BY STEVE RUSHIN

N A JANUARY DAY

in 1952, in a conference room in White Sulphur Springs, West Virginia, an 89-year-old man cleared his throat and announced to the NCAA's rules committee that football had entered its Golden Age. "The game is the best it has ever been," said Amos Alonzo Stagg, who argued against meddling with the liberal substitution rule that brought two-platoon football to glorious life, and the game into its sudden prime. No one dared argue with the man. At the time, football had been played for 83 years, and Stagg had been a coach for the last 62 of them.

And he was right. Within seven years of Stagg's declaration, football would eclipse baseball as America's favorite game, and professional football would eclipse college football as its favorite iteration of its favorite game, and the 1958 NFL title game between the Colts and the Giants would be called—in the headline on Tex Maule's story in that week's SPORTS ILLUSTRATED— *The Best Football Game Ever Played.*

Ten months later, after that victorious Colts team scored three touchdowns in the third quarter to beat the Packers 38–21 on Oct. 25, 1959, losing coach Vince Lombardi slumped in a chair in the Green Bay locker room and said: "Unitas is the best quarterback I've ever seen." What Lombardi had no way of knowing, as a new decade beckoned, was that he himself would soon be the best coach anyone had ever seen, of the best team anyone had ever seen.

Those who think, in the 21st century, that football has never been better than it is right now should consider that football is always—almost by definition—never better than it is right now. But bear in mind, too, that history is an unbroken string of Right Nows, which slowly fade into Back Thens.

Namath shows who won Super Bowl III.

7

UNITAS

— OR —

MONTANA

If you were in San Jose on Dec. 28, 1943 and opened that day's edition of the *News*, you wouldn't have missed the double-decker headline: SUNDAY'S WIN DEFINITELY PROVES CHI BEARS BEST TEAM EVER. Nor would you have disagreed. But the Bears of the '40s yielded to the Colts of the '50s, who yielded to the Packers of the '60s, who yielded to Dolphins of the '70s: When Miami crushed the Vikings in Super Bowl VIII, 24–7, the team ran its record to 32–2 over the previous two seasons. After the game, the blackboard in the Dolphins' locker room in Rice Stadium in Houston was blank, save for two words hastily scrawled by an equipment manager: BEST EVER.

It was fitting that the message was written in chalk, for Best Ever is an epithet that can never really be set in stone.

Or can it?

THE MOST ENDURING TOP TEN

ever written wasn't written at all, but chiseled onto stone tablets and conveyed down Mount Sinai by Moses, who introduced to the world not just a set of Biblical precepts but a new format for starting arguments: the list of 10 things.

The Ten Commandments aren't a ranking. If they were, murder wouldn't even make the playoffs, clocking in at number 6. But they do raise many questions for the modern football fan, not the least of which is: "Who were the 10 best guys named Moses in NFL history?"

It's a trick question. There have only been 10 men named Moses in the history of the National Football League. In descending order from least-great Moses to most-great Moses—for these lists are always better when counted down from 10 to one, giving them the drama of a rocket launch—they are: (10) Quentin Moses, (9) J.J. Moses, (8) Moses Ford, (7) Don Moses, (6) Kelvin Moses, (5) Moses Gray, (4) Moses Denson, (3) Moses Moreno, (2) . . .

But wait. This is the part of the beauty pageant at which the host always pauses. Two contestants still on stage, but only one can be crowned with a trembling hand the fairest of them all. Will it be former wide receiver Haven Moses, who played 14 seasons for the Bills and Broncos and made the Pro Bowl in 1973?

Or will it be the insuperably named Moses Regular Jr.? He only played in one season, for the 1996 Giants, but his name is so good that statistics scarcely matter here. Moses Regular sounds like a robe size at the Mount Sinai Men's Wearhouse. Moses Regular Jr. is the best name, in or out of football, since Moses Regular Sr. It is entirely possible that Moses Regular is the finest NFL Moses without ever having been an NFL Regular. He only appeared in three games, on special teams.

And this is the difficulty with best-ever. It's a shifting and subjective standard. You say to-*may*-to, I say to-*mah*-to. You say Joe Klecko, I say Joe Flacco. Was Morten Andersen a better placekicker than Gary Anderson? Beauty is in the eye of the tee-holder.

And so these arguments frequently end up here—at the intersection of Irresistible Force and Immovable Object. Who would win a fight between Batman and Superman, or a lion and a shark, or Frankenstein and Dracula?

Or put another way: Was Joe Montana a better quarterback than Johnny Unitas?

THESE QUESTIONS FORM THE bedrock of our barroom arguments. Never mind that the barroom argument was declared dead in the spring of 2010 by *PC World*, whose editors ranked it No. 2 on their list of "10 Things the Internet has Killed or Ruined," on the presumption that smartphones had made the answer to every arcane question instantly accessible. To its credit, the magazine's Top 10 List did not include "The Top 10 List" as something ruined by the Internet, which sometimes seems to consist of little more than pornography and Top 10 lists, often in combination with one another.

No, despite the Internet's best efforts to work it to its death, the Top 10 List (to say nothing of the barroom argument) has never been more robust. Never mind that it's as old as Moses—exactly as old as Moses, who started a craze with that first Top 10. Instantly, the Old Testament was awash with Lists of 10, including the Ten Plagues that visited Egypt (My top 3: Boils, Locusts, Frogs) and the Ten Lost Tribes of Israel (I gotta go: Zebulun, Asher, Simeon). Ten, from the beginning, was established as the proper number of items to include when counting down things of importance, no matter what Casey Kasem might have had you believe.

The list of 10 taps into a deep human need to rank things, including rankings themselves, so that a Top 10 List of Top 10 Lists would have to include David Letterman's Top 10s and the FBI's 10 Most Wanted List. The Bureau likes to point out that their list is not a ranking, per se, but merely a rogue's gallery of the 10 most notorious criminals endangering America. Human nature knows otherwise, and ends up ranking them anyway, which is why we always have a Public Enemy No. 1.

And isn't that what most sports arguments come down to? Who's No. 1? It's the reason for the seasons, for the right index finger Joe Namath raised as he ran off the field after Super Bowl III, and for all those foam-finger replicas worn by fans forever after. *We're Number 1.*

AND SO THIS BOOK SITS AT THE intersection of three American obsessions. It is the T-junction joining football, lists of 10 and our abiding desire to know—at any given time, in any area of human endeavor—who's No. 1.

Ten is the number of perfection—in the Bible, in the Bo Derek movie, in the perfect 10s of diving and dunk contests. That perfection is made manifest on a football field, measured out in 10 segments of 10 yards each, every 10 yards signaling renewal.

WHITE

OR

GREENE

NIGHT TRAIN

OR

PRIME TIME

The word "rank" comes from the Old French *ranc*, "a row of an army," so that in ranking the various rows of an offense or defense—the linemen, linebackers, d-backs etc.—we are essentially ranking the *rancs* of football players, who are already the most ranked athletes on Earth.

Ranking is what scouts do when grading players, what coaches do with their depth charts. These Top 10 lists are, in essence, an alltime depth chart for almost every position—who's more valuable on a D-line, Reggie White or Joe Greene?—plus coaches, franchises, stadiums, plays and individual games: Take the very best of the very best, and decide who's the best of them.

And so the Best Ever Miami Dolphins of 1972–73 yielded, immediately, to the Pittsburgh Steelers, who won the Super Bowl in four of the next six seasons. "I think this is probably the best team ever assembled," Steelers cornerback Mel Blount said after his team beat the Rams in Super Bowl XIV in 1980. "They talk about Vince Lombardi, but I think Chuck Noll is even greater."

Two years later, the San Francisco 49ers of Montana and Walsh began wiping the Best Ever off the Steelers' chalkboard, and by the time those Niners clapped the erasers, and the cloud of dust had settled, out stepped the New England Patriots of Brady and Belichick, winners of three Super Bowls in four years in the first decade of the new millennium.

Among the best of the best, it is not enough to be the greatest for one season. These athletes want to be the greatest for all seasons. There is no popular acronym for the Greatest of One Decade (GOOD). There is for the Greatest of All Time (GOAT).

WHAT FOLLOWS IS AN EFFORT to separate the GOODs from the GOATs, in every conceivable category. To those who say, "How can you compare across eras?"—how can you say if Dick Lane or Deion Sanders was the better defensive back—we say: "How can you not?" And also: "Night Train or Prime Time—which was the better nickname?" (Bartender, we're gonna need another round.)

And let's do it all as Moses would have done, by chiseling them into a list of 10.

Counting down from 10 is a profound act. It is reserved for momentous occasions. Before we send man into space to explore the limits of human knowledge, we count down from 10. Before we go into surgery—as life hangs in the balance—we are instructed by an anesthesiologist to count down from 10. Every year, all around the world, at 10 seconds to midnight on Dec. 31, countless people in countless languages count down from 10, after which there is pandemonium, celebration, occasional anger, the odd riot or two.

May these lists have the same effect. ■

HOW WE RANKED THEM

These Top 10 lists bring together the often-conflicting expert opinions of seven writers and editors who have covered professional football for SPORTS ILLUSTRATED

READ THIS BOOK closely and you'll find statements that might not seem to make perfect sense, given what's around them. On page 46, for instance, it is declared that Walter Payton is "arguably the greatest football player who ever lived." Skipping over the fact that on page 35 it says "the best all-around player ever" is actually the Redskins' Sammy Baugh, there's the more ticklish point that the Bears running back does not even rank as the best at his position. So how could he be the greatest player ever?

It's all a matter of opinion, of course. And contradictions have been given berth to run free because, as the Supreme Court has shown, dissenting views often contain a great deal of wisdom.

For this book seven SPORTS ILLUSTRATED writers and editors who cover the NFL were polled during the 2011 season and asked to submit Top 10 lists for 14 categories, and to defend their choices. Their votes were then tallied, with 10 points being awarded for a first-place vote, nine for a second and so on. The panelists' justifications for their choices are quoted on the pages devoted to each Top 10 finisher, whether or not the opinions fall in line with the consensus results. For example, in the Best Stadiums category, the Seahawks' new home is described by one of its advocates as the best of the recent constructions, even though the panel as a whole chose to give the devil—in the form of Jerry Jones and his Cowboys Stadium—his due and rank it three spots higher.

The book concludes with each panel member creating an individual list for which the choosing was his alone. For example Damon Hack could put together a list of the 10 Best Uniforms and leave off some handsome alternatives like those of the Vikings, or the Broncos' and Patriots' throwback jerseys, without any panel of colleagues overriding his personal tastes. Uniforms are fun to talk about, but they are something anyone can judge with a mere glimpse. For other categories our experts supported their rankings with statistics, testimonials from football legends and knowledge from their years of reporting, observation and analysis—which is why their dissents can feel so compelling. This group has had its collective eyes on the NFL for quite some time. —*Bill Syken*

THE PANELISTS

DON BANKS SENIOR WRITER, *SI.com* | MARK GODICH SENIOR EDITOR, *Sports Illustrated*

DAMON HACK SENIOR WRITER, *Sports Illustrated* | PETER KING SENIOR WRITER, *Sports Illustrated*

TIM LAYDEN SENIOR WRITER, *Sports Illustrated* | MARK MRAVIC ASSISTANT MANAGING EDITOR, *Sports Illustrated*

JIM TROTTER SENIOR WRITER, *Sports Illustrated*

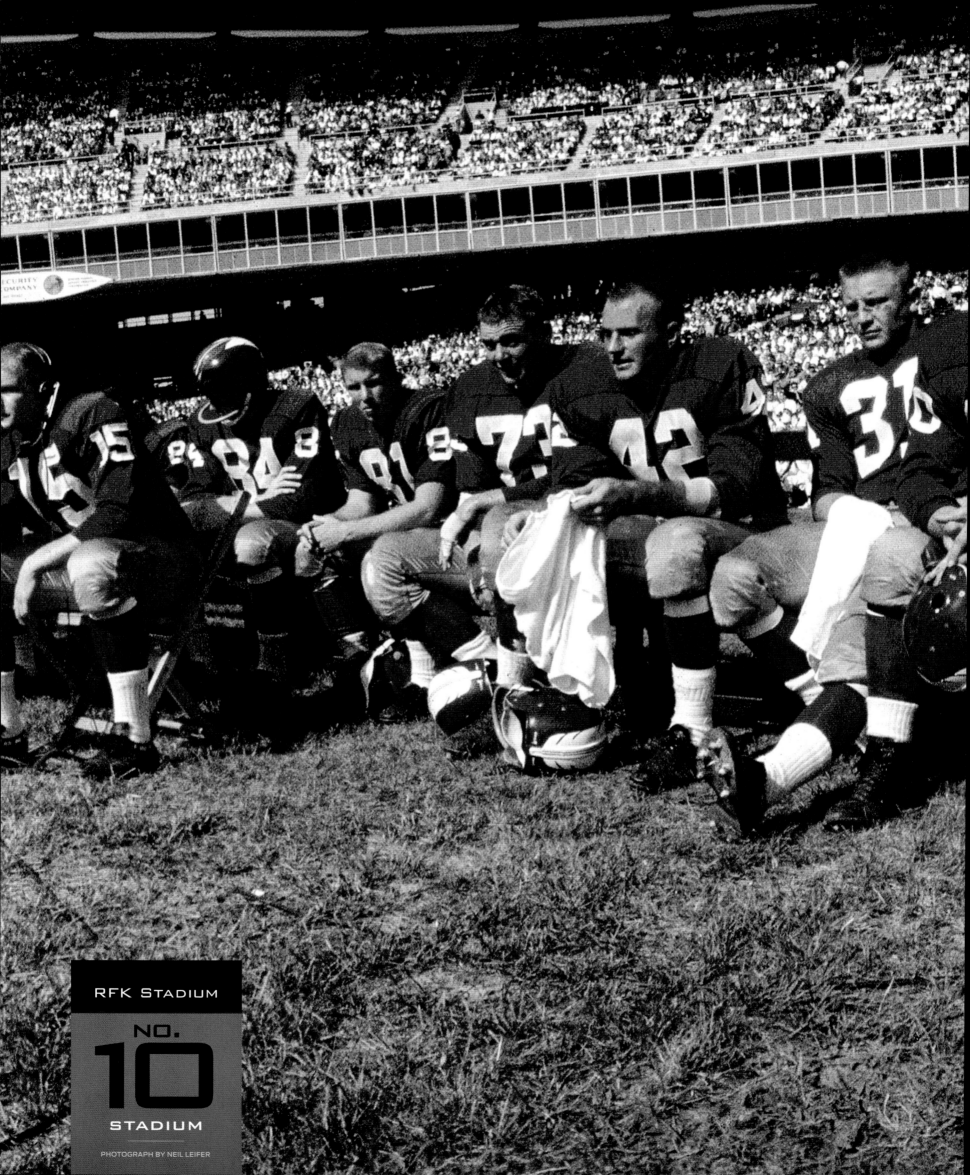

Sports Illustrated

FOOT
GREA

BALL'S
TEST

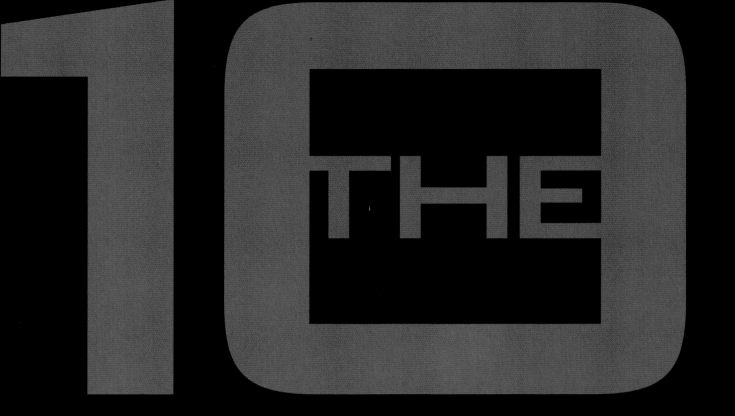

10 THE

BEST QUARTERBACKS

IF JOE MONTANA HAD BEEN DRAFTED BY CHICAGO, AS NEARLY HAPPENED, WOULD HE HAVE BEEN AS GREAT? "WHO KNOWS, IF HE CAME HERE, THAT HE WOULD HAVE HAD THE CAREER THAT HE'S HAD IN SAN FRANCISCO?" BEARS PLAYER PERSONNEL DIRECTOR BILL TOBIN REFLECTED IN A 1990 PROFILE BY PAUL ZIMMERMAN IN SI. "WHAT IF A TAMPA BAY OR A NEW ORLEANS WOULD HAVE TAKEN HIM?" ASKED MONTANA'S HIGH SCHOOL COACH, CHUCK ABRAMSKI. "WHAT IF HE HAD BEEN IN A SYSTEM WHERE HE HAD TO DROP BACK SEVEN STEPS AND THROW 50 YARDS DOWNFIELD?"

BUT MONTANA, OUR TOP PICK AT QB, DID PLAY IN THE OFFENSE OF BILL WALSH, RANKED OUR NO. 3 COACH—AND HE ALSO HAD AS A TARGET OUR NO. 1 RECEIVER, JERRY RICE. HE WAS FORTUNATE, AS WERE MANY OF OUR TOP 10 QUARTERBACKS: SIX PLAYED FOR TOP 10 COACHES, AND FIVE OF THEM THREW TO TOP 10 RECEIVERS OR TIGHT ENDS. IF YOU WANTED, YOU COULD USE THIS TO QUESTION AN INDIVIDUAL'S CREDENTIALS—MAYBE THE COACH AND RECEIVER MADE THE QUARTERBACK GREAT, OR PERHAPS IT WAS THE OTHER WAY AROUND.

MONTANA SAID THAT PLAYING FOR WALSH WAS THE BEST OF ALL POSSIBLE WORLDS: "THERE'S NO COACH I COULD HAVE PLAYED FOR WHO WOULD HAVE BEEN BETTER FOR MY CAREER," HE SAYS. "ABSOLUTELY NONE." AMID A SEA OF HYPOTHETICALS, WE KNOW THIS: THESE PIECES CAME TOGETHER, AND THE RESULTS MADE HISTORY.

1

JOE MONTANA

**49ERS 1979–1992
CHIEFS 1993–1994**

" He had a game that was as cool as his blue eyes. Playing a position at which greatness is often defined by victories, it's no surprise he was 4–0 in Super Bowls. " —JIM TROTTER

▸ THREE-TIME SUPER BOWL MVP
▸ 39 300-YARD GAMES

HE SOMEHOW seems to breathe slower when everyone else breathes fast. Remember that final drive in the 1989 Super Bowl? You fell off the chair. You rolled on the floor with excitement. Was there ever any doubt that he simply was going to move those Niners 92 yards down the field in the final 3:20 to beat the Cincinnati Bengals? Of course not. Didn't you read what he said at the start of the drive? "Hey, check it out," he said to tackle Harris Barton. "Check out what?" Barton asked. "There, in the stands, standing near the exit ramp," Joe said. "There's John Candy." Wasn't that the greatest? Your father remembers reading about someone named Chip Hilton who did the same things Joe does. Your grandfather mentions someone named Frank Merriwell. You don't know any of that. Weren't those characters from fiction? Joe is real. A real Joe.

—*Leigh Montville, SI, December 24, 1990*

Montana threw for 318 career touchdowns.

PHOTOGRAPH BY JOHN IACONO

2

JOHNNY UNITAS

COLTS 1956-1972
CHARGERS 1973

" He was the smartest play-caller of his day (and likely any day), the definition of an on-field commander. He led the Colts down the field to tie the 1958 NFL title game in the final minute and again to win it in overtime. " —PETER KING

▸ THREE-TIME NFL MVP
▸ 40,239 CAREER YARDS, 290 TDS

IN THOSE halcyon days, they didn't have coaches telling quarterbacks what plays to call. Quarterbacks were field generals, not field lieutenants. I never saw war, so that is still my vision of manhood: Unitas standing courageously in the pocket, down amidst the mortals. Lock and load.

—*Frank Deford, SI, September 23, 2002*

Unitas threw TD passes in 47 consecutive games.

3

TOM BRADY

PATRIOTS 2000–PRESENT

" The biggest steal in NFL draft history, the sixth-round pick out of Michigan single-handedly changed the fortunes of the New England franchise as he won three Super Bowl rings in his first four seasons as a starter. " —DON BANKS

▸ NFL RECORD 50 TD PASSES AND ONLY EIGHT INTS IN 2007
▸ BEST WINNING PERCENTAGE OF ANY QB IN SUPER BOWL ERA

WITH HIS VOICE rising as he leaned forward in his chair, Brady said that playing 10 more seasons "is a big goal of mine, a very big goal. I want to play until I'm 41. And if I get to that point and still feel good, I'll keep playing. I mean, what the hell else am I going to do? I don't like anything else." People say, 'What will you do if you don't play football?' Why would I even think of doing anything else? What would I do instead of run out in front of 80,000 people and command 52 guys and be around guys I consider brothers and be one of the real gladiators? Why would I ever want to do anything else? It's so hard to think of anything that would match what I do: Fly to the moon? Jump out of planes? Bungee-jump off cliffs? None of that s--- matters to me. I want to play this game I love, be with my wife and son and enjoy life."

—*Peter King, SI, June 1, 2009*

Brady had 5,235 passing yards in 2011.

PHOTOGRAPH BY SIMON BRUTY

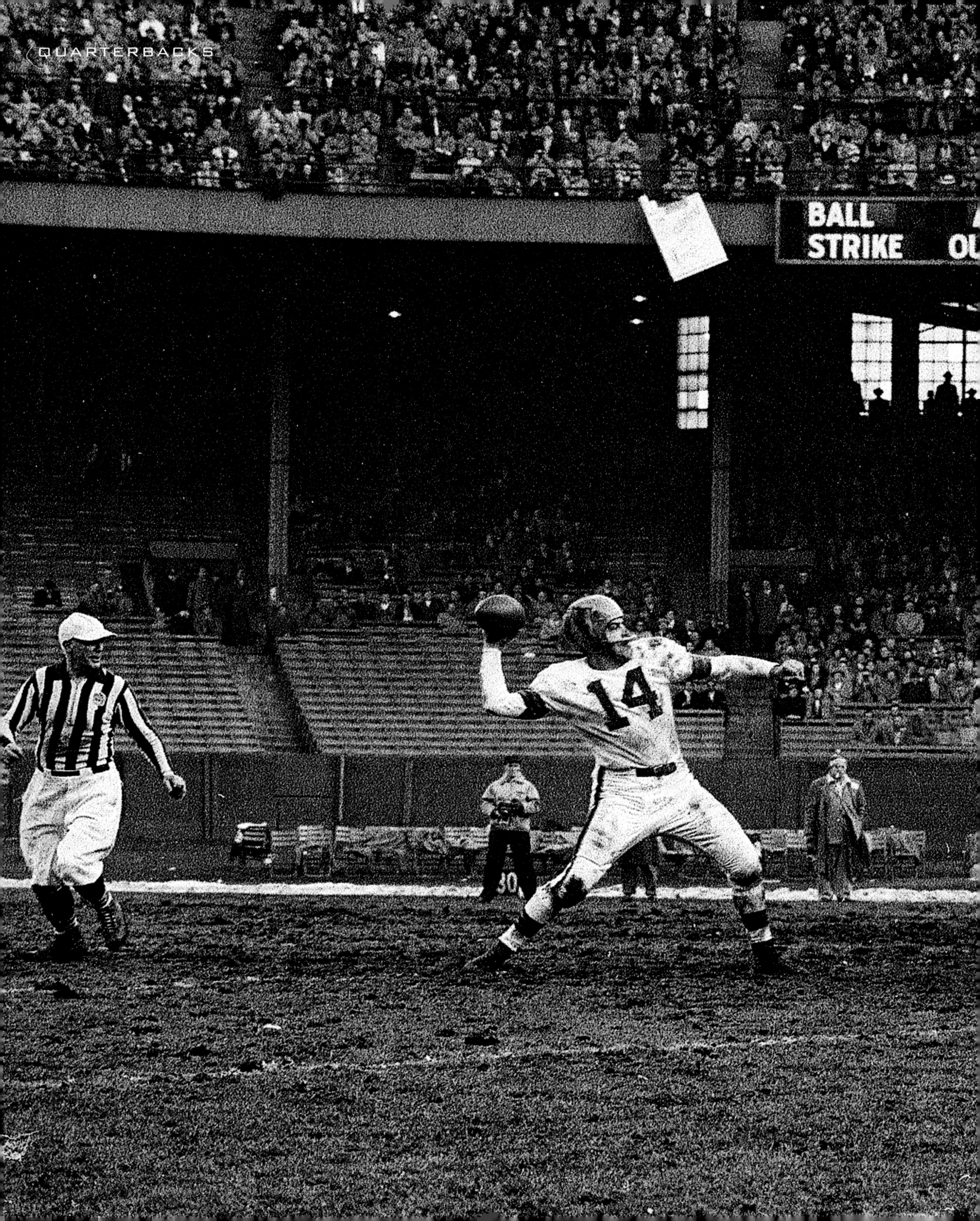
BALL
STRIKE
14

4

OTTO GRAHAM

BROWNS 1946–1955

" He's the greatest winner among
quarterbacks ever, and that cannot [be]
disputed: seven championships in [10]
professional seasons—and he lost i[n]
the championship game the other
three years. " —PETER KING

- ► NINE-TIME ALL-PRO
- ► SIX TOUCHDOWNS IN
  1954 NFL TITLE GAME

WATCHING GRAHAM and his Browns
in the All-America Football
Conference was to see a brand
of football that was way ahead
of its time. The NFL in the late
1940s was shaking off the traces
of the single wing. Pass protection
was primitive, and quarterbacks
completed less than 50% of
their passes. But the Browns,
whose offensive line employed
Paul Brown's technique of cut
blocking and chanted "Nobody
touches Graham" as they broke
the huddle, helped make Otto
the most precise and meticulous
passer the game had ever seen.
Until John Unitas and Joe Montana
arrived, no one was as accurate.
There's a story told about how one
of his teammates bent a wire coat
hanger into a diamond shape one
day and challenged Graham to
throw a football through it from 15
feet away. He went 10 for 10.

—*Paul Zimmerman, SI, December 29, 2003*

Graham was well-protected in the 1954 title ga[me]

PHOTOGRAPH BY EVAN PESKIN

5

PEYTON MANNING

COLTS 1998–2011

" If you were to build a quarterback in a laboratory, there's no doubt you'd get Peyton Manning—a gifted, motivated, masterly thrower. " —DAMON HACK

▸ MOST YARDS, TDS AND COMPLETIONS OF ANY QB IN HIS FIRST 13 NFL SEASONS

IN SEPTEMBER the only thing Manning seemed sure to lead the league in this year was obstacles. Wideout Marvin Harrison was allowed to leave after 11 seasons and into his starting spot had stepped a 2008 sixth-round pick from tiny Mount Union (Ohio) College, Pierre Garçon. Starting wideout Anthony Gonzalez went down with a right-knee injury in the first game, forcing Austin Collie to play much more than planned. Coach Tony Dungy had retired, ceding the job to an unknown, Jim Caldwell. Compounding the problems has been a feeble running game. But Manning, simply, has made Indianapolis slump-proof. The Colts have gone 112 games—seven full seasons—without losing three straight. Indy isn't the winningest regular-season team this decade by accident. Anytime Manning steps behind center and starts gyrating and pointing, history tells us, good things are about to occur.

—*Peter King, SI, November 16, 2009*

The Colts released Manning after 14 seasons in Indy.

PHOTOGRAPH BY DAVID BERGMAN

THE DRIVE TO GLORY

At the top of his game and coming off his Super Bowl win in 2007, Peyton Manning laid bare the inner workings of his mind as he got to talking about the game he loves

BY PETER KING

THERE IS A PEYTON MANNING Fan Club among NFL quarterbacks, a group effusive in its praise and admiration for the Colts passer. Tom Brady dines with Manning a few times every year and considers him a good friend. "Cool guy," Brady says. Carson Palmer has driven from Cincinnati to Indianapolis, incognito, to watch him play. In Kansas City's playoff loss to Indianapolis last year, Chiefs rookie Brodie Croyle kept straying from the offensive area near the bench to get closer to the field so he could watch Manning.

Usually you can find athletes in every sport to dis a great player (off the record) for some kind of perceived fault. Not with Manning. Now that he's won a Super Bowl, he's ascended to a level at which he is practically beyond criticism. SI rates him the No. 1 player in the NFL—big surprise there—and the people he goes up against have no problem with that. "It's not even close," says Broncos coach Mike Shanahan. "He's the best."

His peers see him as a guileless, innovative competitor. As he enters his 10th NFL season, how does Manning see himself? "I play because I love the game, not because it's what I'm supposed to be doing. I think as soon as I'm not excited to be driving to training camp, that's when it'll be over. You know, it's an hour-and-15-minute drive from Indy. I loaded an oldies CD [wife] Ashley just got for me for the drive, then sent out a mass text message to all my teammates whose numbers I have, which is a large majority of them. I wrote, 'Hey boys, let's go bust our asses in camp and do this thing again.' And it was exciting to see all the responses. Booger McFarland saying, 'That's what I'm talking about.' Dwight Freeney goes, 'Hell yeah.' Dungy gave me an 'Amen.' Priceless. So I was excited to be coming up here again. I can't imagine thinking the day before camp, Golly, I wish I didn't have to go.

"I always worry about the teammate that comes up and asks me for an autograph. You don't really want that. I'm like, 'Oh, this is for your brother?' And they're like, 'No, no, it's for me.' And I'm, 'Man, I need you to *block* for me. I don't need you to look up to me. You need to be my equal.'

"I'm just a football meathead. I did *Saturday Night Live* just to have fun. I'm a lot more nervous for a game. On *Saturday Night Live* the people who are nervous are trying to get Alec Baldwin to put them in his TV show. But preparing for *Saturday Night Live* was like preparing for a football game. I told them I wanted it to be funny. I went up there on a Monday. It's the same as a football week: Monday and Tuesday you put the plan in; Wednesday, Thursday and Friday you practice, although you only do each script the one time. The nervous thing is on Wednesday, you sit around with the whole crew, cast, cameras and makeup. They give you a stack of scripts and about 30 minutes to read all 40 of them on your own. Then Lorne Michaels reads the scene, and you have to do the reading. There's nothing about character or whatever, and you sound like a moron in front of these people. That's when they decide what's funny and what's not.

"I'd like to do one of those reality-TV shows on the ultimate debate—what is the toughest job in sports? You'd put a pitcher in there, a golfer, a basketball player, a tennis player, a hockey player, a football player. I wouldn't have to be the football representative. I'd probably put Brett Favre in there, but I'd write his material. And I would say you can't compare anything to quarterback. A pitcher has no time factor, no hurry. He doesn't like the call from the catcher, he steps off, doesn't waste a timeout. I haven't found one job that really compares to what the quarterback has to go through. You take all those things: time, weather, noise and then you get to dealing with the rush, dealing with the speed. And you truly have the game in your hands.

"At the Pro Bowl, Belichick and I had a beer at the pool one day. We talked for a few hours and somebody said, 'All they're doing is telling a bunch of lies to each other.' There's some truth to that. But when we were stretching for practice one morning, we were kind of waiting to see who was going to break the ice first, and he came up to me and said, 'Now, that third-and-two in the championship game when you ran the ball, was y'all going to go for it on fourth down?' And I said, 'Look, on the sideline Tony [Dungy] basically said, 'Don't make me have to decide.' So after that, it was like, 'You asked one, now I have a couple for you.'

"My first question to him? I went back to my rookie year, 1998, against the Jets. We went 3–13, and he's coaching under Parcells and they go 12–4. We beat them at home, my biggest win at the time. We stunk. We had a fourth-and-14 where they were going to blitz like crazy. Our left guard false-starts, but the ball is snapped and you see [the blitz], so we come back and go max protection, thinking they would blitz, and he drops eight [defenders into coverage]. I'm doing what my coach told me—you know, dump it down to your back. So I throw a four-yard pass to Marshall Faulk on fourth-and-19. He gets the first down, and we go on to beat them. I asked Belichick if he remembered that play. Oh, he remembered. 'Damned Mo Lewis missed the tackle.' Unbelievable. We ended up going to dinner. I had an enjoyable week just talking football with the guy.

"The most sincere voice-mail I got after the Super Bowl was from Dan Marino. He did the coin toss that day, and he said it was an honor to be on the field with me. I'll remember that for a long time.

"Once you win, you don't want to quit; you want to win another one. So you have that same hunger, for sure. At least I do. I know I do." ■

6

JOHN ELWAY

BRONCOS 1983–1998

" His greatness was not validated by Super Bowl wins in his final two seasons. It was validated by his taking talent-deficient Broncos teams to three Super Bowls before he ever won a title. " —JIM TROTTER

‣ 47 FOURTH-QUARTER GAME-WINNING OR GAME-TYING DRIVES
‣ RETIRED SECOND ALLTIME IN PASSING YARDS AND COMPLETIONS

THIS YEAR—this gleeful year for Elway—is different. For the first time he may end up not taking a team to the Super Bowl but going *with* one. "This is so great now," he says, beaming. "Before, I'd go into a game just dreading it." His quiver finally full of arrows, Elway is having his sharpest all-around season. Admit it, none of us thought he would be a good *old* quarterback. We figured that howitzer arm or those Energizer legs would be gone by now, and his sandlot shtick would be over. But he's more of a technician than anybody thought. He can be Montana if he wants— checking options 1, 2 and 3 and then dumping—or he can still be 23 years old, the human escape clause, leaving a trail of panting defensive ends in his wake and then throwing the ball from here to February.

—*Rick Reilly, SI, December 30, 1996*

Elway led "The Drive" in the 1986 playoffs (right).

PHOTOGRAPHS BY PETER READ MILLER (LEFT) AND GEORGE TIEDEMANN/GT IMAGES

7

DAN MARINO

DOLPHINS 1983–1999

"The most prolific passer in league history, only the lack of a Super Bowl title mars Marino's record-setting 17-year career in Miami." —DON BANKS

▸ SET CAREER PASSING MARKS IN YARDS, COMPLETIONS AND TDS
▸ SET SINGLE-SEASON MARKS IN YARDS AND TDS

WHEN DON SHULA drafted Marino in May 1983, he was advised by Pittsburgh sportswriter Pat Livingston that in "Danny" he would have a quarterback with "the touch of a Sammy Baugh, the release of a Norm Van Brocklin, the arm of a Terry Bradshaw, the . . ." etc., etc. No reluctant dragon, Pat. Reckless praise doesn't pour so freely from Shula. He got through the 1983 season without conceding much more than how "amazing" it was that "Danny" (ahem) got sacked only 10 times and threw just six interceptions in 306 pass plays, and despite his inexperience was "never indecisive," even in the face of man-eating red-dogs and the best secondary schemes and ploys money could buy. But when Shula was asked what Marino would have to do to improve in 1984, he practically bristled. "Maintain, you mean," he said. It was the Shula equivalent of a standing ovation.

—John Underwood, SI, September 5, 1984

Marino was the first to break the 5,000-yard barrier.

PHOTOGRAPH BY BILL FRAKES

REDSKINS 1937–1952

Quarterbacking was only one of Baugh's skills.

PHOTOGRAPH BY AP

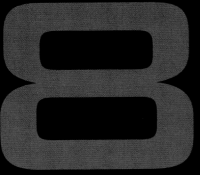

" The best all-around player ever. In 1943 Baugh led the league in punting (45.9-yard average) and completion percentage (55.6 percent) and was second with 23 touchdown passes in 10 games. Plus, as a safety he led the league with 11 interceptions. " —PETER KING

THE PROS were pushovers for Sammy Baugh, fresh out of TCU. He became an All-Pro in his rookie year while taking the Redskins to the NFL championship. Until Baugh, pro football in Texas was a one-paragraph story on the third page of the Monday sports section.

—Dan Jenkins, SI, August 31, 1981

SAMMY BAUGH

‣ SIX-TIME NFL PASSING LEADER
‣ SEVEN-TIME ALL-PRO

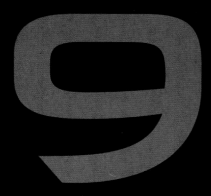

9

BRETT FAVRE

FALCONS 1991
PACKERS 1992–2007
JETS 2008
VIKINGS 2009–2010

" No quarterback had a greater flair for the dramatic. His supreme self-confidence led to impossible completions and, occasionally, monumental mistakes. Case in point: He's the NFL's alltime leader in both career interceptions and touchdowns. " —MARK MRAVIC

▸ NFL'S ALLTIME PASSING LEADER
▸ 297 CONSECUTIVE STARTS

IN THIS AGE of corporate quarterbacking Favre remains a "gunslinger." No Green Bay offensive series of more than four or five plays can be broadcast without the use of that word. In fact the nature and number of clichés Favre attracts would make for a potent drinking game. And since he himself has long since sworn off, hoist a few in his honor. Drink a shot of redeye when you hear *gunslinger*. A dram of rum for *swashbuckler*. A glass of wine whenever an announcer uses the phrase *vintage Favre*. Drink a mug of Ovaltine when you hear *He looks like a kid out there*. Chug whenever you hear *He's just trying to make something happen* or *He threw that one off his back foot*. And if you're a Packers fan, drink a double shot and turn off the TV when you hear *He tried to force that one in there*.

—*Jeff MacGregor, SI, December 4, 2006*

Favre won the NFL MVP award three times.

PHOTOGRAPHY BY JOHN BIEVER

THANKS FOR THE MEMORIES

In 2007 SPORTS ILLUSTRATED *named the quarterback its Sportsman of the Year, and those who have been touched by his generosity recalled their favorite Favre moments*

BY ALAN SHIPNUCK

WHEN BRETT FAVRE decided to return for the 2007 season, even die-hard Cheeseheads must have been hoping only that he would not tarnish his legacy. What no one expected was that Favre would reinvent himself yet again, enjoying one of his best years, at age 38, while cajoling a talented but callow team to a stunning 10–2 record. Along the way he passed two significant milestones for quarterbacks, overtaking Dan Marino atop the alltime list in touchdown passes (436) and John Elway in victories by a starter (157). He should soon pass Marino in passing yards as well.

But one record above all others speaks to what Favre is made of: his Ripkenesque streak of consecutive starts at quarterback—he is more than five seasons ahead of the next player on the list, Peyton Manning. During a recent 37–27 loss at Dallas, Favre was knocked out of the game in the second quarter, when on the same play he separated his left shoulder and took a helmet to his right elbow, causing numbness in two fingers on his throwing hand. Afterward, to no one's surprise, Favre said he expected he would not miss a game. He has rarely been flawless (after all, he leads the NFL in lifetime interceptions, with 283), but he's always shown up. Through pills and booze, through cancer and car crashes and heart attacks, he has played on. Once reckless on and off the field, Favre has matured before our eyes while never losing his boyish love for the game.

Ask people around Green Bay for their favorite Brett Favre memory, and you'll get countless anecdotes but rarely any hesitation. So many elite athletes captivate with their otherworldly physical gifts, but the common theme among the Favre highlights is the human element.

Jennifer Walentowski, mother of Anna, a Make-a-Wish Foundation child that Favre befriended: "In the Super Bowl against the Patriots, Brett threw a beautiful touchdown in the very beginning of the game, and he was so excited, he started running around the field. He had taken off his helmet, and he had both arms in the air, and there was such genuine joy on his face, such realness. Gosh, I'm tearing up right now just thinking about it."

Doug Phillips, whose daughter, Carley, participates in the Miracle League, to which Favre donated $100,000 to help build a baseball facility with a specialized wheelchair-friendly artificial surface: "He hurt his ankle pretty bad against the Vikings [in 1995]. No one knew if he would play the next game [against Chicago]. He was on crutches all week, doubtful right up to kickoff. When he ran out of the tunnel at Lambeau, that was the loudest explosion I have ever heard in my life. And of course Brett threw five touchdowns that day."

Pete D'Amico, cofounder of the Door County Gulf Coast Relief Fund: "I lost my father a month before Brett's dad died. That Monday-night game against Oakland, the day after Big Irv died? I was crying that whole game. Just bawling. I know a lot of other people were too for their own reasons."

Donald Driver, Packers receiver: "My favorite moment is from that Monday night against the Raiders, but it didn't happen on the field. Before the game I went to talk to Brett in his hotel room. He was hurting, obviously, but said he was going to play because we were his family too. It was pure love, pure brotherhood."

Sue LeTourneau of the Brian LaViolette Scholarship Foundation: "On his 30th birthday, I held up a sign in the stands here at Lambeau. When he ran onto the field, he looked at me and gave a thumbs-up. Oh, my God, I thought I was going to die right then and there!"

Mark Tauscher, Packers tackle: "My rookie year [2000] we were at Minnesota late in the year. Big game. At some point in the second half we were facing third down, and [center] Frank Winters misses a linebacker coming on a blitz. Brett gets sacked, but instead of jogging off the field he turns and chucks the ball at Frankie. And Frankie says, 'Well, get rid of the damn ball faster next time!' The whole team was laughing. It kind of loosened us up, and we went on to win."

Mike McCarthy, Packers coach: "In '99, when I was quarterbacks coach, three of the first four games were comebacks in the final couple of minutes. The one that stands out was against Tampa Bay. There's about a minute left, and we call this play where if the rush comes, Brett's supposed to check down to the back. Of course Tampa comes with everything they've got, but Brett just stands in there and throws a strike to Antonio Freeman for the winning touchdown, just as John Lynch and half the defense hits him in the jaw. On the sideline Brett's a little woozy; he's on oxygen; and I go up to him and say, 'What happened to the check-down?' He says, 'Dammit, I forgot all about that. But, hey, I made the throw.' That's Brett Favre in a nutshell—he'll take the beating, but he'll always make the throw."

Ask Favre for his own favorite memory, and he is quiet for a moment. "I've got so many plays running through my mind," he says, finally. "The funny thing is, it's not only about the touchdowns and the big victories. If I were to make a list, I would include the interceptions, the sacks, the really painful losses. Those times when I've been down, when I've been kicked around, I hold on to those. In a way those are the best times I've ever had, because that's when I've found out who I am. And what I want to be." ■

TERRY BRADSHAW

"His stats aren't great (he threw nearly as many interceptions as touchdowns) but his longballs to Lynn Swann and John Stallworth were the difference in three of his four Super Bowl victories, and his .677 winning percentage is third alltime among retired quarterbacks in the postwar era." —MARK MRAVIC

▸ TWO-TIME SUPER BOWL MVP
▸ 1978 NFL MVP

YES, HE IS a smart quarterback, his unfortunate image to the contrary. Although he has been picking NFL defenses to pieces all year, he remains, in the eyes of the ignorant, "dumb." Coach Chuck Noll, who is as outwardly emotional as a throw rug, bristles at any suggestion that his quarterback reads defenses remedially. "That's ridiculous," he snaps. "People who say he's dumb should look in the mirror." Bradshaw calls all of his own plays, often brilliantly. Roger Staubach, supposedly a clever quarterback, calls almost none of his. When the 49ers foolishly tried to blitz him in November, he deftly threw three touchdown passes. He engineered a masterly 11-play, 80-yard drive against Houston that transformed a bitter defensive struggle into a clear-cut Steelers victory. Bradshaw is nobody's fool.

—Ron Fimrite, SI, December 18, 1978

Bradshaw was at his best in big games.

PHOTOGRAPH BY NEIL LEIFER

THE 10

BEST RUNNING BACKS

WHEN IT COMES TO CARS, THE '57 CHEVY REMAINS AN ICON OF EXCELLENCE, NO MATTER HOW MUCH MORE POWERFUL OR EFFICIENT THE NEWER MODELS ARE. SO IT IS WITH RUNNING BACKS. THE CURRENT CROP IS SWIFT AND SLEEK AND VERSATILE, BUT OUR PANELISTS COULD NOT HELP BUT LOOK BACK TO THE PAST.

AND IT WENT BEYOND A FONDNESS FOR JIM BROWN—A ROOKIE IN 1957, INCIDENTALLY—WHO WAS THE NEAR CONSENSUS CHOICE AT NO. 1. WHILE MULTIPLE ACTIVE PLAYERS MADE THE TOP 10 AT OTHER SKILL POSITIONS, WITH RUNNING BACKS THERE ARE NONE AT ALL. MARSHALL FAULK, WHO LAST PLAYED IN 2005, WAS THE MOST RECENT PLAYER CHOSEN. TWO MORE MODERN BACKS, ADRIAN PETERSON AND LADAINIAN TOMLINSON, BOTH EARNED VOTES BUT NOT ENOUGH TO MAKE THE TOP 10.

ONE CULPRIT: THE SPLIT BACKFIELD. MANY COACHES NOW DIVIDE CARRIES BETWEEN TWO OR THREE BACKS, KEEPING EVERYONE FRESH, BUT THEIR RUSHING TOTALS DOWN. THEN THERE'S THE SHIFT TO THE PASSING ATTACK. BEFORE RULE CHANGES BEGINNING IN 1978, RUSHING ATTEMPTS ALWAYS OUTNUMBERED PASSES, BUT SINCE THEN THE BALANCES HAVE FLIPPED. IT'S A LITTLE LIKE THE AUTOMOBILE, WHICH HAS LOST ITS MAGIC IN THE AGE OF FREQUENT FLYING. WHEN IT COMES TO ACCUMULATING POINTS THESE DAYS, WE'RE ALL UP IN THE AIR.

1

JIM BROWN

BROWNS 1957–1965

" Not sure which is more impressive: that he won eight rushing titles in nine seasons and retired in the prime of his career to make movies, or that he got to participate in a love scene with Raquel Welch. "—JIM TROTTER

▸ FOUR-TIME NFL MVP
▸ RETIRED AS NFL'S CAREER RUSHING LEADER WITH 12,312 YARDS

GLENN HOLZMAN, a very good 250-pound tackle for the Los Angeles Rams, recently explained what it is like to face Brown from the wrong side of the line: "He's just the best back in the league . . . fast as the fastest, hard as the hardest. He gets off to the quickest start of any big man I've ever seen. An arm tackle is no soap; he runs right through you. The only way I've found to stop him is hit him right at the ankles with your shoulder . . . otherwise, it's like tackling a locomotive." Brown has tremendous lateral speed and balance; he can be hit, knocked sideways and land on his feet running in another direction, picking up full speed again in a few steps. One league coach made Brown's importance clear after his team had dropped a thriller to the Browns: "If they ever lose Jim Brown, then they'll be even with the rest of us."

—Tex Maule, SI, November 10, 1958

Brown averaged a record 104.3 yards per game.

PHOTOGRAPH BY NEIL LEIFER

2

WALTER PAYTON

BEARS 1975–1987

❝ Arguably the greatest football player who ever lived. He retired as the alltime rushing leader, was likely the best blocker ever from his position, could catch the ball out of the backfield [492 career receptions] and threw eight touchdown passes. ❞ —MARK MRAVIC

▸ HELD RECORDS FOR CAREER RUSHING TOUCHDOWNS (110) AND YARDS IN A GAME (275)
▸ TWO-TIME NFL MVP

"IN THEIR Super Bowl year [1985], we played them at Lambeau," says former Green Bay Packers linebacker Brian Noble. "It was my rookie season, and we were having a great game, up 10–9 late in the fourth quarter. They had the ball at about our 30. I weighed 265 pounds, and Walter came right at me with the ball. I teed up, and there was a huge collision. I hit that man as hard as I hit anybody in my career. I knocked him back about four yards, but he stayed up and just kept going. Touchdown. I was devastated; I cost us the game. Sitting in the locker room afterward, I was ready to quit. But my teammate John Anderson put his arm around me and said, 'Believe me, that's not the first time and it won't be the last time that Walter Payton breaks a tackle like that.' "

—Peter King, SI, November 8, 1999

Sweetness had 77 games of 100 or more yards rushing.

PHOTOGRAPHS BY JOHN BIEVER (LEFT) AND HEINZ KLUETMEIER

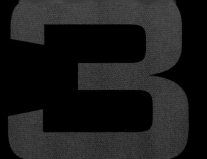

3

"Sanders walked away early, at age 30, having never rushed for fewer than 1,304 yards when he played a 16-game season. No back better combined power between the tackles with breathtaking open-field elusiveness." —TIM LAYDEN

SANDERS IS what people in the NFL call a "freak runner." His style follows no predictable pattern. It's all improvisation, genius, eyes that see more than other people's do, legs that seem to operate as disjointed entities, intuition, awareness of where the danger is—all performed in a churning, thrashing heartbeat.

—*Paul Zimmerman, SI, December 8, 1997*

BARRY SANDERS

▸ 15,269 CAREER YARDS RUSHING
▸ 2,053 YARDS IN 1997

Sanders led the league in rushing four times.

PHOTOGRAPH BY JOHN BIEVER

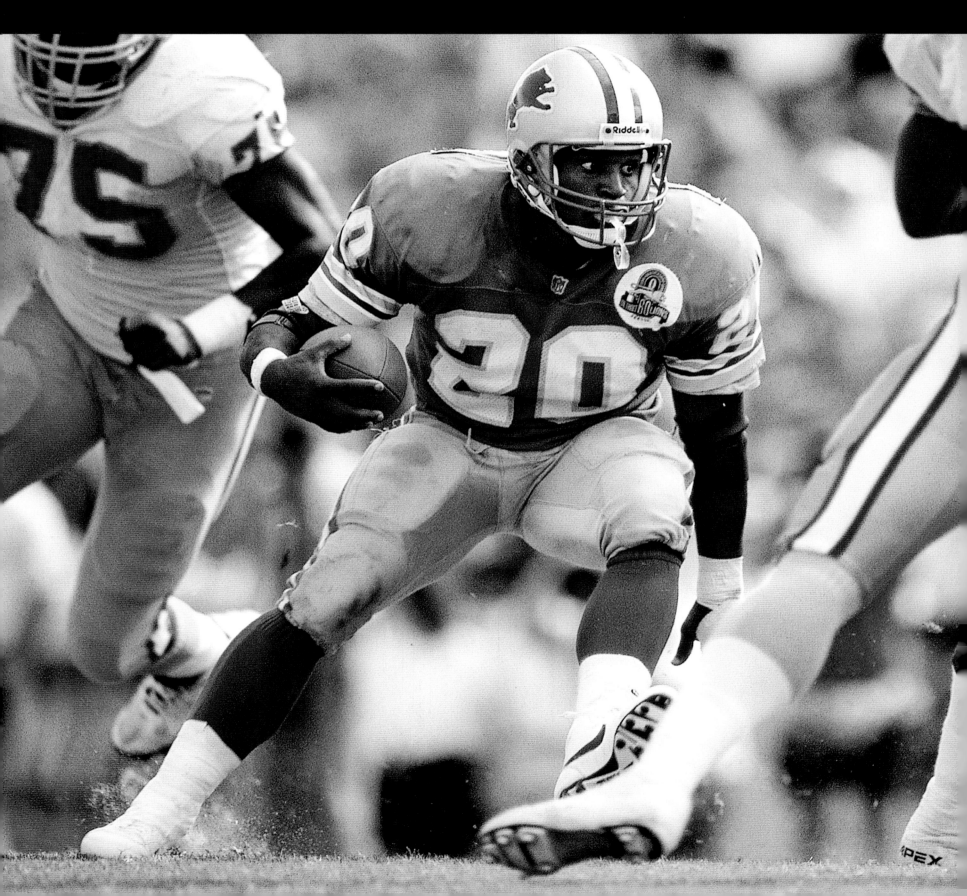

4

O. J. SIMPSON

BILLS 1969–1977
49ERS 1978–1979

"Our job is not to be judge and jury of whatever he did later in life, off the field. It's to judge him as a player—and there aren't three backs in NFL history who combined the electric moves and power of Simpson." —PETER KING

▸ FOUR NFL RUSHING TITLES
▸ FIRST BACK TO RUSH FOR 2,000 YARDS IN A SEASON

IN THE season's opener O.J. set a league record for a single game when he rushed for 250 yards against New England. The Hall of Fame urgently requested his jersey. Twice in the first four weeks he was named AP Offensive Player of the Week. Two weeks ago, against Baltimore, he set another league record with his seventh consecutive 100-yard game. The media began to document his every move. When he left the field briefly in the Philadelphia game the press box was solemnly informed. "Simpson suffered a broken shoelace." . . . The person who seems the least ruffled by all the excitement is Simpson himself. He is not a 26-year-old suddenly encountering fame but a man settling comfortably into a familiar role, O.J. Simpson, superstar. "Being the best is something I've lived with," he says, "and I like living with it."

—*Joe Marshall, SI, October 29, 1973*

Simpson set a record with 23 TDs in 1975.

PHOTOGRAPH BY HEINZ KLUETMEIER

5

GALE
SAYERS

BEARS 1965–1971

❝ His brilliance was relatively brief due to an injury-shortened career, but no one delivered more highlight-reel moves and wow factor than Sayers did in his prime. ❞ —DON BANKS

RECORD 22 TDS AS A ROOKIE
▸ TWO NFL RUSHING TITLES

HIS CAREER has passed into the realm of grainy film mythology, and within that mythology certain assumptions have taken root. Such as this one: He was uniquely great. That assumption is true. "There really has never been anybody else like him, even to this day," says Steelers defensive coordinator Dick LeBeau, who as a defensive back for the Lions played against Sayers 10 times and has been a coach in the NFL for 37 seasons. "He was the best runner with a football under his arm I've ever seen," says Mike Ditka, who played with Sayers and, notably, coached Walter Payton. Here's another assumption: The injuries that blunted Sayers's career left him unfulfilled. That assumption is false. His battered knees ended his football career and started a rich second life, and he offers up two statements, spoken countless times since 1972, to describe this transition, *"As I prepared to play, I prepared to quit. I walked away, and I never looked back."*

—*Tim Layden, SI, August 23, 2010*

Sayers sped through the hole in 1968.

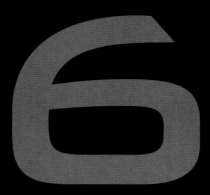

6

EMMITT SMITH

COWBOYS 1990–2002
CARDINALS 2003–2004

" A tough and rugged runner with great vision and underrated speed, Smith always played whether healthy or hurt. " —DAMON HACK

▸ NFL'S ALLTIME LEADING RUSHER WITH 18,355 YARDS
▸ 176 CAREER TDS

PLAYING WITH a nagging tight right hamstring and the most famous shoulder separation in recent sports history, Smith, the reigning NFL MVP, showed America once again that the big game is his playground by leading Dallas to a 38–21 win over the 49ers in the NFC Championship Game. Before leaving the game with 10 minutes to play. Smith had 88 yards rushing, 85 yards receiving, two touchdowns and huge impact. . . . In the game the 49er defense chose to focus heavily on the Cowboy wideouts. "They wanted to see if Emmitt, with his shoulder, could beat 'em," Michael Irvin said afterward. "But you don't challenge Emmitt. Emmitt beat 'em. Emmitt ate 'em up." After the game San Francisco tight end Jamie Williams was worried about Smith's health. "Is Emmitt O.K.?" he wondered. "He'll be fine," a writer told him. "Then Buffalo's in trouble," Williams said.

—*Peter King, SI, January 31, 1994*

Smith led the NFL in rushing four times.

Campbell was lightning and thunder all in one.
PHOTOGRAPH BY RICHARD MACKSON

7

EARL CAMPBELL

" The Tyler Rose was a thorn in the side of every defense he faced. He ran with the power of a bulldozer yet was light enough on his feet to outrace defenders to the corner. He remains the only player to run for 200 yards four times in a season. " —JIM TROTTER

▸ 1979 NFL MVP
▸ 1,934 YARDS RUSHING IN 1980

"HE CAN inflict more damage on a team than any back I know of," says Pittsburgh's Mean Joe Greene. "O.J. did it with speed, Campbell does it with power. He's a punishing runner. He hurts you. There are very few tacklers in the league who will bring Earl Campbell down one-on-one."

—*Bruce Newman, SI, September 3, 1979*

ERIC DICKERSON

1983–1987 RAMS
1987–1991 COLTS
1992 RAIDERS
1993 FALCONS

"Tall, graceful and quick, Dickerson was beautiful to watch darting between the tackles." —DAMON HACK

▸ RECORD 2,105 YARDS RUSHING IN 1984
▸ REACHED 10,000 YARDS IN A RECORD 91 GAMES

WHEN HE showed up at that first minicamp with the Rams, John Robinson and running backs coach Bruce Snyder were expecting this hoss. And that was why, when they discovered what they really had, Dickerson so awed them. "He made no noise when he ran," Robinson says. "You couldn't hear anything," Snyder agrees. "You can usually hear a runner's pads; they'll flop around a little bit. And you'll hear feet on the ground. With a big man, you'll get more sound vocally, a kind of breathing and grunting." There was none of that with Dickerson. "He was so smooth," Robinson said. "If you were blind, he could run right by you, and I don't think you'd know he was there unless you felt the wind. He is an extremely powerful runner, but he's so graceful it's really deceiving. He's the smoothest runner I've ever seen."

—*William Nack, SI, September 4, 1985*

The 6'3" Dickerson rushed for 13,259 career yards.

PHOTOGRAPH BY JON SOOHOO/GETTY IMAGES

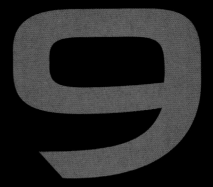

9

MARION MOTLEY

BROWNS 1946–1953
STEELERS 1955

"A punishing runner who was also known for his pass blocking, Motley was a mainstay on the Browns' title teams of the 1940s and '50s, and he led the NFL in rushing in 1950, Cleveland's first year in the league." —MARK GODICH

▸ CAREER AVERAGE OF 5.7 YARDS PER CARRY
▸ TWO-TIME LEAGUE-LEADING RUSHER

MOST OF the world never saw the real Marion Motley. What it saw when the Cleveland Browns entered the NFL in 1950 was a 30-year-old fullback with two bad knees. He was still functional, still capable of running with speed and power— and of picking up pass rushers who wandered through the wall. The real Marion Motley was the 232-pound monster who burst onto the All-America Football Conference scene in 1946 and terrorized the new league. That's the man who fascinated me as a youngster. I can close my eyes and see him running right at me in my seat at Yankee Stadium in the 1947 title game, going 51 yards with Harmon Rowe riding his back and punching him in the face. "Smile, Marion," the photographers said afterward. "I can't," he said. "They knocked out my front teeth."

—Paul Zimmerman, SI, July 5, 1999

Motley ran in the 1950 NFL title game.

PHOTOGRAPH BY AP

10

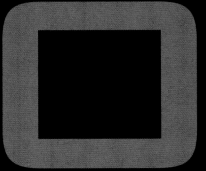

MARSHALL FAULK

COLTS 1994–1998
RAMS 1999–2005

Faulk keyed St. Louis's Greatest Show on Turf.

PHOTOGRAPH BY PETER READ MILLER

" Faulk was so dangerous as a runner, yet equally lethal as a receiver. He could play in the backfield, the slot or at wide receiver, with no drop-off at any spot. " —JIM TROTTER

▸ 2,000 YARDS FROM SCRIMMAGE IN FOUR STRAIGHT SEASONS
▸ 2000 NFL MVP

AL SAUNDERS, the Rams' receivers coach in '99 and 2000, says that in St. Louis's high-scoring offense, Faulk "was like the queen on the chessboard. You can do some damage with your knights and bishops, but nobody does more damage than the queen."

—*Michael Silver, SI, September 3, 2001*

10 THE

BEST WIDE RECEIVERS

WHEN, IN MARCH 2012, HINES WARD ANNOUNCED HIS RETIREMENT, A DISCUSSION FOLLOWED ABOUT WHETHER THE STEELERS WIDEOUT DESERVED ENTRY INTO THE PRO FOOTBALL HALL OF FAME. OUR PANEL HAS A CLEAR OPINION ON THAT QUESTION, BECAUSE WARD MAKES THE LAST SPOT IN OUR TOP 10, AHEAD OF 17 MODERN-ERA RECEIVERS WHO HAVE ALREADY BEEN ENSHRINED.

BUT HOLD ON, DON'T START SCULPTING THAT BUST JUST YET. CRIS CARTER ACTUALLY FINISHED A COUPLE SPOTS AHEAD OF WARD ON OUR LIST, AND HE HAS JUST MISSED OUT ON THE HALL SEVERAL TIMES NOW.

THERE ARE ALSO THREE OTHER PLAYERS IN OUR TOP 10, EITHER RECENTLY RETIRED OR IN THEIR WANING DAYS, WHO WILL COMPLICATE THE RECEIVER VOTE WHEN THEY COME UP FOR CONSIDERATION. AS ONE OF OUR PANELISTS, PETER KING—WHO IS ALSO A HALL VOTER—HAS NOTED IN HIS *MONDAY MORNING QUARTERBACK* COLUMN ON SI.COM, THE WIDE RECEIVER POSITION IS A PARTICULARLY THORNY ONE TO JUDGE, BECAUSE THE MORE TEAMS PASS, THE HARDER IT IS TO COMPARE PLAYERS FROM DIFFERENT ERAS. ONE FACTOR THAT WILL WORK IN WARD'S FAVOR IS THAT HIS CASE DOES NOT HINGE ENTIRELY ON HIS PASS CATCHING. THE PANELISTS WHO VOTED FOR WARD WERE IMPRESSED THAT THE STEELER SHOWED SO MUCH PASSION FOR BLOCKING. IN HIS CASE, IT WASN'T JUST ABOUT PUTTING UP NUMBERS.

1

JERRY RICE

49ERS 1985–2000
RAIDERS 2001–2004
SEAHAWKS 2004

" He owns nearly every major receiving record, not only because of his supreme ability and work ethic, but also because he was blessed to play in San Francisco, with two Hall of Fame quarterbacks in their primes. " —JIM TROTTER

▸ NFL RECORD 208 CAREER TDS
▸ NFL RECORD 22,895
CAREER RECEIVING YARDS

"PEOPLE COME up to me and say, 'I'd love to be in your shoes,'" he says with a sigh. "I say, 'No, you wouldn't.' They don't know what it's like. The pressure. Before games I can't sleep. Before Super Bowl XXIII I woke up at 4 a.m. and just paced. I can't relax. I should be able to enjoy it, but I can't. The table can turn." Someday Rice will probably score his 200th touchdown, which will be 74 more than his closest competitor, Jim Brown, who has been retired for almost 30 years. It's a figure so high, it's crazy. But it may not be enough for this most graceful and obsessive of men. "It's a lot of wear and tear on me," he says needlessly of his intensity down the stretch. "I might not survive," he grimaces. Constant vigilance is required. The table must not move.

—Rick Telander, SI, December 26, 1994

Rice had 14 1,000-yard seasons.

PHOTOGRAPH BY PETER READ MILLER

PACKERS 1935–1945

Hutson invented many standard pass routes.

PHOTOGRAPH BY ROBERT WALSH/AP

2

Don

" With all respect to Jerry Rice, I've valued Hutson as the best receiver ever because of his game-changing speed, and because he set the bar for receiving records so high that many lasted for two or three generations. " —PETER KING

▸ RETIRED WITH 18 MAJOR NFL RECORDS

TWO-TIME NFL MVP

WITH HIS momentum carrying him the other way, Hutson reached back, reached, reached—his arms seemed five feet long—reached past the defender, made the catch, kept his balance and scored. I ran the play back, frame by frame. It was an impossible catch. I've only seen one other like it: Lynn Swann's against the Cowboys in the '76 Super Bowl.

—Paul Zimmerman, SI September 11, 1989

3

RANDY MOSS

VIKINGS 1998–2004
RAIDERS 2005–2006
PATRIOTS 2007–2010
VIKINGS, TITANS 2010

Moss was particularly potent as a deep threat.
PHOTOGRAPH BY DAMIAN STROHMEYER

" At his best, Moss's speed, long limbs and long strides could take over games for weeks at a time. " —DAMON HACK

▸ 14,858 CAREER RECEIVING YARDS
▸ TIED FOR SECOND IN CAREER RECEIVING TDS (153)

"HE JUST doesn't know, just doesn't realize," says Vikings QB Randall Cunningham. "He doesn't understand that when we're playing Kansas City, he's up against the best [secondary]. It hasn't hit him. There's no fright, just this kind of innocence. He's like all of us when we're young, before we do fail. A very few of us never do."

—*Richard Hoffer, SI, September 7, 1998*

4

LANCE ALWORTH

" Alworth was deservedly the first AFL player named to the Hall of Fame, and he dominated that pass-happy league with seven consecutive 1,000-yard seasons. He's still considered one of the most graceful receivers who ever ran a route. " —DON BANKS

best," Alworth says. "Their defenses are not as complex and advanced as ours have become in the AFL. And their cornerbacks are just people. Our top four teams and the NFL's top seven are not far apart. I hope we get to play against them someday and shut them up."

—*Edwin Shrake, SI, December 13, 1965*

▸ 18.9 YARDS PER CATCH
▸ 85 CAREER RECEIVING TDS

Tne brown-eyed Alworth was nicknamed Bambi.

5

RAYMOND BERRY

COLTS 1955–1967

" The first real technician in the modern passing game. " —TIM LAYDEN

▸ RETIRED WITH MOST CAREER CATCHES, RECEIVING YARDS
▸ 12 RECEPTIONS, 178 YARDS IN 1958 TITLE GAME

WHEN I was a skinny kid just out of high school in an east Texas town called Paris, I went to see a movie named *Crazylegs* five times. It was about Elroy Hirsch, who played end for the Los Angeles Rams, and I decided then that the thing I wanted to do most in the world was to catch passes for a professional football team the way Hirsch did. I guess I haven't reached that goal completely. I play end for the Colts, but I don't catch passes the way Elroy did. I've spent hours a day studying game movies of Hirsch and other great offensive ends. But there are things you can't do—I should say I can't do—because I don't have the physical equipment. Some of the moves they make I can copy to a T— all the fakes and feints—but I'm not as fast as some of these guys and not as big or as tall as others, and there's nothing I can do about that. You can't grow and you can't run faster than your physical equipment lets you. All you can do is squeeze the very most out of what you have.

—*Raymond Berry and Tex Maule, SI, October 5, 1959*

Berry was an unheralded 20th-round pick from SMU.

PHOTOGRAPH BY WALTER IOOSS JR.

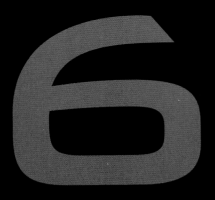

6
TERRELL OWENS

49ERS 1996–2003
EAGLES 2004–2005
COWBOYS 2006–2008
BILLS 2009
BENGALS 2010

❝ His off-field distractions overshadow his historically great performances, such as his 20 receptions in a single game in 2000, and his nine catches for 122 yards in Super Bowl XXXIX with a metal plate and two screws in his ankle. ❞ —MARK MRAVIC

▸ TIED FOR SECOND IN CAREER RECEIVING TDS (153)
▸ 1,078 CAREER RECEPTIONS

"I WAS pretty much the most picked-on guy in high school," says Terrell Owens. "And I took a lot of beatings. Being dark-skinned wasn't in back then, so I'd hear stuff like, 'You should be glad you don't go to night school, because the teacher would call you absent.' Owens can laugh about it now. Having turned 25 on Dec. 7, he's a superstar-in-waiting, a dazzling third-year wideout who has emerged as the successor to Jerry Rice, the greatest receiver of all time. Owens, who has 56 catches for 935 yards and 11 touchdowns, was recently featured in a calendar highlighting the NFL's best bodies. "I want to be a guy everyone notices," Owens says. "I feel like it's just a matter of time before I get a lot of exposure and recognition."

—*Michael Silver, SI, December 14, 1998*

Owens with the third of his five teams.

HAVE 'TUDE, WILL TRAVEL

If the talented, tempestuous wideout and a counterpart from the NBA ever conversed, would they come to appreciate the reasons why their careers came to such unceremonious ends?

BY PHIL TAYLOR

LAST WEEK WAS QUITE A COMEDOWN for a pair of job-hunting former stars, Terrell Owens and Allen Iverson. Owens held a workout at a Los Angeles–area high school, but no NFL teams took him up on his invitation to attend. (T.O. also had to deal with a report that he had tried to commit suicide with an overdose of pills in early October, which he denied through his publicist.) After a year out of the NBA, Iverson, who once said he felt disrespected when asked to come off the bench, told Yahoo! Sports that he's now willing "to help any squad in any capacity." If the temperamental twosome had commiserated with each other, I know just how the conversation would have gone. O.K., actually I don't. But don't you suspect it would have sounded something like this?

T.O.: You get any phone calls yet?

A.I.: Nope. I haven't even heard a rumor. You?

T.O.: Nothing.

A.I.: This is crazy. We're A.I. and T.O.—there's a reason you can't have an alphabet without us. I mean, you have six Pro Bowls in your back pocket, T.O. There's no club that could use a receiver with the second-most yards in NFL history? I know you're 37 and you had ACL surgery in April, but you're healthy now. Teams should be chasing you the way I used to chase my next jump shot.

T.O.: Trust me, you don't have to remind me how fantastic I am. I'm obviously in great shape—that's why I take my shirt off every 20 minutes. But what about you, A.I.? You're an 11-time All-Star guard with four scoring titles, a former MVP. You might be 36, but you could go out there right now and score 20 in your robe and slippers. A future Hall of Famer like you shouldn't have to send out word that he'd do anything for a roster spot. I never thought I'd hear the great A.I. sound so hum . . . so hum . . . .

A.I.: *Humble?* I know, I have a hard time saying it too. I guess you'll have to get used to it, considering the way the whole NFL ignored your workout last week.

T.O.: You should have stopped by. I could have used the company.

A.I.: No, that's not for me, man. A workout sounds too much like practice, and you know how I feel about practice. I mean, *practice?* We're talking 'bout *practice?* Not a game. *Practice.* We're talking 'bout *prac* . . . .

T.O.: Yeah, sorry. I forgot. Didn't mean to get you going on that. I can't figure it out, though. The only team that's shown interest in me so far is from the Arena league, and I'm pretty sure they were just looking for some attention. I hate when people do that.

A.I.: All this free time has given me a chance to think, T.O. What if the only reason teams put up with us all those years was that we were so talented they had no choice? What if nobody seems interested in us now because we're not good enough to be worth the trouble anymore? People always did say that we weren't team players, that we were too wrapped up in ourselves. T.O.? You listening to me?

T.O.: What? Oh, sorry. I was staring at my abs.

A.I.: O.K., turn away from the mirror for a second. Think about it. Guys like us, superstars who happen to be a little high maintenance, don't get to go out on our own terms once we start to slip a bit. Look at Randy Moss. No one signed him because he's moody and demanding and can't give you a 1,200-yard season anymore. Same with Barry Bonds. He didn't want to retire after his Giants career ended, but no one wanted to take on all his baggage. Maybe if we had been easier to handle in our prime . . . .

T.O.: You could be right. It's a shame, though, because there's so much we could teach young players. We're a dying breed, A.I. Where are the prima donnas of tomorrow going to come from? Look at Larry Fitzgerald in Arizona. He hasn't had a quarterback who could get him the ball in two years, but he has to be so classy about it. He should be whining like a preschooler at nap time, the way I used to. I'm pretty sure Donovan McNabb has only 80 percent hearing in his right ear from all my yapping.

A.I.: Yeah, you were the master at that.

T.O.: Same with Calvin Johnson of the Detroit Lions. He made two touchdown catches in Dallas a few weeks ago, and did he once run to the star at midfield and do a look-at-me pose? No. Does he even *own* a Sharpie he can pull out of his sock to autograph the ball after he scores? I mean, how do these guys expect to get their own reality shows if they don't call attention to themselves? They're all about team, team, team.

A.I.: You don't have to tell me. Check out the NBA. You know what's amazing about Derrick Rose of the Bulls? It's not that he's the MVP at age 22; it's that he shows up at every practice. On time. That's wild. All the young stars today, like Kevin Durant in Oklahoma City and the Clippers' Blake Griffin, pretty much play with halos over their heads. It's as if nobody ever informed them that when you're that good, you can get away with doing—or not doing—whatever you want. Maybe they're lucky no one ever told them that.

T.O.: So you're saying that we're the ones who should take a lesson from them? Hmm. Could be. As soon as I get back in the league, I'll be a better teammate. I'll be different. It's never too late to learn.

A.I.: I don't know, T.O. Maybe sometimes it is.

7
PAUL WARFIELD

BROWNS 1964–1969
DOLPHINS 1970–1974
BROWNS 1976–1977

> " It would have been incredible to see him in a wide-open, down-the-field offense. He averaged an astounding 20.1 yards per catch for his career and had 85 touchdowns. Fast, precise and sure-handed, he could not be covered by a single defender. " —JIM TROTTER

▸ EIGHT-TIME PRO BOWL
SELECTION
▸ PLAYED ON THREE
CHAMPIONSHIP TEAMS

IF FRANK RYAN has adequate time to throw, the Colts will be in trouble in the NFL Championship Game. Ryan will then be hitting Paul Warfield and Gary Collins—two excellent receivers—for good gains. Warfield is the best rookie receiver to come up in the last decade. He is not big—6 feet even and 188 pounds— but he has extraordinary moves for a rookie, plus speed. He is almost impossible to cover man for man— witness the Giants' difficulties with him—and he has sure hands. Beyond all this, he has the rare knack of never letting his eyes leave the ball and also of catching well in a crowd. Finally he compensates for his lack of height by tremendous spring, which lifts him higher than taller defensive backs.

—*Tex Maule, SI, December 21, 1964*

Warfield got by his man in 1968.

PHOTOGRAPH BY AP

Carter overcame early-career personal demons.

PHOTOGRAPH BY ANTHONY NESTE

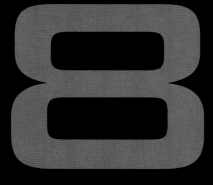

EAGLES 1987–1989
VIKINGS 1990–2001
DOLPHINS 2002

" He was a big receiver with great hands who could make plays wherever you threw him the ball. " —DAMON HACK

▸ FOURTH ALLTIME IN CAREER RECEPTIONS AND TDS
▸ EIGHT CONSECUTIVE PRO BOWL SELECTIONS

CARTER SAYS, "I tell people that when they see alcoholics and drug addicts, they should think about me. People don't want to believe that's who I am because it's so easy to create another image—NFL Man of the Year, a man who loves God. Yes, those things are part of the picture, but so are the others. They're all part of how I got to where I am."

—*Jeffri Chadiha, SI, July 3, 2000*

CRIS CARTER

9

MARVIN HARRISON

COLTS 1996–2008

" Peyton Manning's go-to guy for a decade. The two understood each other completely. " —MARK MRAVIC

▸ NFL RECORD 143 SINGLE-SEASON CATCHES
▸ 1,102 CAREER RECEPTIONS

HARRISON SOMETIMES goes several weeks without agreeing to do even the most perfunctory postgame interviews. Personal information is treated as if it were a state secret. He declines to give a reporter contact information for his mother, saying, with a smile, "She talks too much." Teammates and coaches see him at practices and team meetings but seldom anywhere else. "He's like Batman," says linebacker Cato June, "I don't know if I've ever seen him sit down and eat a meal." There will come a time, however, when Harrison will be forced to stand alone in the spotlight. Five years after he retires, he can expect a call from the Hall of Fame. "I'm not going to talk at the podium. I don't want to do it," Harrison says, his voice rising uncharacteristically. "When people talk about the Hall of Fame, the first thing I say is, 'Do I have to give a speech?' If [I'm not inducted], that will be fine with me because that means I'm not going to give a speech."

—Nunyo Demasio, SI, January 8, 2007

10

HINES WARD

STEELERS 1998–2011

> " Any receiver who catches 1,000 balls, as Ward has done, has to be respected as one of the greats. Any receiver who does that, plus blocks downfield as well as Ward did for so long, has to be in a serious argument for Canton. " —PETER KING

▸ STEELERS FRANCHISE LEADER IN RECEPTIONS, RECEIVING YARDS AND TDS

"I DON'T look at myself as a prototypical wide receiver," Ward says. "I look at myself as a hell of a football player." Ward, whose mother is Korean and father is African-American, then joked that he had a chance to become the "first Asian Super Bowl MVP." He fulfilled that prophecy by making five catches for 123 yards, including a sublime shoestring grab of a Ben Roethlisberger pass; by delivering a crushing block on cornerback Andre Dyson during Willie Parker's touchdown burst; and by gaining 18 yards on a reverse that ended with him and free safety Marquand Manuel crashing into the Seahawks' bench area. "I wanted to hit him," Ward said later of Manuel, who suffered a pulled left groin on the play and did not return. Later, during a timeout, Seahawks rookie middle linebacker Lofa Tatupu sauntered up to Ward and said, "I normally don't respect receivers, but I respect you."

—*Michael Silver, SI, February 13, 2006*

Ward gained 12,083 receiving yards in Pittsburgh.

10

THE

BEST TIGHT ENDS

NOT THAT OTHER POSITIONS HAVEN'T EXPERIENCED THEIR OWN EVOLUTIONS, BUT TIGHT ENDS HAVE HAD A PARTICULARLY PAINED CRAWL FROM THE PRIMORDIAL OOZE. IT'S NOT JUST THE AWKWARD PULL BETWEEN THE NOT-OBVIOUSLY-COMPATIBLE TASKS OF BLOCKING AND RECEIVING. AT TIMES THE POSITION'S VERY EXISTENCE HAS BEEN THREATENED. IN A 1992 SI STORY EXCERPTED ON THE PAGE DEVOTED TO NO. 6 TIGHT END OZZIE NEWSOME, ONE EXECUTIVE ACTUALLY PREDICTED THE EXTINCTION OF THE POSITION.

THE TIGHT END'S MUDDLED ROLE IS ONE REASON WHY, IN THIS CATEGORY, THERE'S A NOTABLE DISCONNECT BETWEEN RANK AND STATISTICAL PRODUCTION. MANY OF THESE GREATS MADE THEIR MARK ON HISTORY NOT JUST WITH CATCH TOTALS, BUT ALSO BY CHANGING THE WAY THE POSITION ITSELF WAS VIEWED.

THANKS IN PART TO THE THREE ACTIVE PLAYERS IN THIS TOP 10 LIST, TIGHT ENDS TODAY ARE MORE IN FASHION THAN EVER. DURING THE 2011 SEASON, WHEN OUR PANELISTS WERE POLLED, EMERGING PLAYERS SUCH AS ROB GRONKOWSKI OF THE PATRIOTS AND JIMMY GRAHAM OF THE SAINTS PUSHED THE POSITION'S EVOLUTION FURTHER STILL, PRODUCING EYE-POPPING STATISTICS THAT WOULD BE THE ENVY OF MOST WIDE RECEIVERS. THOSE YOUNG STARS DIDN'T MAKE THIS LIST, BUT GIVEN TIME THEY MAY SOMEDAY BE VIEWED AS NATURAL SELECTIONS.

1

JOHN
MACKEY

COLTS 1963–1971
CHARGERS 1972

"Unlike many of today's pass-catching tight ends, Mackey was the complete package—not only a speedy, gifted receiver who averaged 15.8 yards on 331 catches, but also a nasty, devastating run blocker." —JIM TROTTER

▸ SIX TDS OF 50 OR MORE
YARDS IN 1966
▸ INFLUENTIAL PLAYERS
ASSOCIATION PRESIDENT

CENTER BILL CURRY, now the Colts' player rep, vividly recalls the first time Mackey ever opened up at a team meeting. "John has always been a great inspiration on the field," says Curry. "Late in a tough game most of us will be dragging ourselves around, working hard to give 98%. Then we'll see Mackey grabbing the ball and knocking guys down even though he is beat too, and so we all start giving 120% just the way he is. But he never used to say anything, just do it. Then once at a team meeting before an important game Johnny Unitas called on Mackey to say something and this time he did. 'Men,' he said, 'these guys really need their butts kicked and we're going to go out and do just that.' It was simple and yet somehow electrifying and we did just that."

—Gwilym S. Brown, SI, August 30, 1971

Mackey was a rare deep threat for a tight end.

2

KELLEN WINSLOW

CHARGERS 1979–1987

Winslow had three seasons with 88-plus catches.

PHOTOGRAPH BY ANDY HAYT

" In the '80s, there were two tight ends who were as dangerous as wide receivers, and Winslow was just slightly more dynamic than Ozzie Newsome. " —TIM LAYDEN

▸ FOUR-TIME ALL-PRO
▸ 13 CATCHES, BLOCKED FG IN 1982 PLAYOFF GAME AGAINST MIAMI

WINSLOW IS a specimen—not only big, but also amazingly talented. "I've never seen anybody with his athletic ability," says QB Dan Fouts. "I think he may be the best football player in the game, at any position. And I'm not saying that to cause controversy, just as a description. He can throw a football 80 or 100 yards."

—*Rick Telander, SI, September 1, 1982*

3

TONY GONZALEZ

CHIEFS 1997–2008
FALCONS 2009–PRESENT

" A powerful athlete with remarkable leaping ability, Gonzalez's longevity makes him one of the greatest ever. " —DAMON HACK

▸ HOLDS NFL CAREER RECORDS FOR RECEPTIONS, YARDS, TDS AT THE POSITION

GONZALEZ SAYS he was one of the worst players on one of the worst Pop Warner teams in Orange County. The league rules said that every kid whose parents paid the $180 entry fee had to play six downs in every game. That's how many Gonzalez played: six. Off the field his life was even worse. In eighth grade he was stalked by a pair of bullies. At the end of eighth grade, a couple of things changed. First, he stopped worrying about the bullies. Second, he found basketball. He scored 18 points in the first game he ever played, in a rec league in Huntington Beach. Basketball gave him confidence. "The next year, I went out for football at the high school because my brother was playing," he says. "The first day of practice, Eric Escobedo, a friend of mine, looked up and said, 'Gonzalez? What are you doing back out here?' Well, he didn't know I was different. After basketball, well, I got it. I figured it out. I could play football too."

—*Leigh Montville, SI, December 27, 1999*

Gonzalez is second only to Jerry Rice in catches.

4

MIKE DITKA

BEARS 1961–1966
EAGLES 1967–1968
COWBOYS 1969–1972

" Before there was Rob Gronkowski, an astoundingly precocious tight end early in his career who blocked well and caught touchdowns, there was Ditka. Check out Ditka's 14-game rookie-year numbers for Da Bears: 56 catches, 1,026 yards, and 12 touchdowns. " —PETER KING

▸ 1961 NFL ROOKIE OF THE YEAR
▸ FIRST TE IN HALL OF FAME

DITKA WAS a Bear even at Aliquippa (Pa.) High when, as a scrawny 135-pound sophomore, he got kicked off the practice field for his own protection. Immediately Ditka was cleaning the locker room latrines and pounding out push-ups with such effort at home "you could hear the house rock," remembers his father, Mike Sr. The family was originally from the Ukraine, the grandfather's name was Dyzcko. Two uncles changed it to Disco, but Mike's dad went with the tougher-sounding Ditka. "I wasn't always the best, but nobody worked harder," says Ditka. "One-on-one. You and me. Let's see who's tougher. I lived for competition. Every game was a personal affront. Everything in my life was based on beating the other guy."

—*Curry Kirkpatrick, SI, December 16, 1985*

Ditka was named to five Pro Bowls, all with the Bears.

5

SHANNON SHARPE

BRONCOS 1990–1999, 2002–2003
RAVENS 2000–2001

" With the skills of a receiver, Sharpe retired as the game's most prolific tight end at the time, with 815 catches, 10,060 yards and 62 touchdowns. "
—DON BANKS

‣ NAMED TO NFL ALL-DECADE TEAM FOR 1990S
‣ THREE 1,000-YARD SEASONS

Sharpe led his teams in receptions seven times.

PHOTOGRAPH BY DAMIAN STROHMEYER

"YOU ASKED about my lisp," Sharpe says. "It never embarrassed me. That's just who I am. My lisp didn't make me loud. I was always loud. I was little and skinny as a kid. They called me Pee Wee. I had to be loud. People say, 'Since you got rich and famous, you've become insufferable.' I say, "That's not true. I've always been insufferable."

—*Rick Reilly, SI, February 1, 1999*

6

OZZIE NEWSOME

BROWNS 1978–1990

" He was the most dangerous weapon on those very good Cleveland teams that couldn't quite reach a Super Bowl. " —MARK MRAVIC

‣ RETIRED AS NFL'S FOURTH-LEADING RECEIVER ALLTIME
‣ 7,980 CAREER YARDS, 47 TDS

THE NFL TIGHT END has gone from being a multipurpose weapon of the 1960s, '70s and '80s—a real star—to being treated like a third tackle, the stepchild of the offensive line, in the '90s. Offensive coordinators have gone so far as to diagram tight ends right out of game plans. "At the peak of my career, I was a threat on every down," says Ozzie Newsome, who retired with more catches (662) than any other tight end in NFL history. "But toward the end of my career a tight end was lucky to be in for 60 percent of the snaps in a game." Today the all-around tight end is virtually obsolete. It's going to be up to newcomers like Derek Brown and Johnny Mitchell, this year's first-round draft picks of the Giants and Jets, to prove there's still a place in the game for the classic tight end. A dubious NFL watches. "I don't think there will ever be a classic tight end again," says San Diego player personnel director Billy Devaney. "The position really is extinct."

—*Peter King, SI, September 7, 1992*

Newsome caught passes in 150 consecutive games.

PHOTOGRAPH BY ANTHONY NESTE

7

DAVE CASPER

RAIDERS, 1974–1980, 1984
OILERS 1980–1983
VIKINGS 1983

" The Ghost was a ghastly matchup for opponents. He wasn't blessed with great speed, but his hands were vise grips. " —JIM TROTTER

- FOUR-TIME ALL-PRO
- MADE RENOWNED "GHOST TO THE POST" AND "HOLY ROLLER" PLAYS

ON THE sidelines coach John Madden grabbed running back Mark van Eeghen and gave him a bit of inside information. "Look for Ghost to the post," said Madden, the bard of the Bay. Ken Stabler dropped back, but the 6' 4", 230-pound Casper, who had already scored two touchdowns, had difficulty breaking away from Baltimore linebacker Tom MacLeod. While waiting for Casper to get untracked, Stabler noticed that the Colts had switched into a coverage designed to prevent the Ghost from going to the post. So Stabler wisely lofted the ball not at the left post but rather in the direction of the right corner of the end zone. "I picked up the ball visually when it was halfway to me," Casper said. "When I looked up I realized the ball was going to the corner, not the post, so I just ducked the old head, turned and ran. When I looked up again, it was there."

—Ron Reid, SI, January 2, 1978

Casper slipped by the Colts' coverage in 1977.

PHOTOGRAPH BY WALTER IOOSS JR.

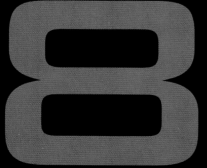

8

ANTONIO
GATES

PHOTOGRAPH BY JOHN W. MCDONOUGH

CHARGERS 2003—PRESENT

Gates was named to the NFL's 2000s All-Decade team.

"Though he's been slowed by injuries the past two years, Gates is a pass-catching machine. He has five seasons of at least 900 yards receiving and three with 10 or more touchdown catches." —DON BANKS

▸ 593 CAREER RECEPTIONS, '76 TDS
▸ TEAM'S LEADING RECEIVER SIX STRAIGHT SEASONS

"THE FIRST touchdown he ever caught was a corner route," says Doug Flutie, the former Chargers quarterback who threw it. "Because he was so athletic, he could keep people's hands off him and get that inside release down by the goal line. I just put it up in the corner and he went and got it. By halftime I realized, This guy's a weapon."

—Damon Hack, SI, October 25, 2010

THE TIGHT END: VERSION 2.0

Antonio Gates's transition from small-college power forward to NFL superstar mirrored a larger transformation at a position that would find revived purpose in the modern offense

BY JEFFRI CHADIHA

THEY HAD GATHERED INSIDE the Kent State Field House on a crisp April afternoon in 2003 for one reason: to judge whether Antonio Gates, the Golden Flashes' All-Conference basketball player, had the tools to play professional football. Scouts from the Colts, Steelers and 49ers, and the tight ends coaches from the Browns and the Chargers took their places on the indoor field as Gates completed his stretching. Once the workout got under way, however, most were wondering why they had come.

Gates plodded through his agility drills, showed little explosiveness on his routes and looked as if he'd added a few unflattering pounds to his 6' 4", 260-pound frame. After he ran an embarrassing 4.8 in the 40, the scouts and coaches had seen enough. At the suggestion of Tim Brewster, then the Chargers' tight ends coach, they ended the workout early.

But as his colleagues gathered their belongings and wished Gates the best, Brewster lingered behind, hoping nobody else knew what he knew: that Gates had sprained his right ankle a week earlier playing in the Portsmouth (Va.) Invitational, a showcase for NBA prospects. For nearly two months Brewster had been in regular contact with Gates, who five years earlier had gotten a football scholarship to Michigan State. From watching tapes of Gates playing power forward, the coach believed he could be a Charles Barkley in shoulder pads.

Brewster emphasized that potential in his report to the San Diego front office. "If I had been truthful to the organization about what I saw that day," says Brewster, now the tight ends coach for the Denver Broncos, "we probably wouldn't have signed Antonio." And all it cost them was a $7,000 signing bonus.

Fast forward to last November, when Gates pulled his Bentley into the lot of the Los Angeles Center Studios to discuss a documentary of the player's improbable journey to NFL stardom. In less than three seasons Gates had become the face of a revolution at his position.

There have always been athletic, pass-catching tight ends in the NFL, but never have there been so many. Look around the league and you'll one on almost every roster. Tony Gonzalez, a power forward and tight end at Cal, was at the forefront of the new era after he was taken by the Kansas City Chiefs in the first round of the '97 draft. Too fast for linebackers to cover and too big for safeties, these players open up space in the passing game and create mismatches in coverage. Indeed, with his size and speed, the new-breed tight end is arguably the most versatile athlete on the field.

For Gates there is, of course, room for improvement, particularly in recognizing coverages, but even there he has made big strides. "The game is slowing down for me," Gates says. "And now I want to see the field in the same way Magic Johnson and Larry Bird saw the basketball court. I want to see plays before they happen."

It's no surprise that Gates draws an analogy to basketball. It was his favorite sport as a child, and he played it endlessly on the streets of Detroit's west side. But coming out of Central High, where he had been a standout in football and hoops, he committed to Michigan State's football program, partly because coach Nick Saban promised he could also try out for the basketball team. Then in the fall of 1998, his first semester at the school, Gates, a Prop 48 qualifier who was sitting out the football season, fell behind in the classroom. In late October, Saban rescinded the basketball portion of their deal.

Gates fumed, but Saban still had high hopes for the young man's football career. He even dug out tape of Gates's performances at Central High and told him, "This is what NFL teams are looking for." But at the end of that semester Gates transferred to Eastern Michigan. He then bounced from the College of the Sequoias, a junior college in Visalia, Calif., to Henry Ford Community College in Dearborn, Mich., before landing at Kent State for his junior and senior seasons. Though undersized, he became a two-time All-Mid-America Conference power forward. Yet by the end of his senior year, in 2003, he realized there wasn't much of a future in the NBA for 6' 4" power forwards. And he knew that NFL scouts, still mindful of his earlier football promise, had been coming to his games to check him out.

Though he hadn't played football since high school, he fit the prototype established by Gonzalez: a wide frame, quick feet, exceptional body control, reliable hands and good instincts. Also, while playing college basketball, he had developed skills that proved to be valuable on the football field. From battling for rebounds against players several inches taller, he had learned how to use his body to hold off opponents. From making cuts off screens, he had discovered how to create the best angles for receiving passes. And he had developed one-on-one moves that were just as effective in the secondary.

Once with the Chargers his production jumped from 24 catches and two touchdowns as a rookie to 81 receptions and 13 TDs in 2004. By last season opponents had grown so wary of him that in one game Gates found two cover guys hovering around him on a play in which his assignment was pass blocking.

In the spring he attended autograph signings around the country with other NFL stars and was surprised that so many fans recognized him in New York, Houston and Chicago. "You never hear people say they come to the game to watch the tight end," Gates says, "but I want to be that guy. I want to be known as the most exciting tight end to ever play this game." ∎

9

JASON WITTEN

" He had eight straight seasons with at least 60 receptions, more than any tight end but Tony Gonzalez, and he's third alltime in receptions at the position. " —MARK MRAVIC

▸ SEVEN-TIME PRO BOWL SELECTION
▸ AVERAGING 945 YARDS PER SEASON AS FULL-TIME STARTER

BILL PARCELLS has never been fond of playing guys right out of college. So the most telling stat about Witten, a 2003 third-round pick out of Tennessee who excels as a blocker and a receiver, isn't that he averaged 63 catches over his first three seasons, but rather that he has 38 starts and just turned 24.

—*Sports Illustrated, September 4, 2006*

Witten has three of Dallas's top five receiving seasons.

PHOTOGRAPH BY DAMIAN STROHMEYER

10

TODD CHRISTENSEN

GIANTS 1979
RAIDERS 1979–1988

❝ This bruiser was a quarterback's best friend, especially on third down. He had a four-year stretch in which he averaged 87 receptions a season. ❞ —MARK GODICH

▸ TWICE LED THE NFL IN RECEPTIONS
▸ FIVE-TIME PRO BOWL SELECTION

TODD CHRISTENSEN'S finger hits the button, and the videotape shoots forward. Raiders quarterback Marc Wilson drops back, buying time, looking, looking, finally hitting his tight end, Christensen, who has somehow wormed his way between two defenders. Christensen makes a diving, rolling catch, and the official throws his arms up with 29 seconds showing on the clock. A sudden silence falls over Cleveland Stadium. "That's what I love best—that massive crowd silence when something bad happens," Christensen says. "I've run this back a million times. It's getting fuzzy. Now watch," he says, hitting the button again. "Watch the cop in the end zone. He takes off his helmet and throws it on the ground." "Where? I didn't see it," says Christensen's eight-year-old son, Toby. "Look closely," Christensen says. "See, he spikes it. There, right there." "Oh yeah," Toby says.

—*Paul Zimmerman, SI, August 10, 1987*

Christensen enjoyed three 1,000-yard seasons.

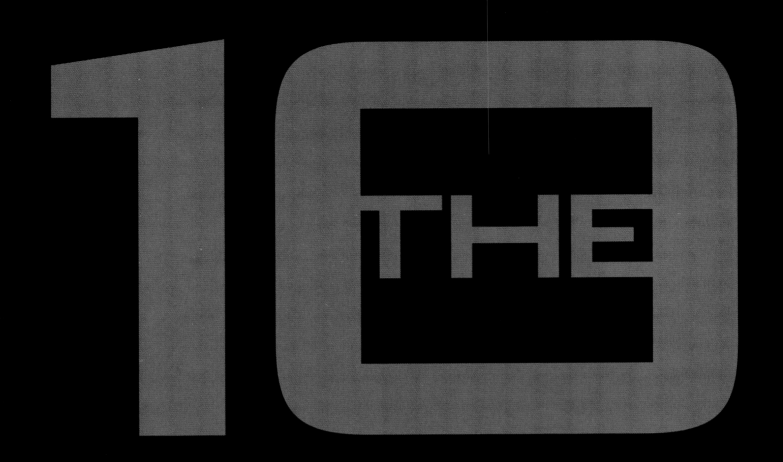

10 THE

BEST OFFENSIVE LINEMEN

IN A POST-*MONEYBALL* WORLD, TALENT EVALUATORS TAKE PRIDE IN BACKING UP THEIR OPINIONS WITH STATISTICAL EVIDENCE. BUT WHEN YOU'RE TALKING ABOUT OFFENSIVE LINEMAN, IT'S MORE ABOUT THE BONE-CRUNCHING THAN NUMBER-CRUNCHING. THERE ARE NO STATS HERE. IF YOU ARE DESPERATE TO QUANTIFY GREATNESS MAYBE YOU CAN TALLY PRO BOWL SELECTIONS, BUT THAT IS REALLY NOTHING MORE THAN A CODIFICATION OF EYEBALL ANALYSIS.

IT'S NO SURPRISE THEN, THAT WHEN OUR PANELISTS SOUGHT TO JUSTIFY THEIR CHOICES FOR TOP LINEMEN, THEY INVOKED, MORE THAN THEY HAD WITH OTHER POSITIONS, THE TESTIMONY OF COACHES—VINCE LOMBARDI SAID THIS, JOHN MADDEN SAID THAT. BECAUSE IF THEY DON'T KNOW, THEN WHO DOES?

IN 1981 PAUL ZIMMERMAN WROTE A COVER STORY, EXCERPTED IN THIS SECTION, THAT BORE THE HEADLINE "THE GREATEST OFFENSIVE LINEMAN OF ALL TIME." IN IT DR. Z ASKED LEAGUE VETERANS TO NAME THE BEST-EVER, AND HE CAME UP WITH A NO.1 AND A NO.2. THOSE SAME PLAYERS WERE SLOTTED BY THIS PANEL NO. 2 AND NO.8. SOME OF THE DISCREPANCY IS OWED TO THE PASSAGE OF TIME—THE NEW NO.1 PLAYER WAS JUST A PUP BACK THEN— BUT IT ALSO UNDERLINES THE SUBJECTIVITY OF OFFENSIVE LINE EVALUATION. THIS IS A BOOK OF OPINIONS, BUT NO PLACE MORE SO THAN HERE.

1

ANTHONY MUÑOZ

BENGALS 1980–1992

" Legendary offensive line coach Jim McNally once said: 'There has never been a lineman as great as Anthony Muñoz, and I doubt whether we will see his equal again.' " —DON BANKS

▸ 11-TIME ALL-PRO
▸ THREE-TIME NFL OFFENSIVE LINEMAN OF THE YEAR

WHEN THE helmet of a Texas Tech player struck Muñoz's left knee in the opening game of his senior season, he required major reconstructive surgery. Desperate to fulfill every Trojan's dream—participating in at least one Rose Bowl—Muñoz made it back for the game. He threw the key block that sprung tailback Charles White for the winning touchdown against Ohio State. At the game were Paul Brown, founder and general manager of the Bengals, and his sons, Mike, the assistant G.M., and Pete, the player personnel director, who were facing a decision: Whatever Muñoz's potential, could they risk using a first-round draft pick on a player with a questionable knee? Muñoz spent the day blowing away Buckeyes and the Brown family's fears. "The three of us sat there and laughed out loud," says Mike. "The guy was so big and so good it was a joke."

—*Jay Greenberg, SI, September 10, 1990*

The agile Muñoz caught four touchdown passes.

2

JOHN HANNAH

PATRIOTS 1973–1985

"John Madden once said he would make Hannah his first selection if he were starting a team. Mind you, Madden coached Hall of Fame offensive linemen Gene Upshaw and Art Shell." —JIM TROTTER

▸ 10-TIME ALL-PRO
▸ NAMED TO NFL ALL-DECADE TEAMS FOR 1970S AND '80S

ONE-BY-ONE, the Patriots' five starting offensive linemen lumbered into the locker room and gathered around a couch. The Pats had just beaten the Bills and the linemen were swapping tales— some a little taller than others— when Patriots offensive line coach Jim Ringo approached with a bottle of Johnny Walker Red in his hand. New England, in the penultimate game of the 1978 regular season, had broken the NFL's single-season team rushing record of 3,088 yards that had been set by the Bills in '73. Ringo poured congratulatory shots for his players, and for more than an hour they sat there together, drinking in their triumph and their whisky. "That season, that day, was as good as it got for me in pro football," says John Hannah. "Our mark [of 3,165 yards] still stands. It was a total team effort."

—Lars Anderson, SI, February 14, 2000

Hannah cleared a path for Sam Cunningham.

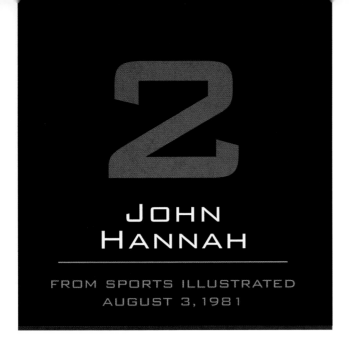

2

JOHN HANNAH

FROM SPORTS ILLUSTRATED
AUGUST 3, 1981

HANNAH DOESN'T FIDDLE AROUND

When Dr. Z evaluated offensive linemen three decades ago,
he concluded that the powerful Patriot was the best ever

BY PAUL ZIMMERMAN

EE NOW, IT'S STARTING. AH, what a parade. Simply magnificent. All the great linemen in NFL history, the offensive linemen, those quiet, dignified toilers in anonymity. Here they come now, Look who's leading the way. Jim Parker. So big, so graceful. God was certainly generous when He created him. And see that little one snorting and pawing the ground, the one with the blood on his jersey? That's Abe Gibron. And there's the Boomer, Bob Brown. Look at those forearms. He once shattered a goalpost with one of them. And that giant blotting out the sun, that's Bob St. Clair, all 6' 9" of him. And there's Mike McCormack, tall, humble, brainy. Yes indeed, this is a parade.

What's that you say? You want to know who's the best of them? The very best? Now how can someone pick something like that? The mere act of it would be an insult to so many players who were so great in their eras. You say I must? O.K., fasten your seat belt. The greatest offensive lineman in history is playing right now and probably hasn't even reached his peak. He is John Hannah, the left guard for the New England Patriots, out of Alabama. He stands 6' 2½" and his weight fluctuates between 260 and 270. (No lineman can honestly claim only one weight.) He is 30 years old and is in his ninth year and is coming off the best season he ever had. He is a pure guard; he's never been anything but a left guard since he started playing in the NFL. He hasn't bounced around between guard and tackle as Parker did, or Forrest Gregg or Bob Kuechenberg; never had to go the offense-defense route like McCormack and Gibron and Chuck Bednarik.

Is it sacrilege to pick a current performer as the greatest who ever lived, in anything? Greatest actor, chef, rodeo rider? Should we wait until he's retired and enshrined and halfway forgotten? Weeb Ewbank, the former coach of the Baltimore Colts and New York Jets, thinks so. "Back off a little, give it some historical perspective," he says. "Let John make the Hall of Fame first."

Weeb's man is Parker, whom he coached for six years in Baltimore. Parker is also the choice of most of the coaches and personnel men who have been around the NFL for a few decades. McCormack generates surprising support, particularly from the Cleveland Browns' faction. Gibron is a dark horse. Hannah's line coach, Jim Ringo, favors a troika of Hannah, Parker and his old Green Bay teammate, Jerry Kramer, but some people feel that although Kramer and right tackle Forrest Gregg were legitimate superstars, they fell under the category of a perfect mesh in a perfect offensive line. The big-name centers of the past—Mel Hein, Frank Gatski, Bulldog Turner, Bednarik, Ringo—receive little support. The opinion is that guards and tackles work in a less protected environment. Only George Halas might remember Cal Hubbard, the legendary giant of the 1920s, and Halas isn't returning phone calls.

But Hannah has his following. Former Denver coach Red Miller says he's the man. So does John Madden, who coached against Hannah when he was with the Raiders. New England general manager Bucko Kilroy, one of the pioneers of modern scouting, who has been rating and evaluating players ever since he lined up against Bronko Nagurski in 1943, says Hannah and McCormack are the only offensive linemen to whom he'd award a perfect "9."

It starts with the firepower, with Hannah's legs, incredibly massive chunks of concrete. "Once we measured John's thighs, and they were

33 inches," says Hannah's wife, Page, a slim ash blonde. "I said, 'I can't bear it. They're bigger than my bust.'"

The ability to explode into an opponent and drive him five yards back was what first attracted the college recruiters to Albertville, Ala., where Hannah grew up and played his final year of high school ball. Hannah says he always had that ability, but it was his first coach at Baylor School for Boys in Chattanooga, a tough, wiry, prematurely gray World War II veteran named Major Luke Worsham, who taught him how to zero in on a target, to aim for the numbers with his helmet, to keep his eyes open and his tail low. Next came the quick feet. Forget about pass blocking if you can't dance. Worsham helped there too.

"Oddly enough," Hannah says, "he helped me develop agility and reactions by putting me on defense in a four-on-one drill. You'd work against a whole side of an offensive line. It was the most terrible thing in the world. If the guard blocked down you knew you'd better close the gap and lower your shoulder. If the end came down and the guard came out, buddy, you grabbed dirt because you knew a trap was coming."

"For all his size and explosiveness and straight-ahead speed," Kilroy says, "John has something none of the others ever had, and that's phenomenal, repeat, *phenomenal* lateral agility and balance, the same as defensive backs. You'll watch his man stunt around the opposite end, and John will just stay with him. He'll slide along like a toe dancer, a tippy-toe. And that's a 270-pound man doing that, a guy capable of positively annihilating an opponent playing him straight up."

Parker, 47 years old now and the owner of a successful liquor store in Baltimore, says he's only gone to three games since he retired in 1967. "I get so flustered watching football nowadays," he says, "so carried away by watching guys making $100,000 a year and making so many mistakes in technique. I get so upset that I wake up with a headache the next morning from banging my head all night in my sleep. But I like to watch Hannah play. He's the only one out there who can do it all—every aspect. If you want me to rate myself, compared to him, I'll say that I sure would have enjoyed playing alongside him.

"I see some things in him that remind me of myself, the way he teases 'em on plays going the opposite way, the way he changes his style on aggressive pass blocking. One time he'll fire out, the next time he'll sit back, lazy, and make 'em think it's a regular pass and then—pow! He'll pop 'em. And on the running plays he's big enough to beat the hell out of them. I've seen him beat them right down into the ground. That's the joy of it, the joy I got out of it."

The joy of being even bigger in a big man's game. And quicker. The joy of being a superior athlete. Parker and Hannah were both gifted in other sports. They were both wrestlers. Parker was a mid-America champion. Hannah won the National Prep Championship and was unbeaten as a freshman at Alabama, before he quit wrestling because it was cutting into spring football. Hannah was also a three-year letterman in the shot and discus at Alabama and his 61' 5" toss in the shotput was a school record at the time. "He didn't even work at

Jim Parker said the only lineman he enjoyed watching was Hannah.

track," says his brother Charles, an offensive tackle for the Tampa Bay Buccaneers. "He'd just show up for the meets. At that time he might have been the greatest large athlete in the world."

The scouts were noting his numbers carefully. In the spring of Hannah's junior year, Bear Bryant, in an unaccustomed moment of generosity, let a combine scout onto the campus to time him in the 40 at the end of a track workout. Hannah weighed 305 pounds. He finished the last five yards falling on his face. "I apologized to the scout for being fat and out of shape," he says. "The guy said, 'Don't apologize. You just ran a 4.85.'"

It is 8:30 p.m. in Crossville, Ala. Hannah's 253-acre cattle and chicken farm is here, 15 miles northeast of Albertville, on a plateau in the Sand Mountain range. It's bedtime for the little Hannahs, nine-month-old Mary Beth and 2½-year-old Seth, except that Seth has no such plans. He's giving a graphic demonstration of what is known as bloodlines.

Seth is running wind sprints—through an obstacle course of chairs and toys. He weighs 37 pounds, not extraordinarily big, but sturdy enough, very solid through the shoulders and chest, big in the legs, like his daddy. He is running at top speed, all-out, but under complete control, with absolutely perfect balance. There's not a trace of a wobble. Every now and then he stops and throws back his head and lets out a loud roar. The Hannahs watch him, waiting for the motor to run down. It shows no signs of it. He turns his head to look at his daddy, and then runs smack into a high chair, bop, forehead first. He blinks, shakes his head and starts running again. "An offensive guard for sure," Page Hannah says.

Like the giant Antaeus, Hannah gets his strength from the earth—those 253 acres of it, 75 planted in feed crops, the rest devoted to livestock. He raises chickens, 43,000 at a time, in two houses. He has a bull and three cows of his own, and a herd of 134 Holstein cattle that he's raising for a breeder in Tampa. Someday he'll have his own herd of Santa Gertrudis, a Shorthorn-Brahman crossbreed developed in Texas. It is a Saturday afternoon in June, and the temperature is in the 90s. Hannah has just finished inspecting his chickens and trimming weeds around half a mile of electric fencing. His shirt is black with sweat, and he sits on the ground, his back against a wooden fence, watching his 2,200-pound Santa Gertrudis bull.

The bull is walking slowly to the water trough, the rich red-brown of his hide gleaming in the afternoon sun, his hindquarters swaying gently, the huge muscles of his shoulders bunching and relaxing. A gentle, magnificent animal. The three heifers at the trough slide sideways to let him through, and then stare at him as he drinks. Hannah laughs and shakes his head.

"Goes anywhere he wants, does anything he wants," he says. "Who's gonna argue with him? People come from all over just to see him. He's still a baby, only four years old. He'll be 2,800 pounds, at least, when he's full-grown. I like to come down here and sit against this fence and just look at him.

"Ain't he something?"

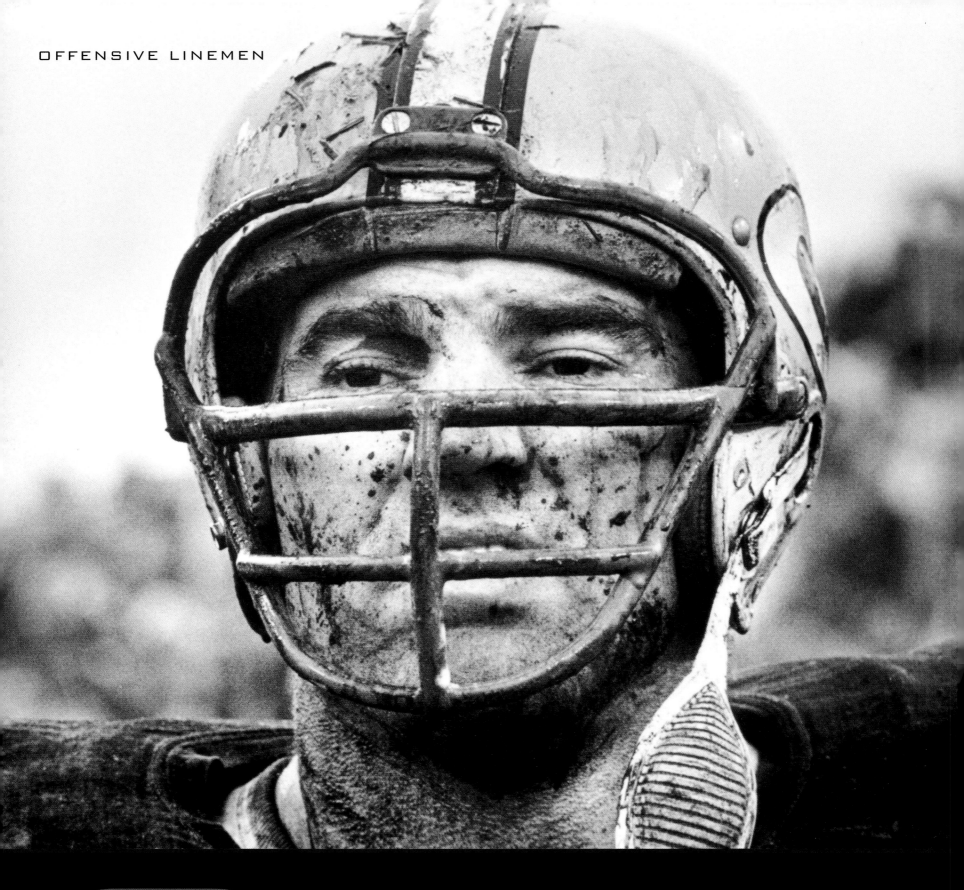

PACKERS 1956, 1958–1970
COWBOYS 1971

Undersized for tackle, Gregg relied on his smarts.

PHOTOGRAPH BY VERNON BIEVER

3

" Vince Lombardi called him the finest player he ever coached. Gregg held the ironman record with 188 consecutive games and paved the way for Paul Hornung and Jim Taylor in the Packers run game. " —MARK MRAVIC

▸ EIGHT-TIME ALL-PRO
▸ PLAYED ON SIX
CHAMPIONSHIP TEAMS

AT 35, Forrest Gregg is one of the oldest players on the team. His assignment was blocking Deacon Jones. Most teams block Jones with two and sometimes three men but for the most part Gregg took on Jones alone. Gregg plays his position with more finesse than any other player in the league.

—Tex Maule, SI, October 28, 1968

FORREST
GREGG

4

BRUCE MATTHEWS

OILERS/TITANS, 1983–2001

"One of the most durable and versatile big uglies of all time, Matthews played 296 games over 19 seasons and started at least one game at every position on the offensive line." —TIM LAYDEN

▸ RECORD-TYING 14 CONSECUTIVE PRO BOWL SELECTIONS
▸ ALL-PRO AT BOTH CENTER AND GUARD

WHEN CLAY and Bruce Matthews get together for a little brotherly competition, it's best to have an ambulance on standby. Boxing matches can turn into knock-down-drag-out fistfights; in Bruce's wedding pictures, you can see a scratch on his forehead that came from roughhousing with his brother. A simple game of one-on-one basketball on Clay's backyard court usually turns into a shouting match, or escalates into so much banging and shoving that one of them gets a black eye, bloody nose or cut lip. "We find losing so disgusting that we refuse, by sheer effort, to lose," Clay says. "With time, effort and the will to win, we prove ourselves in the long run," Bruce says. "No matter what the sport is, if we play long enough, we will beat you."

—*Jill Lieber, SI, September 10, 1990*

Matthews excelled at multiple positions.

PHOTOGRAPH BY US PRESSWIRE

5

MIKE WEBSTER

STEELERS 1974–1988
CHIEFS 1989–1990

> " He seemed to come out of every game a bloody mess. The guess here is it was the opponent's blood. " —DAMON HACK

- ▸ NAMED TO NFL ALL-DECADE TEAMS FOR 1980S AND '90S
- ▸ MISSED ONLY FOUR GAMES IN HIS FIRST 16 SEASONS AND PLAYED IN MORE GAMES (220) THAN ANY STEELER

IT WAS a locker room filled with huge personalities—Mean Joe Greene, mercurial Lynn Swann, Terry Bradshaw, who was always good for a laugh, and Jack Lambert, who'd take out his teeth and growl, just to keep you loose. A reporter could fill a notebook in half an hour with those Steelers during their quadruple Super Bowl run of the 1970s, but if I wanted to know what really happened on the field, if I had technical questions, I went to Mike Webster. I talked to Webster in that Steelers locker room many times, and he never lied or sugarcoated. And after I'd interview him, he'd thank me, then smile and point to the crowded section of the locker room and say, "Better go talk to the superstars." In his mind he was just a workingman who played center. Many people feel no one ever played it better.

—Paul Zimmerman, SI, October 7, 2002

Webster was a Steelers captain.

RAVENS 1996–2007

Ogden dwarfed rushers like Seattle's Okeafor.

PHOTOGRAPH BY SIMON BRUTY

6

JONATHAN OGDEN

" The first draft pick in Baltimore Ravens history could block out the sun with his 6' 9", 340-pound frame. What chance did mere mortals have lining up against him? " —DON BANKS

▸ 11 CONSECUTIVE PRO BOWL SELECTIONS
▸ NINE-TIME ALL-PRO

AS OGDEN slides out he begins pushing Chike Okeafor, who is futilely slapping Ogden's long arms. "It's not only [about] having great hands and strength but also balance," says Ogden. "I have to engage this guy while he's sprinting toward me and I'm moving back. Without balance I'll fall, and he'll be past me."

—Peter King, SI, December 8, 2003

7

GENE UPSHAW

RAIDERS 1967–1981

" One of the first truly athletic pulling guards, Upshaw used his arms and his legs to both outfox and push around defensive linemen. " —DAMON HACK

- ‣ NINE-TIME ALL-PRO
- ‣ 207 CONSECUTIVE STARTS

AL DAVIS was under no illusions about this gentle giant when he drafted him. Upshaw even let Davis know prior to the draft that he thought the Raiders were "too rowdy" and that he would prefer to go to a more upstanding team. "But that's O.K.," Davis says. "When you have enough tough guys on a team, you don't need everybody to be tough. Besides, even if you're not physically tough, you can be tough in other ways, in what you want and how you go after what you want." Davis was quick to see Upshaw's other facets and would often go to him to obtain approval when he was considering bringing in some new crazy; once, in fact, Upshaw gave a thumbs-down on an All-Pro. Moreover, when Upshaw became an annual all-leaguer, his intelligence and perception were discovered by a wider audience.

Tackle Art Shell remembers that after every game, the press gathered about Upshaw "just like he was a quarterback."

—Frank Deford, SI, September 14, 1987

Upshaw led the players' union for 25 years.

PHOTOGRAPH BY WALTER IOOSS JR.

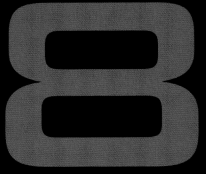

8
JIM

" No offensive lineman accomplished what Parker did—making All-Pro four times at tackle and four times at guard. Anthony Muñoz may well have been a better pure tackle, but Parker and Bruce Matthews would probably duel for the best all-around blocker ever. " —PETER KING

▸ EIGHT CONSECUTIVE
PRO BOWL SELECTIONS
▸ UNITAS'S KEY PROTECTOR

AN OFTEN overlooked sidelight to the famous Giant-Colt championship game in 1958 was the job that Parker did on defensive end Andy Robustelli. His domination of Robustelli was something different, a performance so smooth, so complete, that it was used as a textbook case for many years.

—Paul Zimmerman, SI, September 5, 1994

GIANTS 1931–1945

Hein played linebacker as well as center.

9

MEL

" It's a pretty big honor to be a charter member of the Pro Football Hall of Fame, particularly when men like Otto Graham and Sid Luckman weren't. And though the post-Depression years in NFL history are sketchy, eyewitnesses say he was a block of granite at center. " —PETER KING

HEIN PLAYED in 172 consecutive games. "And I never lost a tooth," he said with pride. An All-Pro eight years in a row, in 1938 he helped the Giants win the NFL title. "He should be barred from football," said Green Bay coach Curly Lambeau. "He's too good."

10

COWBOYS 1994–2005
49ERS 2006–2007

Allen made the Pro Bowl at three positions.

" Maybe the strongest player to ever don shoulder pads and a helmet. He just looked like an interior linemen with his office-building frame, barrel chest and thigh-sized biceps. " —JIM TROTTER

IT'S BEEN a happy time at the Cowboys' summer camp. On timing and measuring day Larry Allen bench-pressed a team-record 600 pounds. Then he ran a five-flat 40, at 320 pounds. "I was embarrassed by the season I had last year," Allen said. "I don't even know why I was picked All-Pro."

—Paul Zimmerman, SI, August 17, 1998

> SEVEN-TIME ALL-PRO
> NAMED TO NFL ALL-DECADE TEAMS FOR 1990S AND 2000S

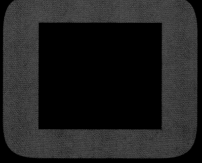

LARRY ALLEN

10 THE

BEST DEFENSIVE LINEMEN

OFFENSIVE PLAYERS MAY ENJOY A DISPROPORTIONATE SHARE OF GRIDIRON GLORY, BUT SAY THIS FOR THE DEFENSE—THEY GET THE BETTER NICKNAMES, AT LEAST AS FAR AS UNITS ARE CONCERNED. JUST IN THIS SECTION ON DEFENSIVE LINEMEN, WE HAVE REPRESENTATIVES OF THE STEEL CURTAIN, THE PURPLE PEOPLE EATERS AND THE FEARSOME FOURSOME. IF ONLY PLAYERS FROM THE NEW YORK SACK EXCHANGE OR THE ORANGE CRUSH HAD MADE IT, THIS SECTION COULD DOUBLE FOR A LIST OF THE BEST UNIT NICKNAMES EVER.

THE CREATIVITY WANES ON THE INDIVIDUAL LEVEL—AMONG THE TOP 10 WE HAVE BOTH A "MINISTER OF DEFENSE" AND A "SECRETARY OF DEFENSE," FOR EXAMPLE. OUR COWBOYS REPRESENTATIVE WAS KNOWN AS "MR. COWBOY." THE MOST MEMORABLE PLAYER NICKNAME HERE IS THE SIMPLEST: MEAN.

WITHIN THE DEFENSIVE LINE THE DIVISION OF LABOR TENDS TO SHINE MORE ATTENTION ON THE ENDS. THEY ARE THE ONES MORE LIKELY TO SACK THE QUARTERBACK—AND THEN DANCE OR POSE IF THE MOOD STRIKES THEM—WHILE THE HUSKIER TACKLES TAKE ON BLOCKERS INSIDE. IN CHOOSING THE TOP 10 LINEMAN THOUGH, THE PANEL, THROUGH NO PLAN OR DESIGN, HONORED TACKLES AND ENDS IN EQUAL NUMBER, WHICH IS A HAPPY COINCIDENCE. ON THIS SIDE OF THE BALL, IT'S ALL ABOUT PUTTING TOGETHER A GOOD UNIT.

1

REGGIE WHITE

EAGLES 1985–1992
PACKERS 1993–1998
PANTHERS 2000

" A physically imposing pass rusher whose forearms sent offensive linemen tumbling. " —DAMON HACK

▸ TWO-TIME NFL DEFENSIVE PLAYER OF THE YEAR
▸ SECOND ALLTIME IN CAREER SACKS WITH 198

WHITE IS the locker room sage to whom the younger Packers turn for inspiration or advice. Older teammates kid him about everything from his habit of calling team meetings—"He calls more meetings than Congress," says safety LeRoy Butler—to his staunch refusal to listen to practically anything but gospel music during his and Butler's shared rides to practice. White's teammates know that his preaching about putting the team first isn't just talk. Despite the meat-grinder nature of the position he plays, until last season he had never missed a nonstrike NFL game. He came into the NFL in 1985 saying that he wanted to be the best defensive lineman ever, and more than a decade later, he's still rolling toward quarterbacks like a wave of lava, burying whatever is in his path. He burns to win. His example has been contagious.

—*Johnette Howard, SI, September 2, 1996*

White was an eight-time All-Pro.

2

JOE GREENE

STEELERS 1969–1981

"The first draft choice of Chuck Noll and the first piece in the Steelers' Super Bowl puzzle. What he did inside made everything work for their defense." —MARK MRAVIC

▸ TWO-TIME NFL DEFENSIVE PLAYER OF THE YEAR
10-TIME PRO BOWL SELECTION

PROFESSOR STUDIES SUPER BOWL, SAYS HAS MYTH QUALITY read the headline in *The* (New Orleans) *Times-Picayune* on Thursday morning before the game. Andy Russell was reading the story aloud at breakfast. "Sociologically speaking," said the lead, "the Super Bowl is a 'propaganda vehicle' which strengthens the American social structure." "I can't stand that stuff!" Joe Greene shouted. "'More than a game, it is a spectacle of mythical proportions which becomes a 'ritualized mass activity,' says Michael R. Real, assistant professor of communications at the University of California at . . . ." "----!" Greene cried. He seized the paper and tore it to shreds. "I'd like to run into that guy," he said of Michael R. Real. The Steelers have a number of stars and leaders of various kinds, but Greene is their sun. The main strength of the team is the defense, of the defense the front four, of the front four, Greene.

—*Roy Blount Jr., SI, February 17, 1975*

Greene was a master at finding angles of attack.

PHOTOGRAPH BY NEIL LEIFER

HE JUST DOES WHAT HE WANTS

He had the skills and he had the size, but it was his outrageous temperament that intimidated opponents, amazed teammates and made Joe Greene a gridiron terror

BY ROY BLOUNT JR.

REENE'S NICKNAME DERIVES from that of his college team, the Mean Green (thought up, incidentally, by a lady named Sidney Sue), but in the pros Greene has done a number of things to deserve it. In his rookie year he was ejected from two games. Once he threw his helmet so hard at a goalpost that pieces of helmet went flying. Another time, after an opposing guard had hit him a good clean block, he seized the offender with one hand on each shoulder pad and kicked him flush between the legs. One day he was glaringly outplaying a good Cincinnati guard named Pat Matson, a 245-pound ball of muscle, until at last Matson developed a bad leg and began limping off the field. Greene ran over and grabbed him before he reached the sideline and tried to coax him back into play, crying, "Come on, I want you out here." "I'll never forget the look on Matson's face," says Steelers defensive captain Andy Russell. There is even a story that once after being thrown out of a game Greene returned to the bench in such a rage that he opened up the equipment manager's tool chest and pulled out a screwdriver. Whatever he intended doing, he had second thoughts and threw it down.

Then there was the time he spit on Dick Butkus. The Bears were humiliating the Steelers. Butkus was blitzing at will, taking long running starts and smashing into the Steeler center just as he snapped the ball, and Greene couldn't stand it any longer. The Steeler offense was on the field. Greene had no business out there, but when Butkus passed within 10 feet of the Steeler bench, Greene bolted out at him, yelling challenges, and drew back and spit full in Butkus's face.

"Butkus didn't look intimidated," says Russell, "but there was Greene obviously wanting to fight him, and fully capable of it, and you could see Butkus thinking, 'This wouldn't be the intelligent thing to do.'" So Butkus turned and walked back into the security of the carnage on the field. When Russell ran into Butkus in the off-season and asked him how he could let a guy spit in his face without retaliating, Butkus said, "I was too busy making All-Pro." Greene—who was himself named All-Pro for the fourth time, and NFL Defensive Player of the Year for the second time, last season—is perhaps the only man alive who could make Butkus come off sounding rather prim.

"Joe's first year," says Russell, "I didn't see how all that emotionalism could be real. It looked like showboating. But I realize now that he's that way. When I get beat I just think, well, I was out of position, I made a mistake, I'll do this to correct it. With Joe, it's in his psyche. It's like it's war, and the other side is winning because they're more violent. And he's the only guy I know, he can be playing a great game himself but if the team's losing he gets into a terrible depression. It could be an exhibition game!"

This season Greene looks different. His upper body is more conventionally muscular, his distinctive spare tire is gone. He has a championship to defend. Does all this mean he will be even better?

"When I dream at night," he says, "I visualize techniques. Some of 'em are just ungodly. It's just cat quickness; run over a guy, hurdle him, jump six feet, put three or four moves on him so he freezes. No flaws in those moves. Perfect push and pull on the guard, jump over the center. Another blocker, slap him aside. Block the ball when the quarterback throws it, catch it and run 99 yards. 'Cause I don't want it to be over quick! The only thing that ever matched the dreams I had was the Super Bowl."

Greene and team founder and owner Art Rooney seemed to enjoy the Super Bowl more than anybody. Rooney, the Chief, was in camp one afternoon this summer, standing beside the practice field. "I knew we were going all the way last year before the playoff game with Oakland when Joe came up to me. He grabbed my hand and said, 'We're gonna get 'em.' That was an emotional moment. I never had a moment like that."

Greene comes over and greets the Chief. They chat for a moment and then Greene moves away, saying, "Enjoy yourself now." It seems an odd thing, but a friendly thing, to say to one's owner.

"That Joe Greene," says the Chief. "He takes you. I've never seen a player lift a team like he does. I just hope he plays out his full years. He's the type of player who wouldn't want to be associated with a team that didn't play all-out."

There was a time when the Chief voiced doubts about Joe Greene. That was when the Steelers had drafted him No. 1 and he was holding out. "Who is he anyway?" the Chief grumbled. "I don't know that he's so good."

A few years later, Art Jr. would gesture at the photographs of old Steeler greats—Ernie Stautner, Whizzer White, Bullet Bill Dudley—covering the walls of his father's office and say, "Someday you'll have to take all these down and throw them away and put up one of Joe Greene."

But he didn't say that when the Chief questioned how good Greene might be. "Joe Greene is as good," is what Art Jr. told his father, "as you can imagine."

And if things stay close enough to being as good as Greene can imagine, pro football may be able to hold on to him—oops, that's the wrong term—may be able to keep him around a while longer. Meanwhile Mean Joe is nervous, and waiting, and doing, one way or another, what he wants to out there. ∎

3

DEACON JONES

RAMS 1961–1971
CHARGERS 1972–1973
REDSKINS 1974

" Thank the Lord for pro football researchers. Studying play-by-play sheets from the era before official sack stats were kept, they found these numbing numbers: In a 14-game season, Jones, from 1963 to 1969, put up 20, 22, 19, 18, 26, 24 and 15 sacks in those seasons. No wonder his old coach George Allen called him the greatest defensive end of all time. " —PETER KING

› TWO-TIME NFL DEFENSIVE PLAYER OF THE YEAR
› EIGHT-TIME PRO BOWL SELECTION

IT SHOULD come as no surprise that when asked about his patented head slap, Jones is only too happy to demonstrate it in slow motion, bringing his left palm flush up against a reporter's right ear, producing a ringing sensation that lingers long after. "You think that rings?" Jones says. "I had a metal plate cut to fit in the palm of my hand." To this day his grin is distilled evil, an offensive tackle's nightmare. "I used to wrap that mother with a wet cast, then let the cast dry. That's what you got upside your head, every 30 seconds."

"I've seen the films," says the Giants' Michael Strahan. "This guy was the best ever. He made defensive end a glamour position."

—SI, August 30, 1999

Jones was credited with inventing the term "sack."

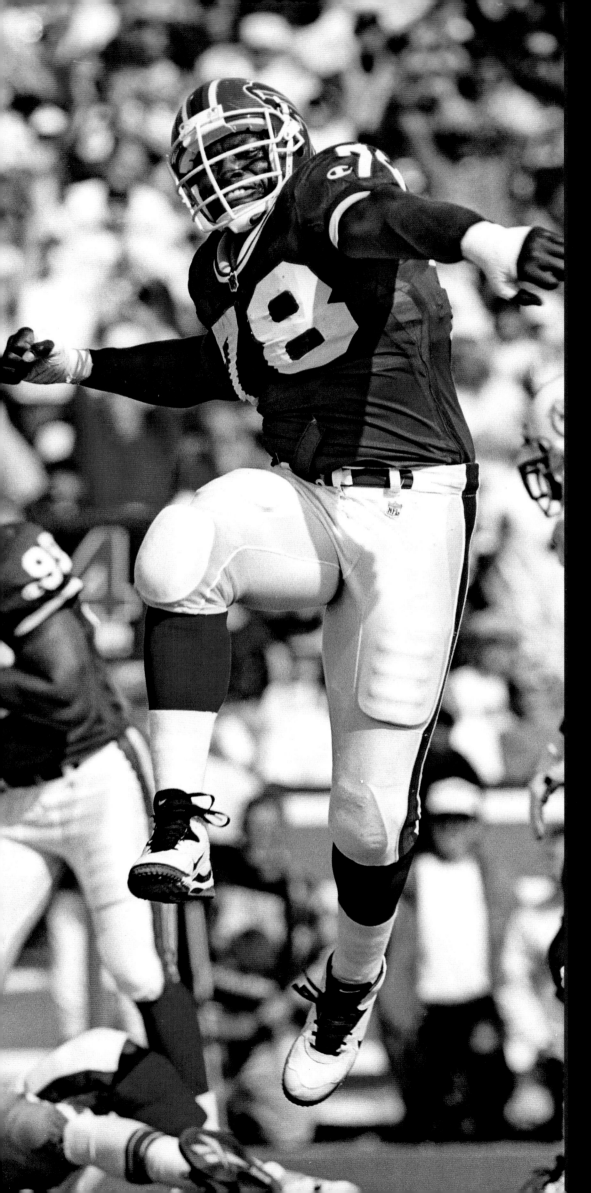

4

BRUCE SMITH

BILLS 1985–1999
REDSKINS 2000–2003

"He may have been 6' 4" and 262 pounds, but his burst off the line was enough to make wide receivers envious." —JIM TROTTER

▸ ALLTIME NFL SACKS LEADER WITH 200
▸ NAMED TO NFL ALL-DECADE TEAMS FOR 1980S AND '90S

"I THINK he's double-jointed," says Bills center Kent Hull. "He'll line up over me, and I'll try to hit him, and there's nothing there—he's going back and coming forward at the same time. There's no way a human being should do what he does." "Sometimes I've been in pass coverage and just laughed," says Bills linebacker Darryl Talley, Smith's good friend and roommate on the road. "The other team will have a tackle and a guard and a back blocking him, and if he beats them, the center comes over to help. It's just funny to see. It's like they're bees and Bruce has got sugar on him, like he's dipped in honey. But the most amazing thing to watch is his rush. Cornelius [Bennett, another Bills linebacker] and I can't figure it out—it's like a speedskater coming around the corner, he's so low to the ground, almost flat, with offensive linemen literally chasing him."

—*Rick Telander, SI, September 2, 1991*

Smith had 13 seasons with double-digit sacks.

PHOTOGRAPH BY RICK STEWART/GETTY IMAGES

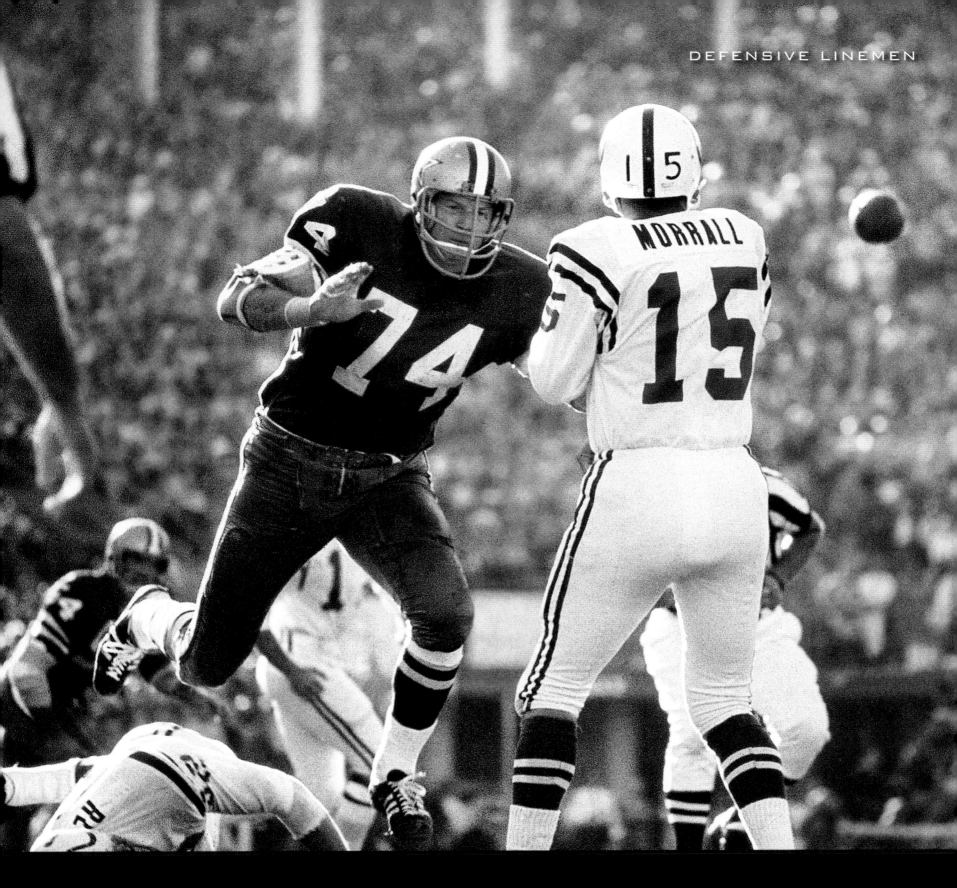

COWBOYS 1961–1974

Lilly was known as Mr. Cowboy.

PHOTOGRAPH BY NEIL LEIFER

5

BOB LILLY

❝ The best defensive tackle in NFL history, Lilly was the interior powerhouse in coach Tom Landry's flex defense. To move the ball on the Cowboys in the '60s and '70s, you had to block Lilly. ❞ —TIM LAYDEN

‣ EIGHT-TIME ALL-PRO, 11-TIME PRO BOWL SELECTION
‣ MISSED JUST ONE GAME IN 14 SEASONS

BOB LILLY IS is one of the very few men who, merely by his personal contribution, can establish the whole character of a game. . . . He is a big, rock-hard man with a face that conceivably could make him a fortune in Western movies when John Wayne retires.

—*Tex Maule, SI, December 18, 1972*

6

ALAN PAGE

VIKINGS 1967–1978
BEARS 1978–1981

"A mainstay of the Vikings' Purple People Eaters, Page punched the clock for 234 consecutive starts, wreaking havoc with an almost controlled fury." —DAMON HACK

▸ FIRST DEFENSIVE PLAYER
VOTED LEAGUE MVP
▸ 173 SACKS, 28 BLOCKED KICKS

THE TURNING POINT was Alan Page. Until he arrived, the Vikings had good outside pressure but were weak at tackle. Page came as an end, a position he had played at Notre Dame, was quickly switched to tackle and went from mediocrity to greatness, and so did the Vikings. "I didn't want to change," Page says, "but now it's the only place I want to play. I was restricted at end. Inside I can do more things, go in more directions." "Carl Eller is probably the premier pass rusher today," says Bob Hollway, the Vikings' defensive coach. "He has strength, quickness and great leverage. Jim Marshall is probably the finest athlete on the defensive team. He has extraordinary balance and quickness. And Page is the most relentless player I've ever seen. He drains himself totally every game, and nobody gets off the ball quicker than he does."

—Pat Putnam, SI, December 14, 1970

Page's Vikings played in four Super Bowls.

THANKS, YOUR HONOR

The author met his childhood hero, who had graduated from being a football star to become a Minnesota Supreme Court justice, and found himself once again flooded with wonder

BY STEVE RUSHIN

THE NATIONAL FOOTBALL LEAGUE was born in an automobile showroom in Canton, Ohio, on Sept. 17, 1920. Alan Page was born in that city nearly 25 years later—on Aug. 7, 1945, in the 72 hours between the bombings of Hiroshima and Nagasaki.

"Born between the bombs," affirms Page, the former Minnesota Vikings and Chicago Bears defensive tackle and 1971's NFL Most Valuable Player, now seated in his office in St. Paul, contemplating the era of his birth. "It's interesting, isn't it, given the significance of those bombs? It's funny you ask, because I *have* thought on occasion about what it all means. I haven't yet come to any conclusions."

Page has the disarming habit of saying "I don't know" when he doesn't know the answer to a question. It's a quality rare among star athletes and unheard of in elected officials. For most of his adult life Page has been one or the other: a gridiron luminary enshrined in 1988 in the Pro Football Hall of Fame—which was under construction in Canton when Page attended Central Catholic High there—and an off-the-field overachiever elected in November 1992 to the Supreme Court of Minnesota, on which he still sits.

"There's a danger for judges to assume they have all the answers," says Page, who seldom submits to interviews, explaining his reluctance to pontificate. "There's a saying one of my former colleagues used quite a bit in talking about this court: 'We're not last because we're right. We're only right because we're last.' I think that's something that you have to keep remembering."

I haven't yet told Page that he was my childhood hero, or that we have met before, nearly 26 years earlier, but I have come here to do just that—to St. Paul, hometown of F. Scott Fitzgerald, who wrote, "Show me a hero and I'll write you a tragedy."

"I've never understood the phenomenon of athlete worship, of how we get our athletic heroes," says Page, 54, when Fitzgerald's line is recited to him. "I can remember from the beginning, by which I mean my sophomore or junior year in high school, being looked on as a good football player, yes, but it went beyond my ability as a football player." People who had never met Page nonetheless began to admire him, and he found this profoundly disquieting. "I like to think that I was a good human being," he continues, "but people couldn't know that from watching me play football. So I kind of rejected the whole hero notion early on.

"There were times," he adds, a trifle unnecessarily, "when I didn't sign autographs."

You couldn't buy a number 88 Vikings jersey in Minnesota in 1974. You could buy the 10 of Fran Tarkenton or the 44 of Chuck Foreman, but if you wanted the 88 of Alan Page your parents had to find a blank purple football shirt and have the numbers ironed on. As far as I know, my parents were the only ones who ever did. The jersey became my security blanket—what psychologists call a "transition object," the item that sustains a child in moments away from his mother. I wore the shirt until it simply disintegrated in the wash.

I grew up in the town in which the Vikings played their home games. Yet even in Bloomington, Minn., in the 1970s, I was alone among my schoolmates in worshipping Page. I knew only that he was genuinely great and that his Afro sometimes resembled Mickey Mouse ears when he removed his helmet. I at once loved Alan Page and knew nothing about him.

Then one unfathomable day in September '74, the month in which I turned eight, a second-grade classmate named Troy Chaika invited me to a Saturday night sleepover at the Airport Holiday Inn, which his father managed and where the Vikings bivouacked on the night before each home game. I could meet the players when they checked in and, if I asked politely, get their autographs.

After an eternity, Saturday came. My mom—God bless her, for it must have pained her beyond words—allowed me to leave the house in my 88 jersey, now literally in tatters.

I took my place in the Holiday Inn lobby—Bic pen in one damp hand, spiral notebook in the other—and recited my mantra rapid-fire to myself, like Hail Marys on a rosary: *"Please Mr. Page may I have your autograph? Please Mr. Page may I have your autograph? Please Mr. Page. . . . "*

Moments before the Vikings' 8 p.m. arrival, my friend's father, the innkeeper, cheerily reminded me to be polite and that the players would in turn oblige me. "Except Page," he added offhandedly, in the oblivious way of adults. "Don't ask him. He doesn't sign autographs."

Which is how I came to be blinking back tears when the Vikings walked into the Holiday Inn.

Page strode purposefully toward the stairwell. I choked as he breezed past; I was unable to speak. Still, I had never seen Page outside a television set and couldn't quite believe he was incarnate, so—my chicken chest heaving, hyperventilation setting in—I continued to watch as he paused at the stairs, turned and looked back at the lobby, evidently having forgotten to pick up his room key.

But he hadn't forgotten any such thing. No, Page walked directly toward me, took the Bic from my trembling hand and signed his name, *Alan Page*, in one grand flourish. He smiled and put his hand on top of my head, as if palming a grapefruit. Then he disappeared into the stairwell, leaving me to stand there in the lobby, slack-jawed, forming a small puddle of admiration and urine. ∎

TEXANS 1952
COLTS 1953–1964, 1966

Marchetti was named to 11 Pro Bowls.

PHOTOGRAPH BY WALTER IOOSS JR.

7

" Lauded as the NFL's best defensive end of its first 50 years, Marchetti was best known for his tenacious pass rush. He broke his leg in the epic 1958 NFL title game, but not before his key stop gave the Colts the chance to win. " —MARK GODICH

► 10-TIME ALL-PRO

GINO MARCHETTI

MARCHETTI developed a new pass rush technique—grabbing and throwing—and relied on quick moves and footwork. "I've heard defensive players say, 'Hell, I didn't even get my uniform dirty playing against Marchetti,'" said Weeb Ewbank, Marchetti's coach with the Colts. "Well, he dirtied a lot of quarterbacks' uniforms."

—Paul Zimmerman, SI, August 28, 2000

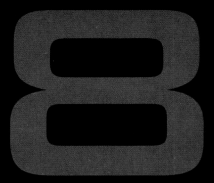

8

MERLIN OLSEN

RAMS 1962–1976

> " Olsen was a dominating defensive tackle whose superb technique and tenacity earned him a record 14 consecutive Pro Bowl selections. " —DON BANKS

▸ PLAYED IN 198 STRAIGHT GAMES
▸ LINCHPIN OF THE "FEARSOME FOURSOME"

AFTER A 15-year career, Olsen went into acting, playing a genial farmer on *Little House on the Prairie*, then an 1870s frontiersman do-gooder in *Father Murphy*. "That's who he was in real life," former Rams teammate Jack Youngblood says. Throughout his career, all in L.A., he took it upon himself to teach new players how to play the right way. A 1982 Hall of Fame inductee, he returned to Canton often to work with Hall of Fame Enterprises, which raises money for indigent former players. "He looked at the game and said, 'Darn it, this is wrong,' " Youngblood says. " 'We've got to treat retired players better.' " As one of the players in the Rams' famed Fearsome Foursome, Olsen's bullish presence helped the men to his left—Deacon Jones and later Youngblood—earn busts in Canton. The mark of a good teammate is to make those around you better, and Olsen did that during, and after, his life in football.

—*Peter King, SI, March 22, 2010*

Olsen dominated through smarts as well as size.

9

LEE ROY SELMON

" He was powerful enough to bull rush interior linemen and quick enough to get around tackles. His greatness was that he made plays with little talent around him, when offenses could game-plan for him almost exclusively. " —JIM TROTTER

THE BUCS are unbeaten, untied and unbelievable. Not bad for a team that has known only one place—last. . . . How do the Bucs take their sudden success? "Well," says Lee Roy Selmon, "I don't have to go to the drive-in window at McDonald's anymore," he says. "Now I feel safe walking right into the restaurant."

—*Joe Marshall, SI, October 1, 1979*

▸ 1979 NFL DEFENSIVE PLAYER OF THE YEAR
▸ 78½ CAREER SACKS

A back injury cut short Selmon's career.

PHOTOGRAPH BY JAMES DRAKE

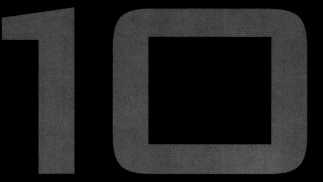

WARREN SAPP

BUCCANEERS 1995–2003
RAIDERS 2004–2007

"A rare interior defensive lineman who could rush the passer and stop the run with equal ability." —DAMON HACK

▸ NAMED TO NFL ALL-DECADE TEAMS FOR 1990S AND 2000S
▸ 96½ CAREER SACKS

HE'S GLIB, and cocky and smart, and as talented as any defensive lineman in football. It has been two months since his 25th birthday and six weeks since the end of his breakout season, in which he had 10½ sacks and displayed both an uncanny ability to play his best in big games and an unwillingness to let anyone else have the last word. Last August, Sapp single-handedly destroyed San Francisco in Tampa Bay's season-opening 13–6 upset. He had 2½ sacks and removed from the game a future wing of the Pro Football Hall of Fame. His first-quarter sack of Steve Young resulted in Young's suffering a concussion; his second-quarter tackle of wideout Jerry Rice, a play on which Sapp was penalized for grabbing the face mask, resulted in Rice's tearing ligaments in his left knee. When word reached him later in the season that Rice was upset because he hadn't called to apologize, Sapp had a question: "What should I be apologizing for?"

—Austin Murphy, SI, March 9, 1998

Sapp was the 1999 NFL Defensive Player of the Year.

PHOTOGRAPH BY GARY BOGDON

10 THE

BEST LINEBACKERS

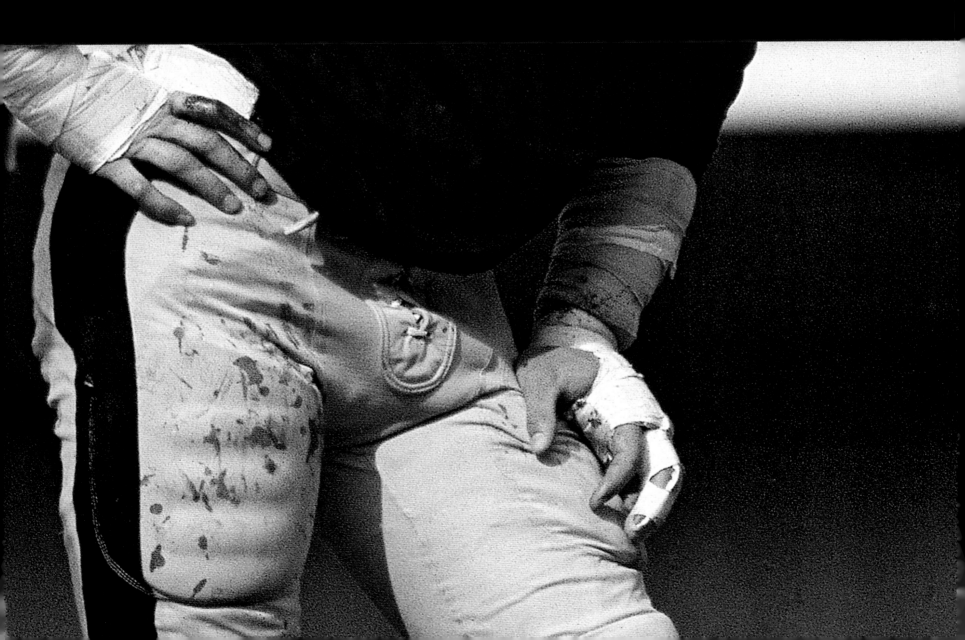

IN MOST OF OUR PLAYER CATEGORIES YOU SEE STYLISTIC DIFFERENCES BETWEEN THE MEN WHO MAKE UP THE TOP RANKS. AMONGST LINEBACKERS, NOT SO MUCH. HERE IT'S A STRAIGHT MONSTER MASH. TRUE, AS OUR PANELISTS NOTED, THESE WERE MONSTERS WHO STUDIED FILM AND WHO IN MANY CASES FUNCTIONED AS THE CEREBRAL QUARTERBACKS OF THEIR DEFENSES. BUT STILL, IT'S A SCARY BUNCH. SOME SAMPLES OF THE ENCOMIUMS OFFERED BY OUR PANELISTS: "AS NASTY AS THEY CAME." "A VIOLENT TACKLER WHO LIVED TO DISH OUT PERCUSSIVE HITS." "THE MOST FEARED HITTER EVER TO PLAY." "A DAWG!"

THE TOP FOUR LINEBACKERS MADE A PARTICULAR IMPRESSION, ATTRACTING VOTES WITH A DEEPER UNANIMITY THAN FOUND IN ANY OTHER CATEGORY. OUR NO. 1 MAN, LAWRENCE TAYLOR, WAS RANKED FIRST ON SIX OF THE SEVEN BALLOTS, AND OUR NEXT TWO FINISHERS, DICK BUTKUS AND RAY LEWIS, DID NOT APPEAR LOWER THAN FOURTH. JACK LAMBERT, AT NO. 4, HAD SIMILARLY BROAD SUPPORT.

YOU MIGHT SAY THAT A GROUP OF 'BACKERS FOR A DREAM 3–4 DEFENSE HAD BEEN CLEARLY IDENTIFIED, IF NOT FOR THE AWKWARDNESS OF HAVING THREE MIDDLE LINEBACKERS IN THE GROUP. WHO WOULD HAVE TAKEN CHARGE—LEWIS, BUTKUS OR LAMBERT? IMAGINE THEM FIGHTING IT OUT. THAT WOULD BE A COMPELLING CONCEPT FOR A PAY-PER-VIEW. AND WE ALREADY HAVE QUOTES FOR THE POSTER.

1

LAWRENCE TAYLOR

GIANTS 1981–1993

" The most frightening pass rusher ever to play the game. " —DAMON HACK

▸ THREE-TIME NFL DEFENSIVE PLAYER OF THE YEAR
▸ 1986 NFL MVP

"WHAT MAKES LT so great, what makes him so aggressive, is his total disregard for his body," says Bill Belichick, the Giants' defensive coordinator. Taylor seems to get a morbid, masochistic delight out of his ferocious tackles. "There's a sack, and then, there's a sack!" LT explains. "You run up behind the quarterback. He doesn't see you. You put your helmet in his back. Wrap yourself around him. Throw him to the ground . . . and the coach comes running out and asks, 'Are you all right?'" And when he's not delivering the hits, he enjoys watching them. "In defensive meetings, while we're studying film, all of a sudden Lawrence will say, 'Ah, Bill. Run that play back again,'" Belichick says. "And I'll realize he's looking at some guy 20 yards away from the ball—a wide receiver who was knocked off the screen by a defensive back. I've even seen him get his thrills watching one of our own guys get dusted."

—Jill Lieber, SI, January 26, 1987

Taylor had 132 ½ career sacks.

PHOTOGRAPHS BY JOHN BIEVER (LEFT) AND JOHN W. MCDONOUGH

2

DICK BUTKUS

BEARS 1965–1973

"His name is synonymous with his position and brutal, old school football. Lost in the very real memory of Butkus's violence is his remarkable athleticism. He played the entire width of the field and also intercepted 22 passes in a career blunted to nine years by knee injuries." —TIM LAYDEN

▸ SEVEN-TIME ALL-PRO
▸ 27 CAREER FUMBLE RECOVERIES

BEARS FANS still think of him as the ultimate in ursine violence. Take the folks at a bar called Chances R on a recent afternoon. The barkeep is a mountainous Irishman named Larry Mahoney, equally adept at bouncing a drunken housepainter or trilling a ballad in his fine tenor. "Hey, let's play a word game," Mahoney chirps to his assembled parishioners on this particular day. "What do you think of when I say 'Dick Butkus'?"

"Killer," say a young long-haired couple named Bill and Dee, whose motorcycle had just been blown over by a line squall. "Bull," says another patron. Others chime in: "Wild boar." "King Kong." "Mayor Daley." "Mean and nasty." "Elizabeth Taylor." Elizabeth Taylor? "I can see it," says Mahoney. "Butkus has the same kind of ego, the same self-dedication or cruelty or something."

—Robert F. Jones, SI, September 21, 1970

Butkus was defined by an unquantifiable ferocity.

3

RAY LEWIS

RAVENS 1996–PRESENT

" He chases down ballcarriers as if he were a human Pac-Man. Plus, his pregame sermons are enough to make spectators want to go out and hit someone. " —JIM TROTTER

▸ TWO-TIME NFL DEFENSIVE PLAYER OF THE YEAR
▸ 13-TIME PRO BOWL SELECTION

WHEN MIKE SINGLETARY took over as Ravens linebackers coach in 2003, Lewis was playing at a level few had ever seen. But Lewis begged for instruction. Whatever Singletary said, Lewis soaked up; once he suggested Lewis play more on the balls of his feet, and in the next practice Lewis collapsed because his calves were cramping.

—S.L. Price, SI, November 13, 2006

4

JACK LAMBERT

STEELERS 1974–1984

" Menacing in demeanor, able to play the run or the pass with equal skill, Lambert was the heart and soul of Pittsburgh's great Steel Curtain defense of the '70s. " —DON BANKS

▸ 1976 NFL DEFENSIVE PLAYER OF THE YEAR
▸ NINE CONSECUTIVE PRO BOWL SELECTIONS

ONE PITTSBURGH sportswriter has called Lambert "the Nureyev of linebackers," a clear reference to his ability and balance in the middle of muddle. "Who's Nureyev?" Lambert asks, deadpan. The ballet dancer is defined for him. "I don't know if that's a compliment or an insult," he says, after pondering the information. "But I guess those guys are pretty good athletes. I'll take it as a compliment." Other oldtime Steelers fans liken Lambert to the tough players of the team's early, losing years—men like Ernie Stautner and Bobby Layne, who hurt you when they played you, win or lose. "I like that comparison better," Lambert says. "That's what I'd really have liked, to play back in those days even though the money was hardly there. They played for the game—and to hit. Cripes, 50 bucks a game, but they loved it."

—*Robert F. Jones, SI, July 12, 1976*

Lambert was Pittsburgh's defensive captain.

PHOTOGRAPH BY WALTER IOOSS JR.

5

WILLIE LANIER

CHIEFS 1967–1977

" His nickname was Contact. Is there a better moniker for a middle linebacker? " —JIM TROTTER

▸ EIGHT-TIME PRO BOWL OR AFL ALL-STAR GAME SELECTION
▸ 28 CAREER INTERCEPTIONS, 17 FUMBLE RECOVERIES

IN THE '67 draft the Chiefs took Notre Dame middle linebacker Jim Lynch (who was white) with the 47th pick and Lanier three spots later. In camp that summer coach Hank Stram told the two that the best player would win the starting job. "I wondered if there was going to be an open competition," says Lanier, "but from the start, it was refreshing to see there was a purity about the competition." That season Lanier become pro football's first black starting middle linebacker. "Imagine if there had been no AFL and no Kansas City Chiefs," says Lanier. "Maybe I have to wait five years for my chance [to play in the NFL], for the chance to play middle linebacker. And five years in football is an eternity." Before he died in 2006, team owner Lamar Hunt said that the Chiefs "never pretended we made a conscious effort to open things up [racially]. We made a conscious effort to go out and find the best players anywhere that we could."

—Peter King, SI, July 13, 2009

Lanier's hitting complemented his great agility.

6

MIKE SINGLETARY

" Singletary is another iconic figure in NFL history, exhaling freezing breath into the Soldier Field air. More importantly, he was the on-field brains in Buddy Ryan's "46" defense and one of the best tacklers ever. " —TIM LAYDEN

▸ TWO-TIME NFL DEFENSIVE PLAYER OF THE YEAR
▸ EIGHT-TIME ALL-PRO

"I DON'T FEEL PAIN from a hit like that," Singletary says [of a punishing shot on running back Eric Dickerson]. "What I feel is joy. Joy for the tackle. Joy for myself. Joy for the other man. You understand me; I understand you. It's football, it's middle linebacking. It's just . . . good for everybody.'"
—*Rick Telander, SI, January 27, 1986*

Singletary's focus showed in his signature stare.

7
CHUCK
BEDNARIK

EAGLES 1949–1962

" Perhaps the last great two-way player, Bednarik was a crushing tackler who laid out Giants halfback Frank Gifford in 1960 in one of the league's most devastating hits ever. " —DON BANKS

▸ ALSO PLAYED CENTER
▸ NINE-TIME ALL-PRO

A TITILLATING sidelight to this game was the possibility that Bednarik, the Eagle linebacker and offensive center, might be left for dead by one or another of the Giant team in revenge for Bednarik's chilling tackle of Frank Gifford two weeks ago. Bednarik, hitting Gifford with a blindside tackle late in the game, left the Giant halfback cold as snow. The Philadelphian danced a happy, heathen victory jig after Gifford's fumble had been recovered by the Eagles, thus ensuring their victory. His histrionics were misconstrued in some quarters as unseemly joy. "I got lots of letters," Bednarik said. "All good except for one from a lady in Texas. Then I got lots of telephone calls including one at 2:30 in the morning from some woman hollering at me. I disconnected the phone. I sent Gifford some fruit in the hospital, and I wrote him a three-page letter. It was a good tackle."

—Tex Maule, SI, December 5, 1960

Bednarik rejoiced over the fallen Gifford.

PHOTOGRAPH BY JOHN G. ZIMMERMAN

CONCRETE CHARLIE

As players become increasingly specialized in their tasks, it only serves to highlight the remarkable achievements of Chuck Bednarik on both sides of the ball

BY JOHN SCHULIAN

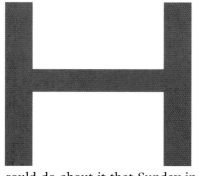

E WENT DOWN HARD, LEFT in a heap by a crackback block as naked as it was vicious. Pro football was like that in 1960, a gang fight in shoulder pads, its violence devoid of the high-tech veneer it has today. The crackback was legal, and all the Philadelphia Eagles could do about it that Sunday in Cleveland was carry a linebacker named Bob Pellegrini off on his shield.

Buck Shaw, a gentleman coach in this ruffian's pastime, watched for as long as he could, then he started searching the Eagle sideline for someone to throw into the breach. His first choice was already banged up, and after that the standard 38-man NFL roster felt as tight as a hangman's noose. Looking back, you realize that Shaw had only one choice all along.

"Chuck," he said, "get in there."

And Charles Philip Bednarik, who already had a full-time job as Philadelphia's offensive center and a part-time job selling concrete after practice, headed onto the field without a word. Just the way his father had marched off to the open-hearth furnaces at Bethlehem Steel on so many heartless mornings. Just the way Bednarik himself had climbed behind the machine gun in a B-24 for 30 missions as a teenager fighting in World War II. It was a family tradition: Duty called, you answered.

Chuck Bednarik was 35 years old, still imposing at 6' 3" and 235 pounds, but also the father of one daughter too many to be what he really had in mind—retired. Jackie's birth the previous February gave him five children, all girls, and more bills than he thought he could handle without football. So here he was in his 12th NFL season, telling himself he was taking it easy on his creaky legs by playing center after all those years as an All-Pro linebacker. The only time he intended to move back to defense was in practice, when he wanted to work up a little extra sweat.

And now, five games into the season, this: Jim Brown over there in the Cleveland huddle, waiting to trample some fresh meat, and Bednarik trying to decipher the defensive terminology the Eagles had installed in the two years since he was their middle linebacker. Chuck Weber had his old job now, and Bednarik found himself asking what the left outside linebacker was supposed to do on passing plays. "Take the second man out of the backfield," Weber said. That was as fancy as it would get. Everything else would be about putting the wood to Jim Brown.

Bednarik nodded and turned to face a destiny that went far beyond emergency duty at linebacker. He was taking his first step toward a place in NFL history as the kind of player they don't make anymore.

He really was the last of a breed. For 58½ minutes in the NFL's 1960 championship game, he held his ground in the middle of Philly's Franklin Field, a force of nature determined to postpone the christening of the Green Bay Packers' dynasty. "I didn't run down on kickoffs, that's all," Bednarik says. The rest of that frosty Dec. 26, on both offense and defense, he played with the passion that crested when he wrestled Packers fullback Jim Taylor to the ground one last time and held him there until the final gun punctuated the Eagles' 17–13 victory.

Philadelphia hasn't ruled pro football in the 33 years since then, and pro football hasn't produced a player with the combination of talent, hunger and opportunity to duplicate what Bednarik did. It is a far different game now, of course, its complexities seeming to increase exponentially every year, but the athletes playing it are so much bigger and faster than Bednarik and his contemporaries that surely someone with the ability to go both ways must dwell among them. And don't try to make a case for Deion Sanders by bringing up the turn he took at wide receiver last season. Bednarik has heard that kind of noise before. "This writer in St. Louis calls me a few years back and starts talking about some guy out there, some wide receiver," he says, making no attempt to hide his disdain for both the position and the player. "Yeah, Roy Green, that was his name. This writer's talking about how the guy would catch passes and then go in on the Cardinals' umbrella defense, and I tell him, 'Don't give me that b.s. You've got to play every down.' Had Green come along 30 years earlier, he might have been turned loose to meet Bednarik's high standards. It is just as easy to imagine Walter Payton having shifted from running back to safety, or Lawrence Taylor moving from linebacker to tight end. But that day is long past, for the NFL of the '90s is a monument to specialization.

"No way in hell any of them can go both ways," Bednarik insists. "They don't want to. They're afraid they'll get hurt. And the money's too big, that's another thing. They'd just say, 'Forget it, I'm already making enough.'"

He nurtures the resentment he is sure every star of his era shares, feeding it with the dollar figures he sees in the sports pages every day, priming it with the memory that his fattest contract with the Eagles paid him $25,000, in 1962, his farewell season.

"People laugh when they hear what I made," he says. "I tell them, 'Hey, don't laugh at me. I could do everything but eat a football.'" Even when he was in his 50s, brought back by then coach Dick Vermeil to show the struggling Eagles what a champion looked like, Bednarik was something to behold. He walked into training camp, bent over the first ball he saw and whistled a strike back through his legs to a punter unused to such service from the team's long snappers. "And you know the amazing thing?" Vermeil says. "Chuck didn't look." ∎

PACKERS 1958–1972

Nitschke was a relentless leader.

" One of the game's great intimidators, Nitschke was a glowering and fierce presence in the middle of the Packers defense, but he was surprisingly agile and athletic as well, picking off 25 passes in his career and tackling from sideline to sideline. " —DON BANKS

BALDING, almost toothless, playing in a seemingly perpetual rage, Nitschke would have been a caricature of the maniacal middleman except for how well he performed. He ran the defense for all of Vince Lombardi's five championship teams. It was Nitschke's traffic-cop command and surprising athleticism that defined their take-no-prisoners defense.

—Paul Zimmerman, SI, March 16, 1998

▸ 1962 TITLE GAME MVP
▸ 23 CAREER FUMBLE RECOVERIES

RAY
NITSCHKE

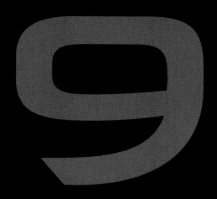

9

BRONKO NAGURSKI

BEARS 1930–1937, 1943

" A two-way player who was punishing as a running back and a linebacker. He came out of a five-year retirement to help lead Chicago to the 1943 title. " —MARK GODICH

‣ SEVEN-TIME ALL-PRO
‣ THREW TWO TDS IN 1933 NFL TITLE GAME

I ASKED a former teammate, quarterback Sid Luckman, about Nagurski. "A monster," Luckman said. "The neck, the hands. They measured him for a championship ring in 1943, when he made his comeback, and his ring size was 19½." I watched film of Nagurski. He would get into rages. He would attack people, both offensively and defensively, where he played end or backed up the line. After I had read about how he was impossible for one man to stop, one thing puzzled me. Where were the big numbers? He averaged less than 10 carries a game. I asked him about that. "[George] Halas stockpiled backs," Nagurski said, "and he believed in spreading it around. Plus he wanted to keep me fresh for defense, where I'd put in a full afternoon. How many of today's 1,000-yard runners would like to spend half the game playing defense?"

—Paul Zimmerman, SI, November 24, 1997

Nagurski defined ruggedness in the early NFL.

PHOTOGRAPH BY AP

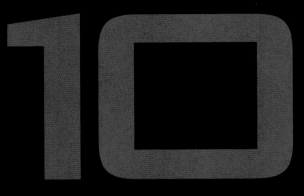

JOE SCHMIDT

LIONS 1953–1965

"A seventh-round draft choice of the Lions, Schmidt helped revolutionize the middle linebacker position. He had an uncanny ability to read plays. Always around the ball, he recovered eight fumbles in 1955, a record for a 12-game season." —MARK GODICH

▸ NINE-TIME ALL-PRO
▸ 24 CAREER INTERCEPTIONS

FOR A WEEK Schmidt had been tempting me to try the fake 11 in the game in Pontiac—a quarterback draw play it is, and it means the quarterback accepts the horror that comes when the linebackers recover from the fake and pick him up. There weren't many quarterbacks around who called this play. Schmidt did a little pantomime there in the training room of a nervous quarterback working the fake 11— poised behind his center, then dancing back in his stockinged feet, pumping his arm hard, then running fast in place, head down, emulating the dash for the line, then looking up and screaming as the imaginary linebackers converged, following it all with a concussive sound he made by exploding his palms together and the expiring, anguished cry of a broken quarterback. "Oh, yes," he called out. "You got to get him to try that one."

—*George Plimpton, SI, September 7, 1964*

Schmidt was the original defensive quarterback.

PHOTOGRAPH BY MARVIN E. NEWMAN

10

THE

BEST DEFENSIVE BACKS

THE YOUNGEST ATHLETE IN THIS BOOK, BY FAR, IS A DEFENSIVE BACK. WHILE OUR PANELISTS GENERALLY HESITATED TO EMBRACE HOT YOUNG THINGS, THIS IS THE ONE INSTANCE IN WHICH THEY CONFERRED ALLTIME GREATNESS ON A PLAYER WHOSE RÉSUMÉ IS SO FLAGRANTLY PARTIAL.

THIS SPEAKS TO THE TALENT OF JETS CORNERBACK DARRELLE REVIS, WHO HAD BEEN IN THE LEAGUE ALL OF FIVE SEASONS AT THE TIME OF THE VOTE ("HE USES PHYSICAL PLAY TO TURN RECEIVERS INTO REAL-LIFE LON CHANEYS—INVISIBLE MEN," DECLARED ONE ADMIRER, JIM TROTTER) BUT ALSO TO THE RISING VALUE OF DEFENSIVE BACKS IN A PASS-HAPPY LEAGUE. REVIS IS ONE OF THREE ACTIVE PLAYERS TO MAKE THIS LIST, WHILE A FOURTH, PITTSBURGH SAFETY TROY POLAMALU, FINISHED JUST OUTSIDE THE VOTING. THE CATEGORIES OF QUARTERBACK, WIDE RECEIVER AND TIGHT END ARE ALL STOCKED WITH CURRENT OR RECENTLY RETIRED PLAYERS, SO IT ONLY MAKES SENSE THAT THE MEN WHO STOP THEM SHOULD BE HERE AS WELL.

IN REVIS'S CASE, HE HELPED MAKE A NAME FOR HIMSELF IN THE AFC TRENCHES, SHORT-CIRCUITING THE OTHERWISE ELECTRIC CONNECTION BETWEEN THE PATRIOTS' TOM BRADY AND RANDY MOSS. THOSE MEN WERE OUR NO. 3 QUARTERBACK AND RECEIVER, RESPECTIVELY. WHAT BETTER WAY FOR A DEFENSIVE BACK TO MAKE A CASE THAT HE BELONGS IN THE TOP 10 TOO?

1

RONNIE LOTT

49ERS 1981–1990
RAIDERS 1991–1992
JETS 1993–1994

"An All-Pro at three distinct secondary positions—cornerback, free safety, strong safety—Lott was capable of playing man-to-man defense on the best receivers or getting the best running backs to the ground. He deserves to be in the argument for best alltime player, regardless of position." —TIM LAYDEN

- ▸ 63 CAREER INTERCEPTIONS
- ▸ NAMED TO NFL ALL-DECADE TEAMS FOR 1980S AND '90S

LOTT LAUGHS when asked about his hardest hit, a head-on-collision with Falcons running back William Andrews in 1982. "I ran 10 yards straight at him, as hard as I could," he recalls. "He didn't see me. The whole time I was saying to myself, This is it! Then, boom. I slid off of him like butter. I hit the ground, and he didn't go down. I was thinking, 'What?' People are always asking where I'll be 10 years from now, if I'll be able to walk," continues Lott. "I'm just thankful to be here today. It's not important to be known as someone who hits hard. It's important to be thought of as a guy who gives his all. Sure, I'm taking a risk of getting injured or being burned. But one thing you don't do is sell out on your heart."

—Jill Lieber, SI, January 23, 1989

Lott twice led the NFL in interceptions.

PHOTOGRAPH BY MICKEY PFLEGER

2

DEION SANDERS

FALCONS 1989–1993
49ERS 1994
COWBOYS 1995–1999
REDSKINS 2000
RAVENS 2004–2005

> " A showman whose playmaking ability at cornerback was without peer. When he made an interception, the fun was just beginning. " —DAMON HACK

▸ NAMED TO NFL ALL-DECADE TEAM FOR 1990S AS BOTH CORNERBACK AND PUNT RETURNER
▸ 1994 NFL DEFENSIVE PLAYER OF THE YEAR

ISAAC BRUCE, the Rams rookie receiver, looked at Sanders across the line, and what he saw was something altogether different from what he had been expecting. Standing there as mute as a scarecrow in a deep winter field, Sanders was smiling.

He was smiling as if he and Bruce were old pals, linked to each other in ways too mysterious to describe.

"That's all he did," Bruce says. "Smiled. Then later I'm running my routes, and instead of giving me a hard time, he's kind of coaching me. He's saying, 'Look, you need to stay low when coming out of your cuts, so I won't be able to tell where you're going.' " Bruce took Sanders's advice, but alas, he finished the game without any catches while Sanders was covering him.

—John Ed Bradley, SI, October 9, 1995

Sanders personified the shutdown corner.

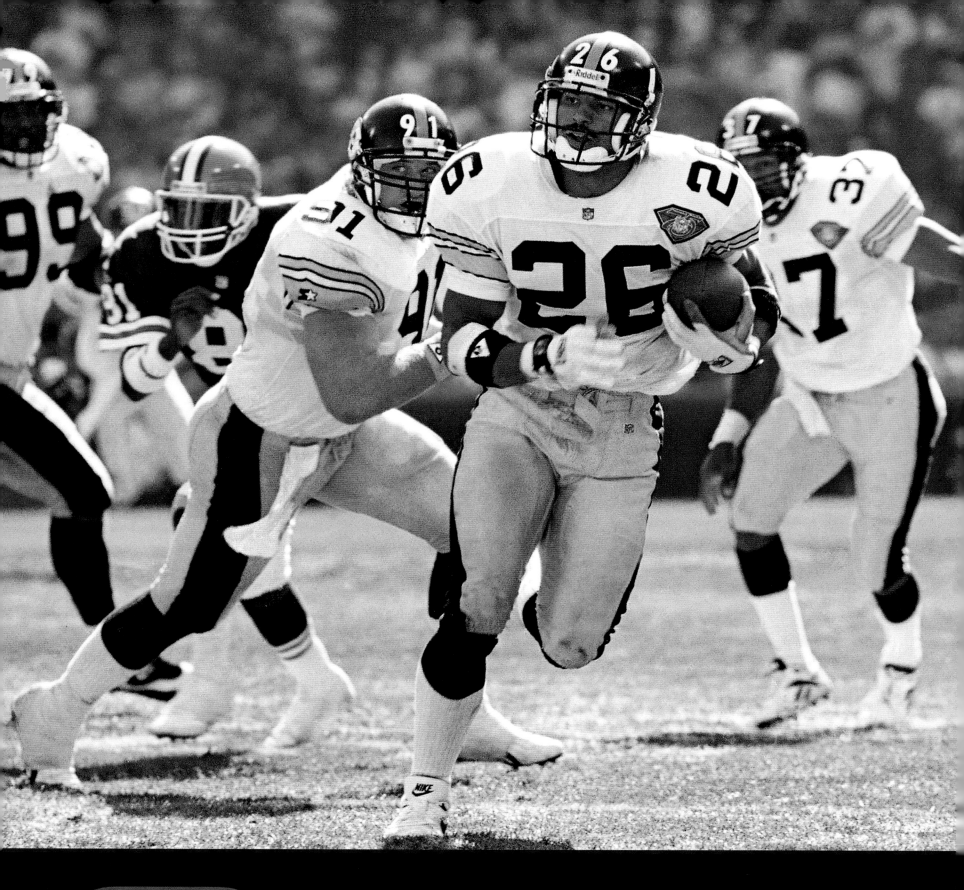

Woodson was the 1993 NFL Defensive Player of the Year.

STEELERS 1987–1996
49ERS 1997
RAVENS 1998–2001
RAIDERS 2002–2003

" He was Charles Woodson before Charles Woodson. When he lost a half step later in his career, he moved to safety and became a Pro Bowl performer there. " —JIM TROTTER

WOODSON WAS magnificent, returning two interceptions for a total of 73 yards, deflecting three other passes and making seven tackles. Playing left corner, Woodson looked like a combination blitzing outside linebacker, sticky-coverage corner and punishing strong safety.

—Peter King, SI, September 14, 1992

ROD WOODSON

▸ CAREER LEADER IN INTERCEPTION RETURN YARDS

4

DICK LANE

RAMS 1952–1953
CARDINALS 1954–1959
LIONS 1960–1965

" He set an early standard for NFL defensive backs with his record 14 interceptions in the 12-game season of 1952, and his blend of height and athleticism made him one of the game's most spectacular playmakers. " —DON BANKS

▸ SEVEN-TIME PRO BOWL SELECTION
▸ 68 CAREER INTERCEPTIONS

HE CAME up in an era when cornerbacks were still called defensive halfbacks. He played a style of football that was born of poverty and desperation. Years later Night Train Lane's technique would acquire the catchy name bump and run, but when he came into the NFL, in 1952, his approach was as elemental as the game itself. Lock on a receiver, rough him up down the field, try to knock him off his pattern, and if he still caught the ball, take his head off. Lane was the most feared corner in the game. A big guy at 6'2" and more than 200 pounds, he was known for the Night Train Necktie, a neck-high tackle that the league eventually banned. "I've never seen anyone hit like him," Packers Hall of Famer Herb Adderley once said. "I mean, take them down, whether it be Jim Brown or Jim Taylor."

—*Paul Zimmerman, SI, February 11, 2002*

Night Train was a devastating tackler.

PHOTOGRAPH BY BETTMANN / CORBIS

CHARLES
WOODSON

RAIDERS 1998–2005
PACKERS 2006–PRESEN

" Woodson broke in with the Raid
as a lockdown defender. As the
leader of the Packers a decade lat
he became a blitzer and freelanc
ball hawk. " —TIM LAYDEN

▸ 2009 NFL DEFENSIVE
  PLAYER OF THE YEAR
▸ EIGHT-TIME PRO BOWL
  SELECTION

SITTING ON the couch in his town
house, he gestures to the TV scree
and says, "That's my man right ther
He's referring to Victor Newman, h
favorite character on *The Young an
the Restless*, whom Woodson admi
for obvious reasons. "The more criti
the situation gets," says Eric Braede
the actor who portrays Newman, "t
more ice-cold Victor becomes." Th
scary thing is, Woodson expects t
get colder as he gets older. He say
his rookie year was "very average
and views the Hall of Fame as a
plausible destination. "I don't thin
that's too heavy," he says. "I can't se
happening any other way." You look
a grin, a hint that the hyperbole is f
effect, but instead his eyes narrow a
his voice turns frosty. "Put a bull an
a cat in an arena and have them ru
at each other," he says. "What do y
think the bull is thinking? When I co
somebody, that's what I'm thinkin

—Michael Silver, SI, August 30, 1999

Woodson has scored 11 touchdowns off interce

ED REED

RAVENS 2002–PRESENT

n elite ball hawk, Reed has scored 12
er touchdowns and is the only player
eague history to reach the end zone
n interception, fumble recovery, punt
k and punt return." —DON BANKS

▶ 2004 NFL DEFENSIVE
PLAYER OF THE YEAR
7 CAREER INTERCEPTIONS

REED IS no less than "a unique,
nce-in-a-lifetime football player,"
according to Ravens defensive
coordinator Greg Mattison, and
his career statistics bear out
that claim. His 61 combined
regular-season and postseason
terceptions rank him 12th alltime.
e has played three fewer seasons
than anyone else in the top 18.
More important, says Mattison, is
ow Reed's experience rubs off on
his teammates—how he explains
to them the way a quarterback
hinks and an offense works; how
e can create all those turnovers
without gambling outside the
ructure of the defense. In 2010 his
mportance to the Ravens has been
s evident as ever. In the six games
eed missed while recovering from
his hip surgery, Baltimore, with a
patchwork secondary, produced
ust three interceptions. In the 10
games Reed played, the Ravens
picked off 16 passes.

—Ben Reiter, SI, January 17, 2011

d has returned interceptions 106 and 107 yards.

PHOTOGRAPH BY SIMON BRUTY

LOOK AT ME NOW

A difficult decision to leave his parents' home as a teenager and move in with a high school secretary set Ed Reed on the path to becoming to one of the best safeties in NFL history

BY JEFFRI CHADIHA

OUTSIDE A MOVIE THEATER IN La Place, La., a middle-aged white woman was ranting at a police officer, inching closer and closer as if bent on getting arrested. Jeanne Hall rarely exploded in rage, but she'd had it. First the cashier declined to sell tickets to Hall for the six children going to the movie with her. Recent rowdiness, the cashier explained, had prompted the theater to place restrictions on unaccompanied children entering the establishment after 7 p.m. Then the officer, called over by the cashier after Hall protested, told her she could take her daughter and two sons into the theater, but the three teenage black males could not be admitted because Hall was not their parent or guardian.

Never mind that the officer was upholding a theater rule, Hall was cursing him for refusing to accept her explanation that those three boys were around her house so much they might as well have been family. She was digging in for a fight, causing a commotion that startled other customers as they passed by. Then one of the boys, 16-year-old Ed Reed, stepped in. "Let's go," he calmly said to Hall. "We can rent a movie at home."

Even at that age Reed could read a situation and react deftly. He could see that the officer would never understand the relationship he had with this woman he called Mama as easily as she called him Son. It was time to move on. There were bigger obstacles to get past in life.

Early in his junior year he made a decision that would change his life: He asked Jeanne Hall, the secretary for the assistant principal at Destrehan, if he could move in with her family. Hall was a mother figure to many of the school's discipline cases, several of whom were athletes. She offered her home, a modest house in a middle-class neighborhood less than a mile from the Reeds', as an alternative to roaming the streets and getting into more trouble; it was a place where aimless kids could hang out and study, play video games or watch movies. "Ed didn't have the self-discipline to get his academics straightened out by himself," says Hall, who agreed to take him in. "He knew we would challenge him."

Now Reed had to persuade his parents to let him move out. Karen was 13 when she lost her mother to breast cancer and Ed Sr. was 19 when his father died of lung cancer. A close-knit family was important to both parents, but they also wanted the best for their children. Only a few months earlier Ed Sr. had told him, "Son, you don't ever want to make a living doing what I do." He and Karen realized Ed Jr. had a chance to go to college on a football scholarship, and they could see he wasn't going to make it unless his grades—and work habits—improved. After assuring his parents that he would come home often, Reed got their consent for the move. "It was hard to let Ed go, but I didn't want to tell him that," Karen says. "I knew Mrs. Hall, and I knew she wanted to help him."

Jeanne and her husband, Walter, a foreman at an oil refinery, provided Reed with a structured lifestyle. After football practice each night, for example, he usually napped until 9:30, then studied with Jeanne until midnight. His grades gradually improved. He was becoming more confident in his schoolwork, so much so that one night late in his junior year he shooed away Jeanne when she tried to help him with his math homework. When she checked his work later, Jeanne found all correct answers. "I actually can learn," Reed told her.

Since then, Reed says, he's been obsessed with realizing his potential. His motto became: Listen, learn, then lead. "There was something inside of me that [the Halls] brought out," Reed says. "And once I realized what I could do, I wanted to take it to another level. I saw if I did things right, people would follow me."

Reed was recruited by Miami, LSU and Tulane. He chose Miami, where he was a two-time All-America safety, helped the Hurricanes win the 2001 national title and graduated with a degree in liberal arts. By his senior year he had established himself as one of Miami's leaders, on and off the field. Each weekday morning before the season he would wake up at 5:30 and direct his teammates through their conditioning drills. At night he would join his friends and teammates at one of the area's many clubs, usually to make sure they avoided trouble.

After he was selected with the No. 24 pick in the 2002 draft, Reed gravitated to fellow Miami alum Ray Lewis. The two players watched game tapes for hours at Lewis's home, and they trained together in the off-season. Some teammates jokingly called Reed "Ray Jr.," but he didn't mind. He'd found another mentor, another Jeanne Hall.

Today Reed continues to speak almost daily with Hall, who is still generous with advice, and still calls Reed "her son." Last December, Hall and her 24-year-old daughter, Leslie, were waiting for Reed outside M&T Bank Stadium after the Ravens' 37–14 win over the Giants when Leslie's cellphone chimed. It was Reed, who asked them to walk down the street, where he was waiting in his Range Rover. He was worried that fans would recognize him and delay their exit. "Who do you think you are?" Leslie said with a laugh. "You act like you're somebody special."

But when Jeanne and Leslie finally reached the SUV, they heard shrieks and screams behind them. Leslie whirled and saw several fans racing toward Reed's vehicle. A few minutes later, with the stadium in Reed's rearview mirror, Leslie reluctantly apologized. "I have to give you your props, Edward," she said. "You really have become pretty important after all." ∎

7

MEL BLOUNT

STEELERS 1970-1983

" What Joe Greene meant to the Steel Curtain defensive front, what nasty Jack Lambert meant to the Steeler linebacking corps, Blount meant to the Pittsburgh secondary. A ferocious hitter, Blount's downfield muggings of wide receivers forced quarterbacks to throw away from him. In his third season he allowed zero touchdown passes. " —PETER KING

▸ 1975 NFL DEFENSIVE PLAYER OF THE YEAR
▸ 57 CAREER INTERCEPTIONS, 13 FUMBLE RECOVERIES

THE MOST Olympian sports body I've ever seen belongs to Wilt Chamberlain, who, beginning at gracefully slim ankles, broadens in unhurried geometrical progression to shoulders the size of an ox yoke. Mel has the same body only scaled down from 7'1" to 6'3". At the top of Blount's exquisite physique is his calmly erect, completely shaven head, which looks like a highly polished, bearded, semiprecious stone. At age 35 he weighs 205 pounds, about the same as he did at the end of his college career at Southern University. I asked him once whether he ever worried about his weight. "I don't worry about anything, man," he said. "It's not part of my makeup."

—Roy Blount Jr., SI, July 25, 1983

Blount's dominance led to more receiver-friendly rules.

8

DARRELLE REVIS

JETS 2007–PRESENT

"Revis Island doesn't just refer to the Jets' confidence in leaving him alone with an opponent's best wideout. It's also where he stands in relation to the rest of the modern cornerback crop." —MARK MRAVIC

▸ THREE-TIME ALL-PRO
▸ FOUR-TIME PRO BOWL SELECTION

IT'S LESS of a risk to bring pressure when your best cornerback, Darrelle Revis, can blanket Patriots wide receiver Randy Moss wherever Moss goes. Sometimes Revis jammed Moss at the line; other times he faked jamming him and instead backed off. "If [Moss] went to the bathroom, I went too," Revis said.

—*Damon Hack, SI, September 28, 2009*

Few quarterbacks dared to challenge Revis.

PHOTOGRAPH BY PETER READ MILLER

9

DARRELL GREEN

REDSKINS 1983-2002

" A wonder of nature who played 20 seasons with same franchise. Green paved the way for Deion Sanders to become famous as a pass defender. " —TIM LAYDEN

▸ NAMED TO NFL ALL-DECADE TEAM FOR 1990S
▸ NFL-RECORD 19 CONSECUTIVE SEASONS WITH AN INTERCEPTION

TWO VETERANS of past wars met near midfield at Foxboro Stadium. During a midweek interview, Patriots coach Bill Parcells, 55, had given the needle to his old NFC East nemesis, 36-year-old Redskins cornerback Darrell Green. "He's older than I am," said Parcells. So here came Green on Sunday, feigning anger. "Hey, Coach!" he said. "You know you're six months older than me!" Late in the third quarter Green made a play for the ages. Patriots back Curtis Martin broke into the clear near midfield, and Green, despite getting knocked down early in the play, was in hot pursuit. "I looked behind me, and I had about five yards on him," Martin said. "I was in the open field, so I started to put it in another gear. By the time I got in gear, Darrell was on my back." Green is a physical marvel. As a rookie, in 1983, he ran the 40 in 4.33 seconds. Last year he ran it in 4.28.

—Peter King, SI, October 21, 1996

Green was only 5' 8" and 176 pounds.

PATRIOTS 1976–1982
RAIDERS 1983–1989

Haynes had the jets to fly with the best of them.

10

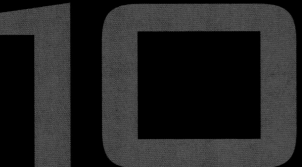

MIKE HAYNES

"A tall, angular cornerback who made the NFL's 75th anniversary team, Haynes had 46 interceptions. What Marcus Allen was for running backs—smooth, durable, classy—Haynes was for defensive backs " —PETER KING

▶ NAMED TO NFL ALL-DECADE TEAM FOR 1980S

IT IS Haynes's inner calm that makes him relish the challenge of man coverage. Raiders secondary coach and former Pro Bowl corner Willie Brown asked Haynes why he liked playing bump-and-run so much. "Because I feel in control," Haynes replied. Brown smiled. "That's how I felt too," he said.

—*Rick Telander, SI, September 24, 1984*

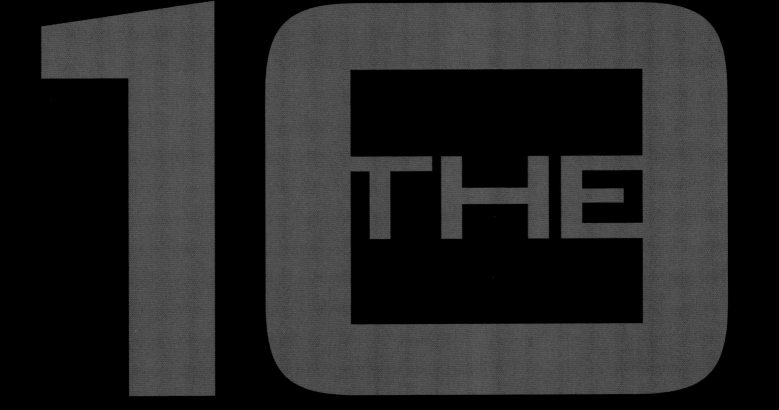

10

THE

Best Coaches

HERE'S A MEMO TO THE COLTS' CHUCK PAGANO, THE BUCCANEERS' GREG SCHIANO, THE DOLPHINS' JOE PHILBIN AND THE RAIDERS' DENNIS ALLEN, ALL OF WHOM ARE BEGINNING THEIR NFL HEAD COACHING CAREERS IN 2012: IF YOU WANT TO BE CONSIDERED ONE OF THE ALLTIME GREATS, THERE'S ONLY ONE WAY TO DO IT. YOU HAVE TO WIN A CHAMPIONSHIP. ACTUALLY, CHECK THAT: YOU HAVE TO WIN MULTIPLE CHAMPIONSHIPS.

NOT THAT A PLAYER'S CASE FOR HISTORICAL VALIDATION ISN'T AIDED BY HOISTING THE LOMBARDI TROPHY, BUT ONLY WITH COACHES DOES IT APPEAR TO BE A REQUIREMENT. AMONG OUR TOP QUARTERBACKS, FOR EXAMPLE, WE HAVE DAN MARINO, WHO NEVER WON A SUPER BOWL. OUR NO. 1 OFFENSIVE LINEMAN'S MASSIVE FINGERS ARE RING-FREE. COACHES, THOUGH, ENJOY NO SUCH LENIENCY.

THE ONLY CHAMPIONSHIP-FREE COACH TO EVEN MERIT A MENTION ON ANY OF OUR PANELISTS' BALLOTS WAS DON CORYELL. IN MAKING THE CASE FOR THE FORMER CHARGERS COACH, PANELIST JIM TROTTER PRAISED HIS INNOVATIONS IN THE PASSING GAME AS WELL AS THE SUPER BOWLS WON BY FORMER ASSISTANTS SUCH AS JOHN MADDEN AND JOE GIBBS.

GIBBS, WHO WON THREE TITLES, MADE THE TOP 10. MADDEN, WITH ONLY ONE, DID NOT. IT'S ANOTHER REMINDER THAT FOR THIS CLUB, THE ENTRANCE REQUIREMENTS ARE PRETTY STIFF.

1

VINCE LOMBARD

PACKERS 1959–1967
REDSKINS 1969

" If the NFL logo were a person, that person would be Vince Lombardi, the most iconic figure in the history of the league. He built the Packers into a model franchise. " —TIM LAYDEN

► WON FIVE NFL TITLES AND
SUPER BOWLS I AND II
► WINNING RECORD IN EACH
OF HIS 10 SEASONS

THE MAN who turned doubt into affirmation is Vince Lombardi, a moody, hoarse-voiced individual of great enthusiasms and lofty contempts. ("If you're within that circle of people important to him and his team," says a man etching circles on a white tablecloth in the Elks club, "there is nothing, absolutely nothing, he won't do for you. If you're not, he doesn't give a damn about you.") In less than two years as general manager and coach, Lombardi has taken a team which gave Green Bay its worst record in history (1-10-1 in 1958) and prodded it into distinction. "All those years of lookin' for somethin' and someone," says a man in a service station, "and this New Yorker"—the phrase was almost a profanity—"comes along and does it."

—*William Barry Furlong, SI, December 12, 1960*

Lombardi celebrates the 1961 NFL championship.

PAUL BROWN

BROWNS 1946-1962
BENGALS 1968-1975

fter he won four All-America Football
Conference titles with his expansion
Browns, his greatest achievement may
ve been Cleveland's first game in the
FL, in which the team clobbered the
defending champion Eagles 35–10.
en he won three NFL titles in his first
six seasons. **"** —PETER KING

NNOVATOR CREDITED WITH
REVOLUTIONIZING GAME
EPARATION AND SCOUTING
THROUGH FILM STUDY
FIRST COACH TO SEND IN
LAYS FROM THE SIDELINE

HIS OWN personal habits and
table manners are impeccable. He
expects the same from his players.
A few years ago we had a big end,"
Brown said. "I heard he chewed
tobacco and spat it on the wall
next to his bed. Can you imagine
that?" He peered over his glasses.
"I went to his room," he said. "I told
him that I would fine him $500
if he didn't wash down the walls.
hen I stood and watched him wash
them. Can you imagine living with
an animal like that?" The player
went on to become All-Pro. Yet
there was always, in Brown's mind,
a reservation about him. "If they're
sloppy, or drinkers, or chasers or
whiners, it will show up eventually."

—*Tex Maule, SI, September 10, 1962*

Brown's career record was 213-104-9.

BILL WALSH

49ERS 1979-1988

" He turned a foundering franchise into a great dynasty. In addition to winning three Super Bowls, he also positioned his successor, George Seifert, to win two more. " —JIM TROTTER

▸ REVOLUTIONIZED MODERN PASSING GAME
▸ 10-PLUS WINS IN EACH NONSTRIKE SEASON FROM 1981 TO 1988

A SPRINT-OUT quarterback in college, Ken Anderson had never dropped straight back to pass. "I knew nothing," he says. Walsh, then a Bengals assistant, showed him how to cradle the ball, how to move back into the pocket, how to set up. "We'd literally walk through the steps, counting out the numbers as we went," says Anderson. What Anderson got was the now famous Walsh teaching blitz, the intense reconstruction process Bengals quarterbacks Greg Cook and Virgil Carter had gotten before him and Dan Fouts, Joe Montana and others would get later. Walsh spoke quietly and rationally, joked a lot and emphasized restraint and discipline in throwing. "I don't advocate the discipline of a Marine drill sergeant," says Walsh. "What I try to get across is the discipline you'll see in a ballerina or concert pianist."

—*Rick Telander, SI, January 25, 1982*

Walsh was also a master drafter as 49ers G.M.

THE TOP OF HIS GAME

Four months before Bill Walsh died of leukemia, SI ran this appreciation which included testimonial from a man who would, four years later, take up the mantle of 49ers coach

BY MICHAEL SILVER

WHEN BILL WALSH acquired Steve Young from the Tampa Bay Buccaneers for second- and fourth-round draft picks before the 1987 season, the lefthanded quarterback was the NFL's version of a wild mustang—swift and untamed. It took years for Young's coaches, including Walsh and future offensive coordinators Mike Holmgren, Marc Trestman and Mike Shanahan, to mold him into the precise passer and methodical decision-maker the 49ers' offense demanded. More than seven years removed from his last NFL game, Young now believes that for all the credit Walsh receives, his genius is nonetheless underrated.

"I get the sense that East Coasters don't see the impact [West Coasters] do," Young says. "I don't know if people realize the innovation he has brought to this game on so many levels. From a business perspective, I'd compare it to Silicon Valley—where Andy Grove, Steve Jobs and some of the other pioneers really changed business. Bill Walsh, around that same time, brought the same kind of mentality to football. In terms of how you deal with people and the kind of environment you create, his was a very enlightened approach."

It's not that Walsh wasn't tough on his employees; tales of his authoritarian antics are numerous. "There was the cardboard-box story," says Walsh, smiling at the recollection. Early in his tenure an offensive lineman had become a problem in the locker room. When the player's agent showed up at the Niners' facility demanding a large pay raise for his client, Walsh had enough. "I said, 'Get his stuff, put it in a cardboard box and put it on his doorstep,' " he recalls. "Word got around."

Once, after a rookie defensive lineman smacked Montana during a training-camp drill, Walsh cut the player on the spot. As the newly unemployed behemoth was led off by a team official, in full view of 100 players and thousands of fans at Sierra Community College in Rocklin, Calif., Walsh paced behind them, screaming, "Don't even let him f------ shower!"

While Walsh's primary job was to win football games, his vision of the coach's role was far more expansive. He had money managers and sociologists counsel his players, delivered speeches on integration and encouraged employees to get involved with charities.

He also seemed aware of the legacy being created by the success of his West Coast offense, the most obvious sign being the wide-open receivers catching Montana's pinpoint passes in stride. Today the West Coast, with its reliance on short passes, precisely timed routes and intricately planned progressions, is the NFL's preeminent scheme. ("Let's call it what it is: the Walshian Offense," Baltimore Ravens coach Brian Billick

insists.) But in the early 1980s it merely drove opposing coaches nuts. Old schoolers, such as the Chicago Bears' Mike Ditka, openly scoffed at the Genius label—a tag Walsh never went to great pains to protest—but his teachings were that innovative. Long before the advent of eBay, copies of his playbooks were being sold on the black market at prices that made him blush.

Walsh was the first coach to script his opening 20 or 25 offensive plays and the first to prowl the sideline with a laminated sheet of plays for specific situations. He recorded his speeches at team meetings and videotaped new plays being installed, creating an archive as a resource for future Niners coaches and players. And with his blessing, his systems were circulated throughout the league by his former assistants and their protégés. "He was proselytizing," Young says. "He was a missionary. I think Bill realized, 'I'm way ahead of the league here,' and he knew the more people he could touch, the more lasting his impact would be."

Two months ago Walsh sat courtside at Maples Pavilion and watched a Stanford basketball game with Jim Harbaugh, the latest in the long procession of coaches he has mentored. As a member of the school's search committee, Walsh had just helped Harbaugh, 43, a former quarterback at Michigan and a 15-year NFL veteran, get hired as the Cardinal's coach. The two men met in the early '90s, when Harbaugh was with the Bears. Harbaugh was competing in *The Quarterback Challenge*, a made-for-TV event in Hawaii for which Walsh was serving as an announcer. The two began discussing passing mechanics, and soon Harbaugh and another quarterback, Bubby Brister, were behind the centerfield wall of an old baseball stadium getting a 90-minute lesson from Walsh on drops and footwork. "He was just so clear and specific," Harbaugh says, "and I was soaking it up like a sponge."

Late last year, even as his leukemia worsened, Walsh, who twice coached Stanford (1977–78 and '92 through '94), remained active in the Cardinal's search. In the energetic and enthusiastic Harbaugh, Walsh saw "a nonstop person" who is "as close to Dick Vermeil"—his longtime friend who coached the St. Louis Rams to the Super Bowl XXXIV championship—"as anyone I've seen."

It's a touching story line—ailing legend guiding protégé—but in Walsh's case so consistent with his past as to be unremarkable. In an era in which many coaches seem to thwart their assistants' opportunities for advancement, it's instructive to remember how far Walsh went to do just the opposite. "I've never known any coach more tireless in his efforts to help the people around him," says Billick, who worked as a 49ers public relations assistant in 1979 and '80 before beginning his coaching career at San Diego State. "I can never repay Bill, but part of his legacy is that I feel compelled to do it for other coaches, and I think we all feel the same way."

∎

4
CHUCK NOLL

STEELERS 1969–1991

" He merely assembled and oversaw what was arguably the greatest dynasty in league history. A genius at identifying and managing talent, his understated but unquestioned authority served as an anchor among some very strong egos. " —MARK MRAVIC

▸ WON FOUR SUPER BOWLS IN SIX YEARS
▸ DRAFTED FOUR FUTURE HALL OF FAMERS IN 1974, A RECORD FOR ONE CLASS

NOLL THE TEACHER has tended to overshadow Noll the innovator, mainly because Noll himself tends to downplay innovation. "If I had to choose between a coach who's a strategy guy and one who's a teacher, it'd be no contest," Noll says. "I'd take the teacher every time." "The key to everything was teaching," says Steelers linebacker Andy Russell. "You'd see him being stopped by some rookie after an afternoon practice during two-a-days, a kid he's got to know is going to be cut in a matter of days. The kid would say, 'Coach, I'm having trouble with this technique,' and Chuck would spend half an hour with him. I think he enjoyed it more than coaching the superstars. He just loves to teach."

—Paul Zimmerman, SI, July 28, 1980

Steelers winning seasons were rare before Noll arrived.

PHOTOGRAPH BY WALTER IOOSS JR.

5

GEORGE HALAS

BEARS 1920–1929, 1933–1942,
1946–1955, 1958–1967
BEARS OWNER UNTIL 1983

" Nicknamed Papa Bear as the patriarch
of the Bears franchise, he was the league's
most enduring face as it transitioned
from leather helmets to national
TV contracts. " —TIM LAYDEN

‣ SIX NFL CHAMPIONSHIPS,
ONLY SIX LOSING SEASONS
IN 40 YEARS
‣ SECOND ON NFL'S ALLTIME
WINS LIST WITH 324

IT IS EASY to forget that this man
across the desk is a certified
institution. Papa Bear was tackled
by Jim Thorpe and struck out by
Walter Johnson. He played six games
in rightfield for the Yankees in 1919
(the Babe settled in that very realty
the next season), and Halas was
also there in Canton, Ohio, sitting
on a running board in a Hupmobile
showroom on Sept. 17, 1920 when
pro football was created. It was a
Friday, one of the last things to be
created in just one day. And this
fellow across the desk was right
there, live. Then Papa Bear won 324
games, 12 more than Stagg, which
at the time was more than anyone
in the history of the pros or the
colleges. He is the only man Vince
Lombardi would embrace and one
of the few he would call Coach.

—*Frank Deford, SI, December 5, 1977*

Halas's sideline tirades were a trademark.

PHOTOGRAPH BY JOHN F. JAQUA

6

DON SHULA

"Nobody did it better or longer than the only coach to lead his team to the Super Bowl in three decades." —DON BANKS

▸ NFL RECORD 347 WINS
▸ SIX SUPER BOWL APPEARANCES, WITH WINS IN SUPER BOWLS VII AND VIII

SHULA HAS thrived in a world of pressure so intense that it has burned out even those who have succeeded at the highest level, or close to it. Joe Gibbs, Bill Walsh, Dick Vermeil, John Robinson, Don Coryell, John Madden—the list is long. Through it all, year after year, Shula marches on.

—*Paul Zimmerman, SI, December 20, 1993*

Shula celebrated the wins record in 1993.

PHOTOGRAPH BY GEORGE WIDMAN/AP

7

BILL BELICHICK

BROWNS 1991–1995
PATRIOTS 2000–PRESENT

" After inventing defensive schemes for the two-time Super Bowl champ Giants a generation ago, he had a clunker of a head coaching trial in Cleveland. Patriots owner Bob Kraft smartly gave him a second chance. Thus far he's averaged 12.9 wins per year, including playoffs. " —PETER KING

▸ THREE SUPER BOWL WINS
▸ TRAILS ONLY HALAS AND SHULA IN WIN PERCENTAGE (MINIMUM 150 WINS)

HE WAS devoted to his father, a longtime assistant coach and scout at Navy. When Bill was nine or 10, he tagged along to the weekly Monday-night meeting, at which players were given the scouting report for the next game. "Imagine what Bill must have absorbed," says Joe Bellino, that team's standout running back. "He'd sit in the back of the room listening to his father give the scouting report. He's a youngster hanging out at the Naval Academy. Midshipmen in uniform, parades, the brass, the visiting presidents, the football team with two Heisman winners [Bellino and 1963 recipient Roger Staubach]. And he saw his father's work ethic. He saw everyone in that room soak up what his dad was telling us, believing if we did what he said, we could beat anybody.

—*Peter King, SI, August 9, 2004*

Belichick set a record for wins in a 10-year span.

PHOTOGRAPH BY DAVID BERGMAN

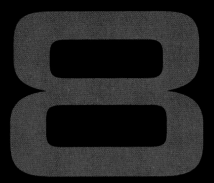

TOM LANDRY

COWBOYS 1960–1988

" No coach has ever done more with a modern expansion franchise, turning the nascent Dallas franchise into an every-year championship contender. He was instrumental in framing the 4–3 defense that ruled the NFL for two decades. " —TIM LAYDEN

‣ WON SUPER BOWLS VI AND XII
‣ 270 CAREER WINS, THIRD-BEST ALLTIME

IN 1956, Landry coached the defense and Vince Lombardi oversaw the offense, giving the NFL champion Giants the most dynamic pair of assistant coaches ever to grace one staff. A visitor to the Giants that season described a walk down the corridor where the coaches' offices were located. "The first office I passed belonged to Landry," he said. "He was busy putting in a defense, running his projector, studying film. The next office was Vince Lombardi's. He was breaking down his own film, putting in an offense. The next office was head coach Jim Lee Howell's. He had his feet up on the desk, and he was reading a newspaper." Upon seeing the visitor, Howell quipped, "With guys like Lombardi and Landry in the building, there isn't much for me to do around here."

—*Paul Zimmerman, SI, February 21, 2000*

Landry made five Super Bowl appearances.

9

JOE GIBBS

" His most notable accomplishment is not that he won Super Bowls in three of his four trips to the Big Game. It's that he won each title with a different starting quarterback. Not many coaches could do that " —JIM TROTTER

- 17–7 IN POSTSEASON
- 171–101 CAREER RECORD

IN THE [Super Bowl] press room they mentioned to Gibbs that in one three-week series he had beaten a trio of legends: Bud Grant, Tom Landry and Don Shula. "The truly great people in this profession are great for years and years," Gibbs said. "Let's see how I am in 10 years."

—*Paul Zimmerman, SI, February 7, 1983*

Gibbs instructed Joe Theismann in Super Bowl XVII.

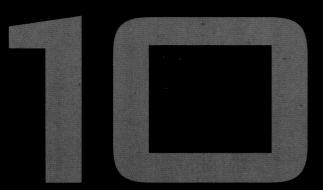

BILL PARCELLS

GIANTS 1983–1990
PATRIOTS 1993–1996
JETS 1997–1999
COWBOYS 2003–2006

> " His abilities to motivate and to scheme made him one of the great teachers of the game. " —DAMON HACK

▸ WON SUPER BOWLS XXI AND XXV
▸ ONLY COACH IN NFL HISTORY TO REACH PLAYOFFS WITH FOUR FRANCHISES

PARCELLS WAS brought up in an environment in which coaches got in athletes' faces. "Everybody who ever coached me was on me, coaching me hard," he says. "But, see, if you respect a player and he respects you, then you have a relationship, and in a relationship all commentary is allowed. I can say anything to Pepper Johnson, and he will understand where I'm coming from. Man, the things coaches used to say to me. . . . " Parcells is usually sparing in talking about his past. But, as coaches often do, he enjoys talking about *his* coaches, the men who shaped his life. With an almost childlike delight—and with laundered language—he remembers the day that a coach yelled to him during football practice, "Parcells, I wish you were a piece of crap out there because then at least somebody might slip on you."

—Jack McCallum, SI, December 14, 1998

Parcells celebrated after Super Bowl XXI (left).

10

THE

BEST GAMES

THE HEADLINE THAT RAN WITH SI'S ORIGINAL STORY ON THE 1958 CHAMPIONSHIP BETWEEN THE COLTS AND THE GIANTS WAS *THE BEST FOOTBALL GAME EVER PLAYED.* TWO WEEKS LATER THE MAGAZINE RAN A FOLLOW-UP WITH THE SOMEWHAT DEFENSIVE TITLE, *HERE'S WHY IT WAS THE BEST FOOTBALL GAME EVER.* AND NOW, MORE THAN FIVE DECADES AND THOUSANDS OF GAMES LATER, THE JUDGMENT HAS BEEN REAFFIRMED. AN ALTERNATIVE TITLE FOR THIS CHAPTER: "IT'S STILL THE BEST GAME EVER."

OF THE 10 SELECTIONS IN THIS SECTION, SIX WERE LEAGUE CHAMPIONSHIP GAMES, AND ALL WERE FROM THE PLAYOFFS— WHEN BOTH THE STAKES AND THE VIEWERSHIPS ARE HIGHER. BUT IN COMPOSING THEIR LISTS, PANELISTS SOMETIMES INVOKED THE MEMORIES OF LONG-FORGOTTEN REGULAR SEASON GAMES. REMEMBER THAT MONDAY NIGHTER WHEN VINNY TESTAVERDE THREW A TD TO JUMBO ELLIOTT AND THE JETS MADE THIS BIG COMEBACK AND BEAT THE DOLPHINS IN OVERTIME? YEAH, KIND OF. NOW THAT YOU MENTION IT.

EVERY GAME THAT MADE A VOTER'S LIST—AS WELL AS ANYTHING THAT RATED A MENTION IN ANY OTHER CATEGORY—APPEARS IN AN APPENDIX IN THE BACK OF THIS BOOK. IT'S WORTH A PEEK, TO SEE WHAT MEMORIES COME SEEPING BACK.

1

1958 TITLE GAME

COLTS 23, GIANTS 17

"Johnny Unitas had to lead Baltimore 73 yards in the final two minutes of regulation for the tying field goal. He then drove the Colts 80 yards in OT for the win. The game was also memorable because it was broadcast by NBC and showcased the league to a national audience." —JIM TROTTER

- KNOWN AS "THE GREATEST GAME EVER PLAYED"
- FIRST PLAYOFF GAME TO GO TO OVERTIME

JUST BEFORE the [winning] touchdown a deliriously happy Baltimore football fan raced onto the field during a timeout and sailed 80 yards, bound for the Baltimore huddle, before the police secondary intercepted him and hauled him to the sideline. He was grinning with idiot glee, and the whole city of Baltimore sympathized with him. One Baltimore fan, listening on his auto radio, ran into a telephone pole when Steve Myhra kicked the tying field goal, and 30,000 others waited to greet the returning heroes. Ray Berry, a thin, tired-looking youngster still dazed with the victory, seemed to speak for the team and for fans everywhere after the game. "It's the greatest thing that ever happened," he said.

—Tex Maule, SI, January 5, 1959

Alan Ameche won the game with this one-yard run.

PHOTOGRAPH BY NEIL LEIFER

2

1981 AFC PLAYOFFS

CHARGERS 41, DOLPHINS 38

"The lingering image of an exhausted Chargers tight end Kellen Winslow being almost carried off the field by two San Diego teammates tells you all you need to know about this overtime classic." —DON BANKS

▸ CHARGERS SURRENDERED AN EARLY 24–0 LEAD
▸ MIAMI'S SCORING INCLUDED A 40-YARD HOOK-AND-LATERAL TOUCHDOWN TO CLOSE FIRST HALF

IN OVERTIME Winslow searched for the oxygen behind the Chargers' bench. It was gone, removed for unknown reasons by maintenance men. When Rolf Benirschke finally kicked the winning field goal, Winslow was blocking and didn't see it. He dropped facedown on the sod, cramping from neck to calf, "ready to cry." He assumed the Chargers had won only because of the silence in the stadium. A Dolphins player asked Winslow if he wanted a hand getting up. Winslow said no thanks and stayed where he was. Eventually two Chargers helped him off the field. In the locker room, trainers covered him with cold towels to bring down his temperature, which was more than 100°, and Winslow fell asleep for a while. Despite drinking constantly throughout the game, he had lost 12 pounds.

—*Rick Telander, SI, September 1, 1982*

Winslow did everything except walk off on his own.

NO ONE SHOULD HAVE LOST

The Dolphins and Chargers battled to exhaustion, trading apparent knockout blows, but the game went on and on as their field goal kickers struggled to finish the job

BY JOHN UNDERWOOD

T IS THE ONE GREAT IRONY OF PROFESSIONAL football that magnificent games such as San Diego's wonderful, woeful 41–38 overtime AFC playoff victory over Miami are almost always decided by the wrong guys. Decided not by heroic, bloodied men who play themselves to exhaustion and perform breathtaking feats, but by men in clean jerseys. With names you cannot spell, and the remnants of European accents, and slender bodies and mystical ways. Men who cannot be coached, only traded. Men whose main objective in life, more often than not, is to avoid the crushing embarrassment of a shanked field goal in the last 30 seconds.

There, at the end, in a moist, numbed Orange Bowl still jammed with disbelievers after 74 minutes and 1,030 yards and 79 points of what San Diego coach Don Coryell called "probably the most exciting game in the history of pro football," was Dan Fouts. Heroic, bloodied Fouts, the nonpareil Chargers quarterback. His black beard and white jersey crusted with dirt. His skinny legs so tired they could barely carry him off the field after he had thrown, how many? A playoff-record 53 passes? And completed, how many? A playoff-record 33? For a playoff-record 433 yards? And three touchdowns? Fouts should have decided this game.

Or Kellen Winslow. There, at the end, his magnificent athlete's body battered and blued by a relentless—if not altogether cohesive—Miami defense, Winslow had to be carried off. Time after time during the game he was helped to the sidelines, and then, finally, all the way to the dressing room, the last man to make the postgame celebration. Staggering, sore-shouldered, one-more-play-and-let-me-lie-down Winslow, looking as if he might die any minute (the only sure way he could have been stopped), catching, how many? A playoff-record 16 passes? For a playoff-record 166 yards?

Winslow is listed as the tight end in the San Diego offense. The Dolphins know better. Like the 800-pound gorilla, Winslow plays just about wherever Winslow wants to play: tight end, wide receiver, fullback, wingback, slotback. Even on defense, as Miami discovered when he blocked what would have been the winning field goal and thereby spoiled what Dolphins guard Ed Newman called—another drum roll, please—"the greatest comeback in the history of professional football." Winslow should have decided this game.

Or there, on the other side, Don Strock, the gutty, heroic, 6'5" Miami relief pitcher. Strock coming in with the Dolphins submerged at 0–24 and not only matching Smilin' Dan pass for pass, but doing him better than that for so long a stretch that it looked for sure the Dolphins would pull it out. Throwing (42 times, 28 completions) for 397 yards and four touchdowns, and getting Miami ahead and into position to win at 38–31, and then at the threshold of victory twice again at 38–38.

Strock is 31, a golden oldie amid Don Shula's youth movement, and in his 10th year as a Dolphin it is his business to bail out 23-year-old child star David Woodley. He did so again Saturday when Woodley suffered a first-quarter malaise—sacks, misfires, interceptions—right out of Edgar Allan Poe. In the end breakdowns not of his doing cost Strock exactly what Newman said it would have been—the greatest playoff comeback in the NFL's history. "Strock," said Fouts, "was awesome." Strock should have decided this game.

Fittingly, all of the above helped make it what Fouts himself called "the greatest game I ever played in." (See? It's catching.) But, typically, none of them had even a bit part in the final scene. Overtime games almost always come to that because the objective shifts to a totally conservative aim: The first team close enough tries a field goal. Be cool, play it straight, pop it in. Thus, after a day-into-night parade of exquisite offensive plots and ploys, the final blow was a comparative feather duster, struck by a former 123-pound weakling in a dry, spotless uniform. A tidy little 29-yard love tap that Rolf Benirschke put slightly right of center, 13 minutes and 52 seconds into overtime. It takes nothing away from him, however, to say that the denouement was more negative than positive, not a question of which team would deliver the knockout punch, but which team's kicker would not miss one more easy field goal.

Six minutes into the overtime Benirschke missed a 27-yarder that would have won it then and there. "Fortunately," he said, "I got a second chance." The Dolphins' Uwe von Schamann had two chances too. He missed both. With four seconds to play in regulation, Shula sent in Von Schamann to try a 43-yarder. Winslow, a defensive ringer, leaped and batted it away. Von Schamann went down to the far end of the Dolphin bench, away from everybody and meditated as the overtime started. After Benirschke's life-giving miss, he got his second chance. On fourth down at the Charger 17, in went Von Schamann. The snap was true, the hold good—but in his eagerness to get under the ball, Von Schamann dipped his left side a little too much and his right foot, sweeping across, scraped the ground behind the ball. Von Schamann turned away disgustedly almost as soon as he finished his follow-through. The ball disappeared into a sea of dirty white shirts.

San Diego's drive to the winning field goal was all the more impressive because it came at a time when Miami was apparently the stronger team. The setup play was a beauty. Wide receiver Charlie Joiner, in motion, cut across the field at the snap and saw that Miami had switched from a three-deep to a two-deep zone. He broke his pattern and split the defense up the middle. Fouts looked right, then left, then saw Joiner—"and I had all the time in the world to get it to him." The play covered 39 yards to the Miami 10, and Coryell immediately sent in Benirschke. Lights out, Miami. ∎

1967 TITLE GAME

PACKERS 21, COWBOYS 17

"The game was special not only because it was a rematch of the previous season's NFL title game, but also because of the cold, and the ending. With 16 seconds remaining, Bart Starr stunned everyone with a game-winning QB sneak from inside the one. The Packers could not have gotten off another play if he had failed." —JIM TROTTER

▸ KNOWN AS "THE ICE BOWL"
▸ GAME-TIME TEMPERATURE WAS -15°, WITH A WIND CHILL OF -48°

THE FIELD, now in the shadow of the stands, was fast becoming an iced-over pond. "I knew Donny wasn't getting any footing," Starr said after the game. "I figured I wouldn't have as far to run and I wouldn't have as much chance to fumble, so I called the wedge to [guard Jerry] Kramer's side." "When he called the play, I knew he would be following me," Kramer explained. "[Cowboys lineman Jethro] Pugh was playing on my inside shoulder—to my left—and I took my best shot at him. That may have been the biggest block I ever made in my life." The block moved Pugh in and back. Starr came hard behind him and slid into the end zone, and suddenly, for 50,000 people, spring came.

—Tex Maule, SI, January 8, 1968

Lambeau's "frozen tundra" lived up to its nickname.

4

SUPER BOWL III

JETS 16, COLTS 7

> " From a dramatic standpoint, this game doesn't hold up, but that's insignificant. This one gave the AFL credibility and made Joe Namath a folk hero. " —TIM LAYDEN

> ‣ AFL TEAMS HAD LOST FIRST TWO SUPER BOWLS BY WIDE MARGINS
> ‣ ONE-LOSS COLTS WERE 18-POINT FAVORITES

BROADWAY JOE NAMATH is long hair, a Fu Manchu mustache worth $10,000 to shave off, swinging nights in the live spots of the big city, the dream lover of the stewardi—all that spells insouciant youth in the Jet Age. Besides all that, Namath is a superb quarterback who in the Super Bowl proved that his talent is as big as his mouth—which makes it a very big talent, indeed. Almost no one thought the Jets could penetrate the fine Baltimore defense, but Namath was sure of it and said so. "We're a better team than Baltimore," he said before the game. He was lying by the pool at the Gait Ocean Mile Hotel, where the Jets stayed, tanned and oiled against the sun. It was called loudmouthing, bragging, but as it turned out, Super Joe told it the way it was. In a surpassing display of passing accuracy and mental agility, he picked the Colt defense apart.

—*Tex Maule, SI, January 20, 1969*

Field general Namath was the game's MVP.

5

SUPER BOWL XLII

GIANTS 17, PATRIOTS 14

"The Patriots were gunning for the first perfect season since the 1972 Dolphins until the Giants' pass rush and a miracle catch by David Tyree stopped them cold." —DAMON HACK

▸ GIANTS MADE PLAYOFFS
AS WILD-CARD
▸ UNDEFEATED PATRIOTS
WERE 12-POINT FAVORITE

IT WAS to have been a historic night. The Patriots would win their 19th consecutive game and become only the second NFL team to complete a season unbeaten and untied. They would fortify the legacy of a modern professional dynasty with a fourth Super Bowl title in seven years. They would prove themselves perfect. Instead, the Giants completed an unexpected and emotional postseason run. It was history cut from another cloth, a performance built on the sturdy underpinnings of a ferocious defensive effort, sustained when Eli Manning and David Tyree combined on one of the most memorable plays in NFL history. At the victory party Manning worked the room, bouncing among groups of friends. "It's just surreal," Eli said over the noise. Past midnight he joined with his oldest brother, Cooper, and together they sang. The selection, of course, was *New York, New York*.

—*Tim Layden, SI, February 11, 2008*

MVP Manning (left) surged while Tom Brady struggled.

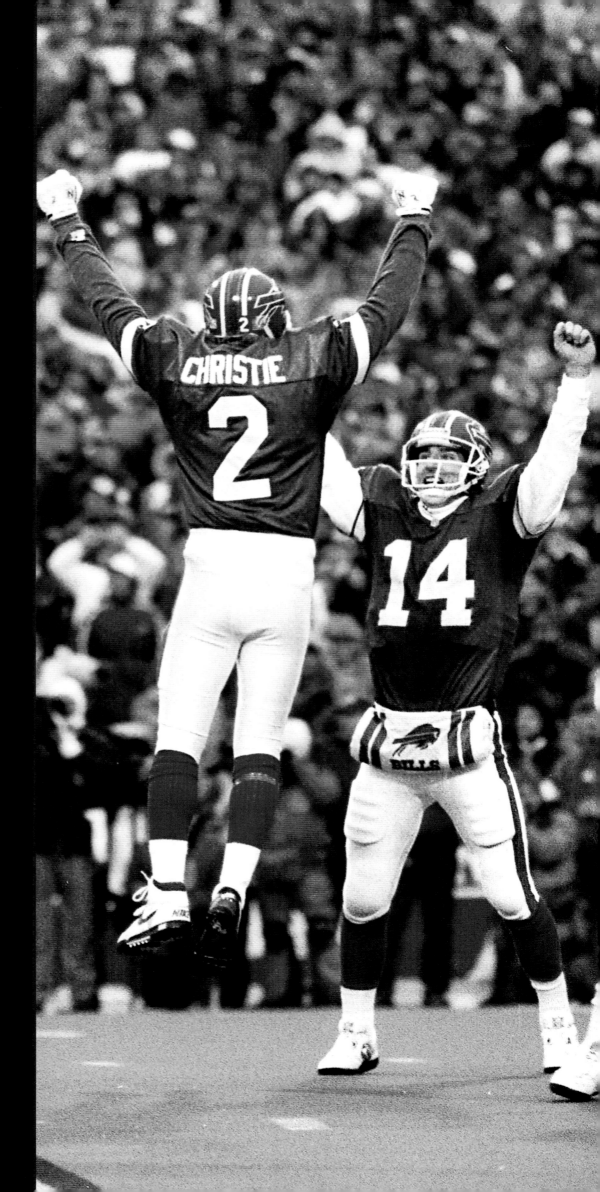

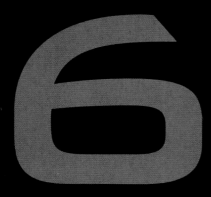

6

1992 AFC WILD CARD

BILLS 41, OILERS 38

" The Bills proved all things were possible with a 32-point second-half comeback. " —DON BANKS

▸ BILLS STARTING QB JIM KELLY MISSED GAME WITH KNEE INJURY
▸ STEVE CHRISTIE HIT A 32-YARD FIELD GOAL TO WIN IT IN OT

FRANK REICH had thrown only 47 passes in the regular season, mostly in garbage time, so no one could have expected him to complete 21 of 34 for 289 yards and four touchdowns with one interception. Now he has the distinction of having led what at the time was the biggest major-college comeback in history as well as pro football's greatest comeback. He brought Maryland back from a 31–0 deficit at the Orange Bowl to beat Miami 42–40 on Nov. 10, 1984. "A lot of the thoughts I had that day came back today," he said, finally alone in the locker room after 90 minutes of bedlam. "I remember thinking the same thing I thought that day in Miami—one play at a time. You don't have to play bombs away. Your defense has to give the ball back to you every time, and you have to be protected well. Our defense was great, and my line was magnificent." Magnificent. A good word to describe the entire day.

—*Peter King, SI, January 11, 1993*

Reich's passes set up Christie's winning field goal.

PHOTOGRAPHS BY JOHN BIEVER

SUPER BOWL XLIII

STEELERS 27, CARDINALS 23

" It contained not one but two of the greatest plays in NFL history. Arizona scored 16 points in five minutes of the fourth quarter, but Ben Roethlisberger directed a 78-yard drive that culminated in Santonio Holmes's tiptoe touchdown catch. " —MARK MRAVIC

▸ JAMES HARRISON CLOSED FIRST HALF WITH A 100-YARD INTERCEPTION RETURN
▸ LARRY FITZGERALD CAUGHT TWO TDS FOR ARIZONA

AT HALFTIME Mike Tomlin talked about honoring the legacy of the players who'd come before, players like Lynn Swann and Jerome Bettis, both of whom were on the field before kickoff. There were reminders of Steelers football everywhere in Tampa. Tens of thousands of towel-waving, black-and-gold-clad fans had descended upon the area, escaping a harsh winter and a harsh economy for a few days at least. And the football on the field was both familiar and magical. Harrison's mad dash recalled Franco Harris's Immaculate Reception. Holmes and Hines Ward channeled the dramatics of Swann and John Stallworth. Ben Roethlisberger pulled halfway to Terry Bradshaw's four rings with a mettle that, like Bradshaw's, might not be truly appreciated until after he's gone.

—Damon Hack, SI, February 9, 2009

MVP Holmes caught this TD with 35 seconds left.

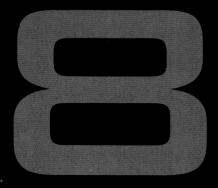

1981 NFC CHAMPIONSHIP

49ERS 28, COWBOYS 27

> " This win broke the Cowboys' stranglehold on the NFC and introduced the nation to Bill Walsh, Joe Montana and the wizardry of the West Coast offense. " —DAMON HACK

▸ DWIGHT CLARK MADE "THE CATCH" OF MONTANA'S SIX-YARD TD PASS WITH 51 SECONDS LEFT
▸ DALLAS'S FINAL DRIVE WAS QUASHED BY A FORCED FUMBLE IN 49ERS TERRITORY

IT HADN'T BEEN the 49ers' day. They had coughed the ball up six times, two of the turnovers leading to touchdowns. Two interference penalties against their brilliant rookie cornerback, Ronnie Lott (one of them on a very questionable call), had led to 10 more points. A tough game. The lead had already changed hands five times. The 49ers had moved smartly up and down the field, but Dallas had knocked them out of their last three playoffs, and as the 49ers took the ball on their own 11-yard line, down 27-21 with 4:54 left, a deep gloom settled over the Candlestick fans. "I looked down the field and I saw that patch of grass between our huddle and their goal posts," San Francisco center Fred Quillan said, "and I thought, 'That's it. That one patch of grass between us and the Super Bowl.'"

—Paul Zimmerman, SI, January 18, 1982

Montana's masterpiece concluded with Clark's catch.

PHOTOGRAPHS BY ANDY HAYT

SUPER BOWL XIII

STEELERS 35, COWBOYS 31

" Meeting in the Super Bowl for the second time in four years, the two best franchises of the era traded body blows, each scoring 14 points during a thrilling fourth quarter. The Steelers held on for their third championship in five seasons. " —MARK GODICH

▸ MVP TERRY BRADSHAW THREW FOUR TOUCHDOWNS
▸ JACKIE SMITH'S END-ZONE DROP HURT DALLAS

ALL GAME LONG it was Bradshaw who was the dominant presence, who was mainly responsible for turning XIII into the best Super Bowl game of all as well as the highest scoring. It was Bradshaw who took ferocious licks from a Dallas defense that sacked him four times. It was Bradshaw who kept playing with an injured shoulder. It was Bradshaw who kept finding Lynn Swann and John Stallworth and tight end Randy Grossman just when he needed them. And it was Bradshaw who escaped a Cowboy rush and improvised the touchdown pass to Rocky Bleier that put the Steelers ahead to stay 21–14 just before halftime. "Today I relaxed, felt good and had fun," said Bradshaw, who was the unanimous choice for MVP. "I just tried to go out there and help win a football game." Which he did—and how.

—*Dan Jenkins, SI, January 29, 1979*

Bradshaw escaped Dallas's Doomsday Defense.

10

2006 AFC CHAMPIONSHIP

COLTS 38, PATRIOTS 34

" Peyton Manning and the Colts rallied from being 21–6 down at halftime, scoring 15 points in the third quarter and 17 in the fourth to defeat their archrivals. Indy went on to win the Super Bowl. " —MARK MRAVIC

▸ JOSEPH ADDAI'S THREE-YARD TOUCHDOWN RUN WITH ONE MINUTE REMAINING WAS THE GAME-WINNER
▸ THE COLTS' DALLAS CLARK HAD 137 RECEIVING YARDS

AS THE PLAYERS sat glumly in their RCA Dome locker room at halftime, coach Tony Dungy strode among them, delivering a message that even the team's biggest star had trouble swallowing. "I'm telling you, this is our game," Dungy proclaimed, fixing his eyes on Peyton Manning, whose playoff struggles mirrored Dungy's own. "It's our time." Manning, who before this game might as well have had CAN'T WIN THE BIG ONE tattooed on his forehead, was still obsessing over the 39-yard interception for a touchdown he'd served up to cornerback Asante Samuel. It's our time? Had these words come from anyone other than Dungy, Manning would have tuned him out. "But Tony is one calm customer," Manning said later, "and he has a way of making you believe."

—*Michael Silver, SI, January 29, 2007*

Harrison (left) and Manning rallied against the Pats.

PHOTOGRAPHS BY DAMIAN STROHMEYER (LEFT) AND AL TIELEMANS

THE 10

BEST PLAYS

AS ANYONE WHO HAS TAKEN HIGH SCHOOL HISTORY KNOWS, THE PASSAGE OF TIME CAN REDUCE GREAT SWATHS TO TINY BITS. THE FIRST HALF OF THE PREVIOUS MILLENNIUM OF WESTERN HISTORY IS REPRESENTED BY THE *MAGNA CARTA* AND THE GUTENBERG BIBLE. IT'S THE SAME WITH SPORTS HIGHLIGHT PACKAGES, IN WHICH THE 1970S BECOME LITTLE MORE THAN CARLTON FISK'S HOME RUN, BRUCE JENNER'S FLAG WAVE AND LYNN SWANN'S LEAPING GRAB.

SWANN'S CATCH EXEMPLIFIES THE DISTORTING POWER OF THE HIGHLIGHT. SO ACROBATIC AND PICTURESQUE, IT IS SHOWN BEFORE EVERY SUPER BOWL. BUT READ SI'S ORIGINAL GAME STORY, AND IT MAY TAKE YOU A WHILE TO REALIZE THAT THE SWANN CATCH DESCRIBED FOR PARAGRAPHS IS A DIFFERENT PLAY, IN WHICH SWANN SCORES A DECISIVE TOUCHDOWN—ONE THAT HAS BEEN FORGOTTEN BECAUSE IT'S NEVER SHOWN. THE HIGHLIGHT CATCH, WHICH ONLY SET UP A MISSED FIELD GOAL, MERITS A MERE SENTENCE.

ANOTHER '70S HIGHLIGHT ON OUR LIST IS THE MIRACLE AT THE MEADOWLANDS, AND IT'S AN OUTLIER IN EVERY WAY. INSTEAD OF TRIUMPH, IT IS TRAGEDY. OUR OTHER PLAYS ARE ALL IN THE POSTSEASON, WHILE THE MIRACLE CAME IN A PEDESTRIAN REGULAR-SEASON GAME. BUT FOOTBALL FANS SEE TRIBUTE TO IT WHENEVER A QUARTERBACK TAKES A KNEE. WE ARE REMINDED OF IT EVERY WEEK, AND THUS DOES IT BECOME PART OF HISTORY.

1

IMMACULATE RECEPTION

1972 AFC PLAYOFFS

" Franco Harris's last-minute touchdown reception against Oakland not only launched the Steelers dynasty, but remains the most famous, and disputed, play in NFL history. " —DON BANKS

▸ STEELERS WERE BEHIND 7–6 AND ON THEIR OWN 40 ▸ OAKLAND ARGUED THE CATCH WAS A CAROM FROM ONE RECEIVER TO ANOTHER, WHICH WAS ILLEGAL THEN

SCRAMBLING, TERRY BRADSHAW spotted Frenchy Fuqua at the Oakland 35 and desperately heaved the ball in his direction. Fuqua and Oakland safety Jack Tatum collided. The Steelers' hopes were dashed, the game was over . . . until, suddenly, from out of nowhere, came rookie fullback Franco Harris. "When the play got messed up," Harris later said, "I was running toward Fuqua, hoping he'd get the ball and I could block for him." The ball headed right for Harris, who, in full stride, scooped it up just above the grass. He raced down the left sideline and scored. Raiders coach John Madden, for one, was a disbeliever and argued—in vain—with officials. "Tomorrow morning when I wake up and read the paper," said Madden, "I still won't believe it."

—Steve Wulf, SI, October 16, 1991

Harris's fourth-down catch came with 22 seconds left.

2

MANNING-TO-TYREE

SUPER BOWL XLII

" Not only was David Tyree's third-and-five reception the most significant play in the Giants' taking down the unbeaten Patriots, it was a physically implausible act that would have been remarkable even if it had occurred in an exhibition game. " —TIM LAYDEN

▸ 32-YARD COMPLETION
▸ SET UP WINNING SCORE

THEY CAUGHT Eli Manning in a squeeze. He was a dead duck, but somehow he escaped. "My man had his jersey," left guard Rich Seubert said. "I yelled, 'Go, Eli, go!'" "I had a good view because nobody rushed over me," right guard Chris Snee said. "I turned around, and there were a couple of guys mugging Eli. Somehow that scrawny body got away." "No one pulled me down. . . . I felt a tug," Manning said. "I tried to stay small." He got off a pass that went 32 yards to Tyree, a special teams whiz and the No. 4 receiver. "I guarantee you," Peyton Manning said, standing by his brother's locker afterward, "there were guys on that Patriots defense who thought the play was already over. He gets sacked, that's it, it's over. Fourth-and-15." Giants fullback Madison Hedgecock said, "Most amazing play I've ever seen on a football field."

—Paul Zimmerman, SI, February 11, 2008

Harrison's hit clamped the ball in tight on Tyree's helmet.

PHOTOGRAPH BY DAMIAN STROHMEYER

AN ESCAPE AND A MIRACLE

Super Bowl XLII had seemed on track for its expected result, but that was before a great escape by Eli Manning and an improbable catch by David Tyree turned conventional wisdom on its head

BY TIM LAYDEN

THE PLAY LIVES ON, SPRINKLING its magic over the weeks and months. Many of the New York Giants got their first clear look at it when they returned to Giants Stadium from Arizona after their epic Super Bowl victory; shouts and screams emanated from film rooms and bounced through the dark hallways. Some of them watched it again nearly three months later at a routine, off-season video session in late April, when players split up by positions to review cut-up digital video of offensive and defensive situations from the entire season.

On that day quarterbacks and wide receivers studied plays in which the Giants used four-wideout formations during their two-minute drill. In the middle of the session—"Just mixed in with the rest of them," says quarterback Eli Manning—up popped the play that defined a game and a season, and perhaps much more. A quarterback escapes a sure sack, a wideout leaps into the night, a football is pinned impossibly against the surface of a helmet and brought safely to earth. The Patriots' unbeaten season ends soon after.

Just as quickly, another play pops up on the screen. But the memory lingers. "The more you look at it," says David Tyree, "the more it doesn't make sense from a logical standpoint. The velocity of the throw, the defender draped all over me, the curved surface of the ball against a round helmet, the way we came down to the ground. It just doesn't make sense."

Manning sees it in simpler terms. As he watched the video in darkness, he measured the distance between victory and defeat. "If we don't make that play," he says, "it's fourth down and at least five yards, and you don't know what can happen then. You watch that play and you realize how close we came to not winning the Super Bowl."

The wonder of Manning-to-Tyree remains. It was improvisational brilliance at best, sandlot good luck at worst. It still doesn't make sense, and that is part of its enduring beauty. "It's the greatest play in Super Bowl history," says Steve Sabol, the NFL Films president who has been chronicling the league since his father, Ed, started the company in 1962. Considering the play's stage and subplots, perhaps it's fair to see Sabol's claim and raise him: Call it the greatest play in NFL history.

The Giants, down 10–7, faced third-and-five at their 44 with 1:15 left. The call came into Manning's helmet receiver: 62 Y Sail Union.

"It's one of our basic two-minute plays," says Manning. "We probably ran it 10 or 12 times during the season." The play calls for a four-wideout formation. Y Sail tells the Y receiver, right slot Steve Smith, to run a corner route while the right wideout, Tyree, runs a post pattern. "A dummy route," says Tyree, "just to take the top off the coverage."

The Patriots came out in dime coverage and spread four DBs across the field. Manning went to the line of scrimmage and called signals: "Five-eighty, five-eighty [meaningless numbers], set, hut!"

Manning's first read was to the right, where free safety James Sanders lined up over Smith and cornerback Asante Samuel over Tyree. If Sanders sat hard on Smith, Tyree needed only to get inside of Samuel and he'd be open to the post deep. "The safety sat pretty hard," says Manning. "I probably would have thrown it to David anyway."

In fact Sanders and Samuel appeared to bungle the coverage. "Tyree and Smith were both open," says NFL Films senior producer Greg Cosell, who has watched the video many times.

Manning, however, had other concerns. At the snap Patriots linebacker Adalius Thomas beat Giants left tackle David Diehl with a speed rush to the outside, forcing Manning to step up early; nosetackle Jarvis Green beat center Shaun O'Hara to O'Hara's left; and right defensive end Richard Seymour looped to his left behind Green. O'Hara tried to come off Green and cut off Seymour, and left guard Rich Seubert tried to pick up Green. Both failed. Seymour was the first to get to Manning, briefly grabbing the quarterback's jersey. Green's grip was more substantial—a meaty forearm across the top of Manning's back and then a handful of jersey as Manning tried to escape.

History will remember Manning's great escape, but much credit on the play goes to Giants linemen O'Hara and Seubert, who were badly beaten initially but stayed with the play, heeding the order delivered on football fields every day: Play to the whistle. As Seymour grabbed Manning, O'Hara reached across under Seymour's chin and tried to drag him off Manning. Likewise, Seubert thrust a forearm under Green's left arm, making it more difficult for Green to get leverage on Manning.

The act of breaking free spit Manning out of the scrum and away from the line of scrimmage. He ran five steps to his right and back to the 33-yard line toward the Giants' sideline, caught a glimpse of Tyree, squared his shoulders and let fly. "If it had been the third quarter and that play happened, I would not have thrown the ball," says Manning. "You don't throw a 40-yard pass into the middle of the field, kind of up for grabs. But it was third-and-five, I almost got sacked, so you either throw it away or you give Tyree a shot. I gave him a shot."

Manning's throw traveled 42 yards in the air, and it was no moon ball. "People said it hung up," says Tyree. "Take a look. It was a pretty hard throw." Tyree went nearly straight up and got two hands on the ball. The Patriots' safety, Rodney Harrison, first tried to bat the ball through Tyree's hands, pushing it against the receiver's helmet. Then Harrison took Tyree down by his right biceps, which had the effect of clamping the ball tighter against the headgear. "As it was happening, I almost felt like I could hear music," says Tyree. "It was fast, but it was slow too." ∎

3

THE CATCH

" Dwight Clark changed the fate of two franchises when he skied for a six-yard TD catch from Joe Montana. The Cowboys, who had won eight of their previous 11 playoff appearances, won only two postseason games in the nine years that followed. Meanwhile San Francisco went on to win five Super Bowls in 14 years. " —JIM TROTTER

▸ THE CATCH WAS THE 13TH PLAY OF AN 89-YARD-DRIVE ▸ 58 SECONDS REMAINED

CLARK REMEMBERS only fragments of The Catch—the fear he'd jumped too soon; the way the ball bounced off his fingertips, obliging him to recatch it; the thought that maybe Montana was heaving the ball out-of-bounds. The Catch propelled San Francisco into the Super Bowl and has made a famous and much-photographed man of the dashing, white-toothed Clark. He still can't quite get a handle on what happened that day, on how a midair 10th of a second could mean so much to so many. But whenever the crush of the autograph hounds and the praise of the writers and the flacks threaten to inflate Clark's opinion of himself, he knows enough to ask himself one question. "I just say, 'Dwight, what if you'd dropped that thing?'"

—Rick Telander, SI, September 1, 1982

Clark was Montana's second option on the play.

PHOTOGRAPH BY WALTER IOOSS JR.

4

THE HOLMES TD

SUPER BOWL XLIII

" Santonio Holmes caught the pass while falling, nearly parallel to the ground, to finish off a game-winning 78-yard drive engineered by Ben Roethlisberger. " —TIM LAYDEN

▸ SIX-YARD CATCH GAVE PITTSBURGH A 27–23 LEAD
▸ 35 SECONDS REMAINED

FIRST-AND-GOAL, 48 seconds to play. Roethlisberger whistled a pass to the back of the end zone that slipped through the leaping Holmes's hands. On the next play, with the Steelers' line keeping the Cardinals' rush at bay, Roethlisberger had time to run through his progression. His first read, running back Willie Parker, was covered in the flat. His second option, receiver Nate Washington, also had too many red jerseys around him. So Roethlisberger looked to his third option, Holmes, and saw him racing to the right corner of the end zone. Three defenders were in front of the receiver, but Roethlisberger fired the ball anyway, high and outside. Holmes snagged it with his fingertips and touched the grass with both sets of outstretched toes. His fourth catch of the drive and ninth reception of the night was the game-winner.

—Damon Hack, SI, February 9, 2009

Holmes was named Super Bowl MVP.

PHOTOGRAPHS BY AL TIELEMANS (LEFT) AND PETER READ MILLER

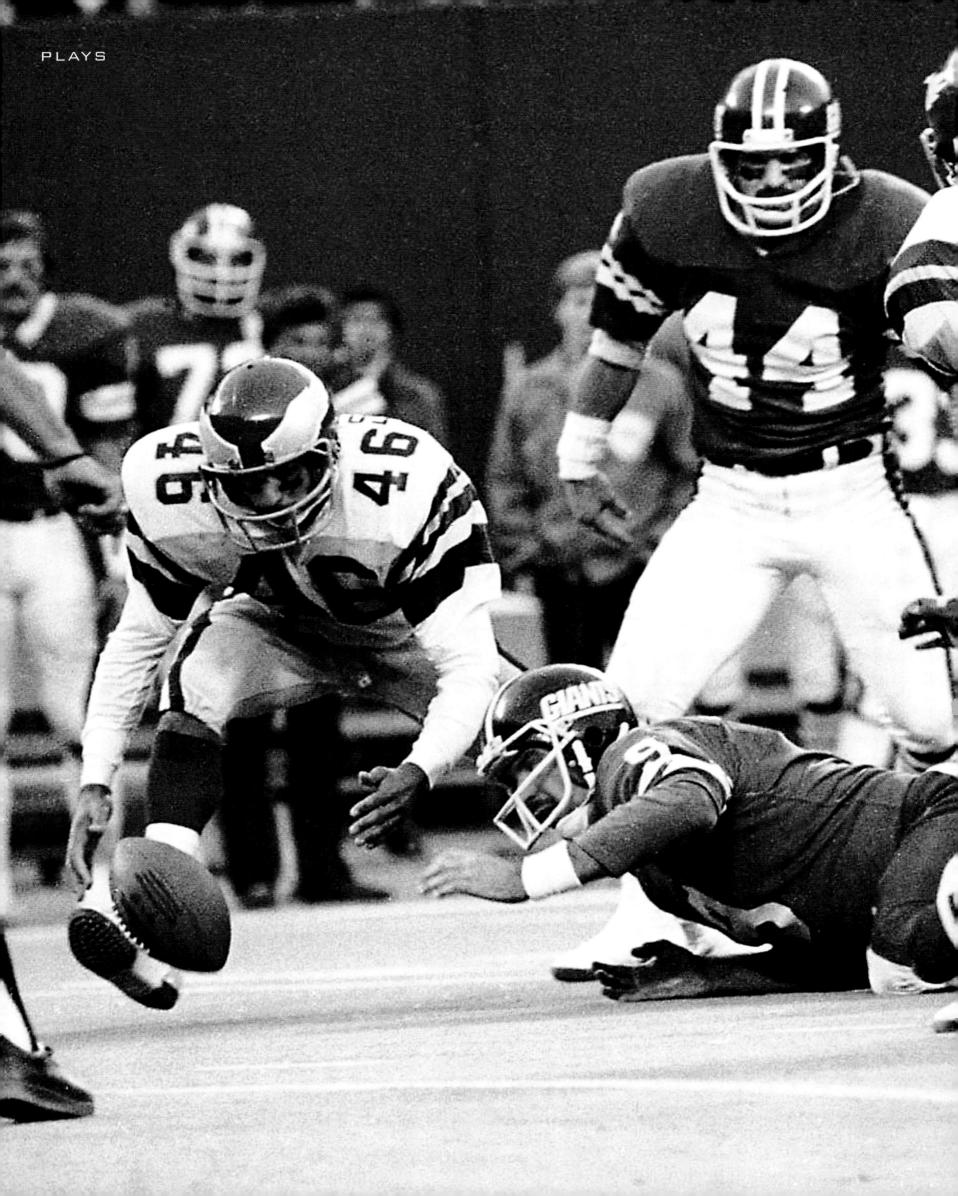

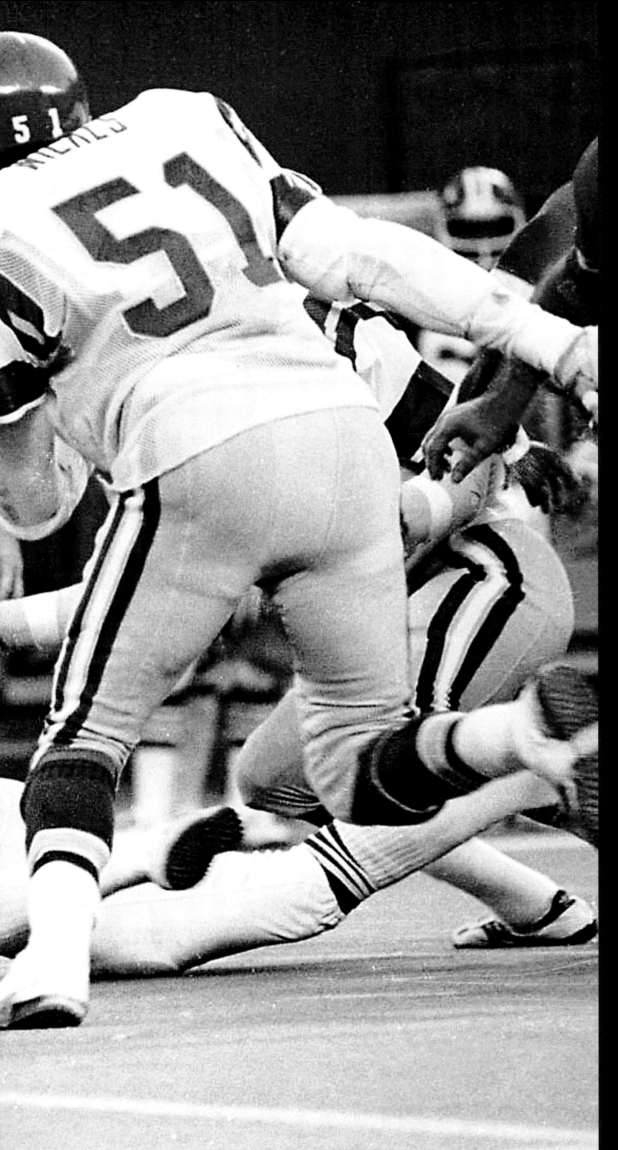

5

MIRACLE AT THE MEADOWLANDS

NOVEMBER 12, 1978

" It still boggles the mind that the Giants attempted to run the ball instead of taking a knee. " —JIM TROTTER

▸ GIANTS LED 17–12 WITH 31 SECONDS LEFT
▸ EAGLES HAD NO TIMEOUTS

"JUST FALL ON IT" his teammates implored in the huddle. The game was over, for God's sake. But Joe Pisarcik had no choice. A week earlier, in a loss to the Washington Redskins, Giants offensive coordinator Bob Gibson had screamed at his quarterback for changing a play. So on this frigid afternoon at Giants Stadium, Pisarcik followed Gibson's instructions and called a handoff to the fullback. Pisarcik mishandled the ball and made a clumsy handoff to Larry Csonka, who dived for the football after it bounced off his right hip and fell to the turf. Eagles cornerback Herman Edwards picked it up and raced 26 yards into the end zone. Now the game was over. "It was just one play," Pisarcik says, "but it changed the fortunes of an organization, and it changed people's lives." The play's greatest victim was Gibson, who was canned the day afterward and never worked in football again.

—Albert Chen, SI, July 2, 2001

Edwards ran in the third-down fumble by Pisarcik (9).

PHOTOGRAPHS BY G. PAUL BURNETT/AP

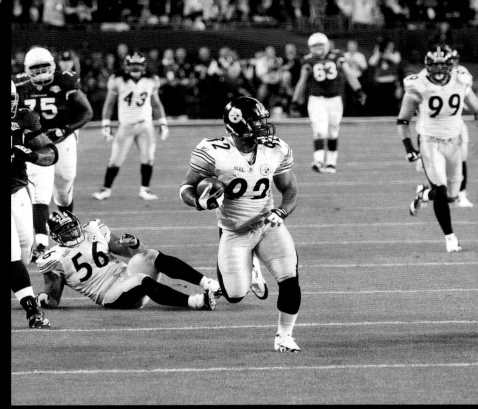

Harrison's TD remains the Super Bowl's longest.

PHOTOGRAPHS BY JOHN BIEVER (3); BILL FRAKES (1); AND HEINZ KLUETMEIER (3)

6

HARRISON'S RUNBACK

" A 14-point swing that might be the greatest individual Super Bowl play ever. The intuition to read the play, the hands to snag the pass, the stamina to slalom through tacklers, and the strength to drag Larry Fitzgerald the final yards into the end zone—amazing. " —JIM TROTTER

▸ RUNBACK WENT 100 YARDS
▸ PLAY CLOSED FIRST HALF

FOR SEVERAL long moments James Harrison lay on his back, palms up, toes pointing skyward. Coach Mike Tomlin headed for the end zone, where he helped him to his feet and walked him off the field. "It was tiring," Harrison said of his historic run, "but it was all worth it."

—Damon Hack, SI, February 9, 2009

MUSIC CITY MIRACLE

" Frank Wycheck's pass to Kevin Dyson remains controversial—was it a forward lateral?—but also truly miraculous. " —DAMON HACK

▸ BILLS HAD JUST TAKEN A 16–15 LEAD
▸ 16 SECONDS REMAINED

AFTER VIEWING a replay for the first time, Titans coach Jeff Fisher put down his wine glass, dropped his head and looked humbled by the magnitude of the feat. Yet Dyson's 75-yard catch and dash—which came after fullback Lorenzo Neal had fielded a short, high kickoff and handed off to tight end Frank Wycheck, who ran to his right before throwing across the field to Dyson behind a wall of blockers along the left sideline—was anything but supernatural. True to his methodical nature, Fisher had anticipated just such a situation, chosen a viable escape route, made sure his team knew the drill and practiced the play at the end of each Saturday's special teams session. "Another one of Jeff Fisher's crazy setups," quipped Blaine Bishop, the Titans' veteran free safety. "You name the situation and we'll practice it. Guys'll be tired and rolling their eyes, saying, 'Yeah, like this'll ever come up.'"

—Michael Silver, SI, January 17, 2000

Once Dyson caught Wycheck's pass, he had a free run.

PHOTOGRAPH BY BOB ROSATO

8
JONES'S TACKLE

SUPER BOWL XXXIV

"For all the hype and glitz and the attention that goes to the big names, sometimes a Super Bowl comes down to one textbook tackle by an unheralded player with the game on the line." —MARK MRAVIC

▸ TITANS HAD BALL ON 10-YARD LINE WITH TIME FOR ONE PLAY
▸ RAMS LED 23–16

TENNESSEE CALLED its final timeout with six seconds remaining, and the season came down to one precious play. The Titans sent tight end Frank Wycheck into the end zone, hoping to draw several defenders to the area and hit Kevin Dyson on an underneath slant with room to run. Dyson, whose kickoff return off a Wycheck lateral had given Tennessee a stunning wild-card victory over the Buffalo Bills, had another Music City Miracle in reach. He caught the ball in stride inside the five and had only one man between him and the first overtime game in Super Bowl history. Rams linebacker Mike Jones, however, wrapped up the wideout, and Dyson's lunge for the goal line fell short. "It seemed like slow-motion," Jones said. "I couldn't see [Steve] McNair throw the ball, but I could feel it."

—*Michael Silver, SI, February 7, 2000*

Dyson's reach was short by one precious yard.

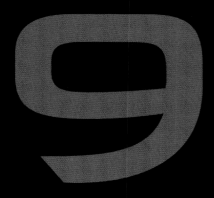

SWANN'S CATCH

SUPER BOWL X

❝ Lynn Swann's acrobatic catch came on a ball that he tipped to himself after it was deflected by Cowboys cornerback Mark Washington. ❞ —MARK GODICH

▸ SWANN'S 53-YARD GRAB HELPED STEELERS OUT OF BAD FIELD POSITION
▸ SWANN WAS NAMED GAME MVP AND HAD FOUR CATCHES FOR 161 YARDS

FOR ALL of those gaudy things that happened throughout the afternoon, memories of the 1976 Super Bowl will keep going back to the Pittsburgh Steelers' Lynn Swann climbing into the air like the boy in the Indian rope trick, and coming down with the football. He didn't come down with very many passes last Sunday, really, only four, but he caught the ones that truly mattered. That is why it will seem that he spent the day way up there in the crisp sky, a thousand feet above Miami's Orange Bowl, where neither the Dallas Cowboys nor even a squadron of fighter planes could do anything to stop him. When it was all over Lynn Swann and the Steelers had won 21–17 and had repeated as the champions of professional madness.

—*Dan Jenkins, SI, January 26, 1976*

Swann and Washington both tipped at the ball.

PHOTOGRAPHS BY KEN REGAN / CAMERA 5 (LEFT) AND HEINZ KLUETMEIER

HAIL MARY

" Roger Staubach's desperation bomb to Drew Pearson against the Vikings is as momentous for its contribution to the language as for its impact on the field. " —MARK MRAVIC

▸ 50-YARD THROW GAVE DALLAS A 17–14 WIN
▸ STAUBACH: "I CLOSED MY EYES AND SAID A HAIL MARY"

USUALLY it only happens in those novels written for young readers. It is cold and gloomy and all hope seems to be gone, but the good guy who loves his wife and family and country has gone back to try one more long pass against the evil villains who throw bottles and garbage at football officials. The ball sails high and far, straining to be seen against the feeble lights that glow through the gray Minnesota sky. Now the ball is coming to earth as the scoreboard flickers away the final seconds of the game. There are two men underneath the ball and suddenly one of them slips and falls, and the one who is supposed to catch it and complete the grandest of comebacks and upsets and fairy tales does exactly that. Roger Staubach has thrown a pass to Drew Pearson and the Dallas Cowboys have used up a lifetime of good fortune in a single play.

—*Dan Jenkins, SI, January 5, 1976*

The Vikings argued that Pearson (88) had pushed off.

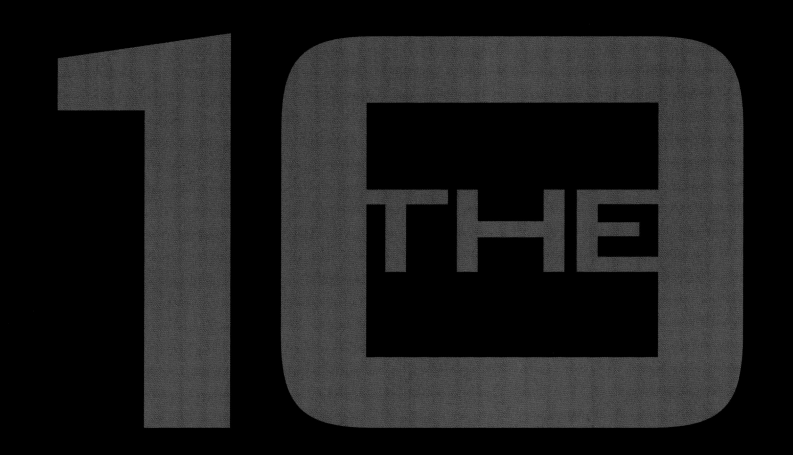

10 THE

BEST SINGLE-SEASON TEAMS

SHOULD ONE BAD SUNDAY DEFINE A TEAM? NOT ACCORDING TO OUR PANEL. THE GROUP WAS FORGIVING OF THE OCCASIONAL STUMBLE, AND NOT JUST IN WEIGHING THE CLASSIC FAN'S DEBATE AT THE TOP OF THE POLL, BETWEEN THE UNDEFEATED BUT UNSPECTACULAR 1972 DOLPHINS AND THE MORE DOMINANT, ONE-LOSS 1985 BEARS.

THE GENEROSITY ALSO SPILLED OVER TO THE 2007 PATRIOTS, WHO PLOWED THROUGH 18 STRAIGHT WINS, UNTIL THEY RAN INTO DAVID TYREE AND HIS MAGIC HELMET. THE PATRIOTS MAKE THE LIST, BUT THE GIANTS TEAM THAT KNOCKED THEM OFF EARNED ONLY ONE VOTE, AND THAT WAS FOR 10TH PLACE.

TAKING THE LOGIC TO THE EXTREME WAS NFL EDITOR MARK MRAVIC. PITTSBURGH WON FOUR SUPER BOWLS IN THE 1970S, BUT NOT IN THE 1976 SEASON—AND HE SAYS THE BICENTENNIAL STEELERS WERE THE BEST OF THEM ALL: "YES. THE BEST STEELERS TEAM OF THE '70S DIDN'T EVEN MAKE THE SUPER BOWL. THE DEFENSE HAD A RECORD FIVE SHUTOUTS AND THREE MORE IN WHICH IT DIDN'T ALLOW A TOUCHDOWN. BOTH FRANCO HARRIS AND ROCKY BLEIER SURPASSED 1,000 YARDS RUSHING. UNFORTUNATELY, BOTH WERE INJURED FOR THE AFC TITLE GAME, WHICH PITTSBURGH LOST TO OAKLAND." EVERY LOSER HAS A STORY—SOME ARE JUST BETTER THAN OTHERS.

1
1985
BEARS

15-1 REGULAR SEASON

" Their one loss came to Dan Marino's Dolphins on the road, with starting quarterback Jim McMahon on the bench. The defense was the most ferocious ever, pitching two playoff shutouts and overwhelming the Patriots in the Super Bowl. Defensive guru Buddy Ryan left following the season, and the level was never matched. " —MARK MRAVIC

▸ LED NFL IN TOTAL DEFENSE AND SCORING DEFENSE
▸ SECOND IN SCORING OFFENSE

IT WILL be many years before we see anything approaching the vision of hell that Chicago inflicted on the poor Patriots in Super Bowl XX. It was near perfect, an exquisite mesh of talent and system, defensive football carried to its highest degree. It was a great roaring wave that swept through the playoffs, gathering force and momentum, until it finally crashed home in New Orleans' Superdome. The game wasn't exciting. So what? Go down to Bourbon Street if you want excitement. The verdict on Chicago's 46–10 victory was in after two Patriot series. Don't feel cheated. Louis-Schmeling II wasn't very competitive, either. Nor was the British cavalry charge at Balaklava, but Tennyson wrote a poem about it.

—*Paul Zimmerman, SI, February 3, 1986*

McMahon and William Perry (72) shone for Chicago.

PHOTOGRAPHS BY WALTER IOOSS JR. (LEFT) AND JOHN BIEVER

1972
DOLPHINS

14-0 REGULAR SEASON

"You can't do any better than perfection, and this rugged team beat back all challenges." —DAMON HACK

▸ LED NFL IN TOTAL OFFENSE
AND DEFENSE
▸ LARRY CSONKA AND
MERCURY MORRIS BOTH HAD
1,000-YARD RUSHING SEASONS

ALMOST EVERYWHERE across the pro football landscape there was a heartfelt vote for the Pittsburgh Steelers, a team so snakebitten that it had suffered its whole long life, 40 years, without a single championship. But after weeks of favoring her with bountiful blessings, the fairy godmother suddenly failed to touch Cinderella with her magic wand. Instead, she strung along with the inexorable Miami Dolphins, that acquisitive bunch of opportunists that she has been dating steadily.

And so it is the Dolphins who will now meet Washington in the Super Bowl. This was Miami's 16th consecutive victory. To the very end it seemed that Pittsburgh might be able to employ the same kind of wicked lightning that it had used in the last seconds to execute the Raiders. But Miami's No-Name Defense precluded another miracle by twice intercepting Terry Bradshaw in the waning minutes of the game.

—*Ron Reid, SI, January 8, 1973*

Csonka ran for 112 yards in Super Bowl VII.

3

1984
49ERS

15–1 REGULAR SEASON

" They had Hall of Famers on offense, defense and the sideline, allowed the fewest points in the league, including holding seven opponents to 10 points or less, and gave up just 10 points in their first two playoff games combined before shutting down the high-scoring Dolphins and Dan Marino in the Super Bowl. " —JIM TROTTER

> ▸ NFL'S FIRST TEAM TO WIN 15 REGULAR-SEASON GAMES
> ▸ ALL FOUR STARTING DBS MADE PRO BOWL

THEY'RE EFFECTIVE on any level, from working on a cerebral plane, with Joe Montana running one of the NFL's most complicated passing attacks, to brutalizing opponents with a very rough and effective ground game. There's only one thing missing. The magic. The beautiful rose-colored glow of 1981, when the 49ers came from nowhere and won it all. In a way it's unfair to compare the two teams. What can compare with your first kiss, your first sip of wine? "Ask anyone and he'll tell you there's no question that this team's better than the one we had in '81," says Ronnie Lott. "And it's fun now, too . . . don't get me wrong . . . but it's more professional. In '81 it was a different kind of fun, bubbly fun, rookie fun, you know what I mean?"

—Paul Zimmerman, SI, November 26, 1984

WR Freddie Solomon snagged one in the NFC title game.

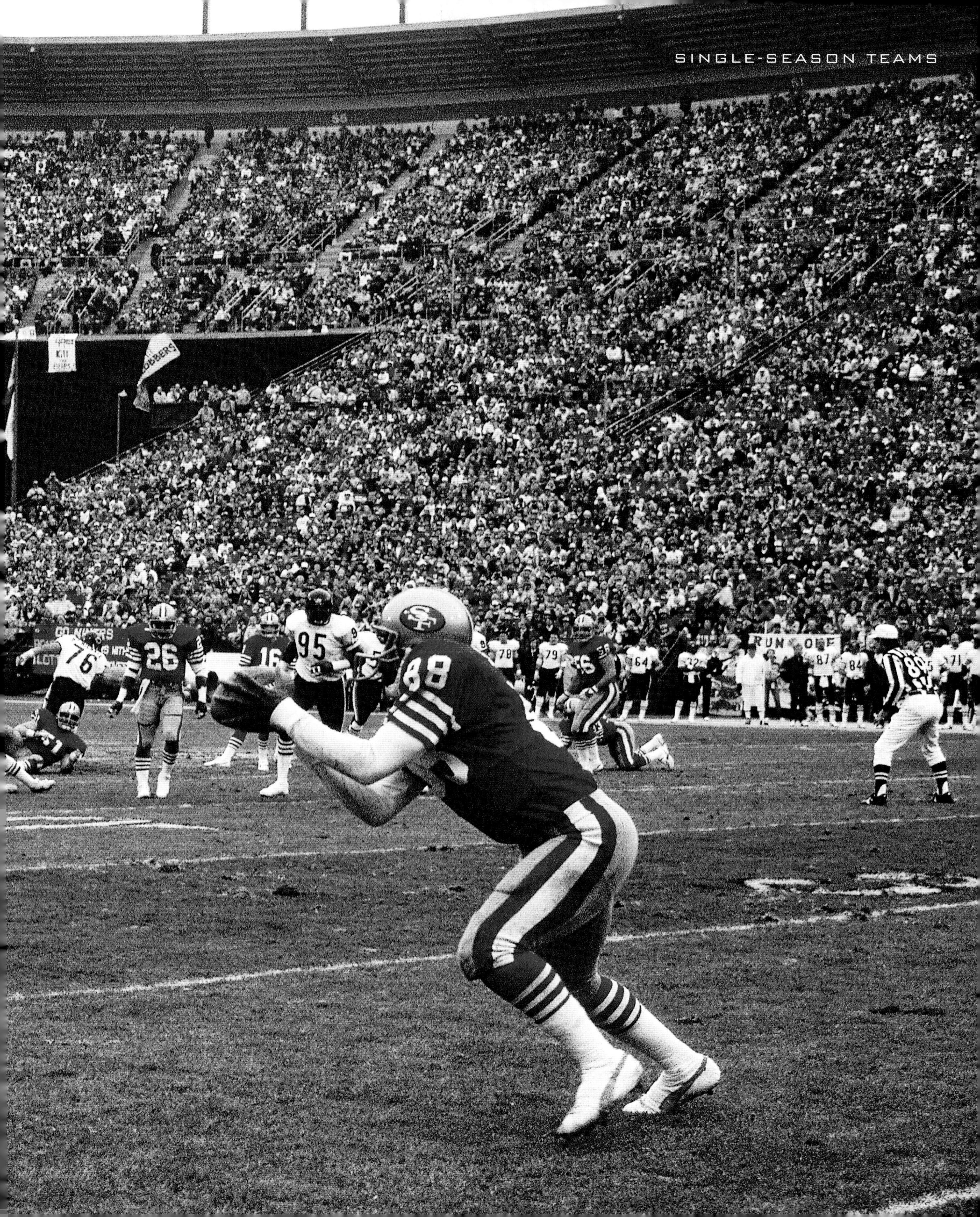
GO NINERS

4

1962
PACKERS

13–1 REGULAR SEASON

" The best team in the Lombardi dynasty, this version of the Packers led the league in offense, defense and scoring margin. " —TIM LAYDEN

▸ OUTSCORED OPPONENTS
415–148
▸ 10 HALL OF FAME PLAYERS

PARTLY BECAUSE of the weather and often because New York coach Allie Sherman and his players wanted to prove that they could whip the Packers where the Packers are best, the Giants ran against the right side of the Packers line—Henry Jordan at right tackle and Bill Quinlan at right end. It was the Giants' misfortune that they did not succeed. Jordan and Quinlan played heroically, and the Packers linebackers— Ray Nitschke, Dan Currie and Bill Forester—were, as they have been all year, the best in the league. Giants backfield coach Kyle Rote pointed that out. "The Packers won because they have a fine offense and a great line," he said. "But most of all, they have three magnificent linebackers. After everyone else had gone home, Sherman said his farewell: "We weren't humiliated. There was no humiliation this year."

There wasn't. The Giants were good. Green Bay simply was better.

—Tex Maule, SI, January 7, 1963

Bart Starr led the NFL with a 90.7 passer rating.

5

1989
49ERS

14–2 REGULAR SEASON

" Joe Montana, Jerry Rice and Ronnie Lott headlined this team of superstars with no visible flaw. " —DAMON HACK

▸ NFL'S TOP SCORING OFFENSE, THIRD-BEST SCORING DEFENSE
▸ DEFEATED BRONCOS 55–10 IN SUPER BOWL XXIV

WE ARE sailing in uncharted waters with these 49ers. We are seeing power football, defensive brilliance, and execution so precise it's scary. . . . So what must coach George Seifert fear as his Niners head to New Orleans for their Super Bowl date with Denver? Complacency? A false sense of invincibility? Arrogance? Greed? All the evils the rich and powerful are heir to? He'll take them, as long as he can keep Montana on his side. "Joe's been phenomenal all year," said Seifert, "but it seems that he's elevated his performance for the playoffs. His concentration, his 'into-it-ness'—it's mind-boggling. You look at him from the sidelines, and you're almost in awe. You find yourself watching like a fan would. You fight to get out of a mode like that. In this game if you let your guard down, pretty soon you're fighting for your life. But today, in the heat of battle, I couldn't help saying, 'Damn, we're pretty good.' "

—*Paul Zimmerman, SI, January 22, 1990*

WR John Taylor (left) and RB Roger Craig added power.

6

1992
COWBOYS

"The first of Dallas's three title teams of the 1990s was also its best. Blessed with playmakers on both sides of the ball, the Cowboys stormed through the playoffs with a balanced attacked that averaged 38.7 points a game, while an opportunistic defense forced a total of 15 turnovers in three-double digit victories." —MARK GODICH

▸ LED NFL IN TOTAL DEFENSE
▸ DEFEATED BUFFALO 52–17 IN SUPER BOWL XXVII

GET USED to the Cowboys, folks, because they're going to be with us for a long time. Troy Aikman and Emmitt Smith and Michael Irvin and Ken Norton Jr. and Charles Haley—all those implements of destruction are just starting to feel their oats. Coach Jimmy Johnson and his hair spray; Jerry Jones, the owner who hungers for the limelight. You say you're tired of them already? Gee, that's tough. . . . The reporters wanted to know how Johnson had come into the NFL without any experience in pro football and put together, with such clarity, exactly the type of team he wanted. "I like the guy who can walk into a poolroom and pick up a cue stick and sink the 8 ball," said Johnson. "The people I want around me, well, the bigger the game, the more they shine."

—Paul Zimmerman, SI, February 8, 1993

Smith (22) and Irvin (88) spread their wings.

7

2007 PATRIOTS

16–0 REGULAR SEASON

" While the Giants and David Tyree ruined their bid for a historic 19–0 season, Tom Brady led a record-breaking Patriots offense that demolished almost everything in its path. " —DON BANKS

▸ SCORED NFL RECORD 589 POINTS
▸ OUTSCORED OPPONENTS BY RECORD 315 POINTS

THEY SHRUGGED off the blowback from the Week 1 Spygate controversy and averaged more than 40 points a game in the first half of the season, prompting accusations that coach Bill Belichick was needlessly running up scores on defenseless opponents. The last month's more difficult victories have provided a true measure of the franchise's culture. The Pats caught America's attention with glitz and big scores, but have kept it with solid performances more emblematic of their foundation. They do not court Football Nation's affection or scrutiny, but inside their walls they embrace the simplest concepts—selflessness, rigor, tunnel vision—until they are reflex. The concepts are not novel. Every football team at every level from Pop Warner to the NFL seeks the same discipline, but the Patriots have come closest to achieving it.

—Tim Layden, SI, January 28, 2008

Brady (left) and LB Tedy Bruschi flirted with perfection.

PHOTOGRAPHS BY JOHN BIEVER (LEFT) AND BOB ROSATO

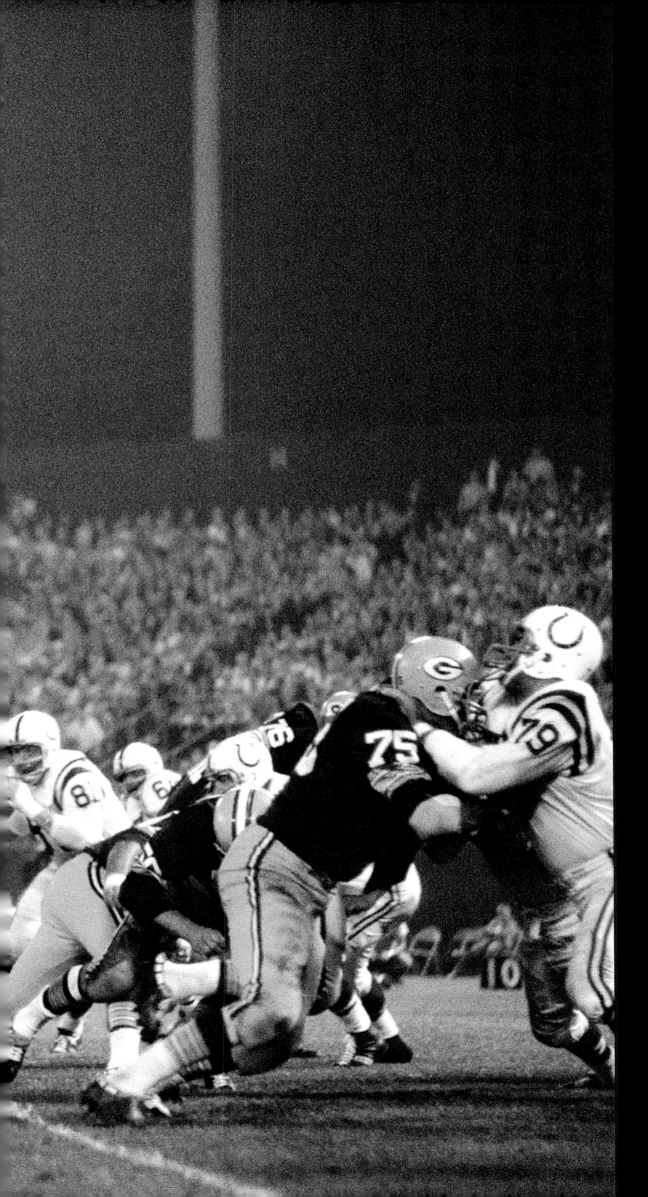

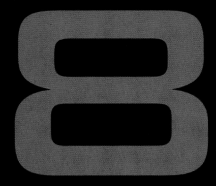

8

1966 PACKERS

12–2 REGULAR SEASON

" The first-ever Super Bowl winner won its fourth NFL championship in the span of six years. By this point Lombardi's Packers were a finely tuned machine. " —DON BANKS

▸ QB BART STARR WAS NAMED NFL MVP
▸ DEFEATED CHIEFS 35–10 IN SUPER BOWL I

HAVING LIVED luxuriously on poise and control all season, the Packers won their second straight NFL championship in Dallas by defeating the Cowboys 34–27 in a flamboyant display of football histrionics. For pure suspense and unremitting excitement no championship game has approached it for at least eight years. . . . After the win the Packers were too tired to think ahead to the Super Bowl. But in chilly Buffalo, after the Chiefs had defeated the Bills 31–7 to win the AFL championship, Kansas City coach Hank Stram let himself be carried away by the wonder of it all. "Pour it on, boys," he burbled. "There'll be lots more when we tear apart the NFL in two weeks." Told of this rather optimistic statement, Packers guard Fuzzy Thurston shrugged. "Hank Stram can think what he wants," he said. "We just play the game and win."

—*Tex Maule, SI, January 9, 1967*

Paul Hornung (5) blocked for Jim Taylor (31).

PHOTOGRAPH BY WALTER IOOSS JR.

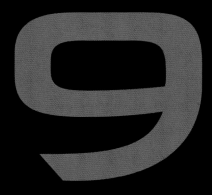

9
1991
REDSKINS

14-2 REGULAR SEASON

" They were five points from an undefeated season, despite playing a grueling schedule. They ranked number 1 in turnover differential, and they outscored opponents 485–224. " —JIM TROTTER

▸ LED NFL IN SCORING OFFENSE
▸ SECOND IN SCORING DEFENSE

MAYBE WE should reflect on the simple fact of Washington's superiority for just a moment. The Skins won 17 games this season and lost only twice. They whipped their NFC playoff foes, the Falcons and the Lions, by a combined score of 65–17. They have the premier offensive line in the league, the best trio of wide receivers (Gary Clark, Art Monk and Ricky Sanders) and the best coach (Joe Gibbs). "If we'd scored before the half," said Bills center Kent Hull after their 37–24 loss in the Super Bowl, "we could have won." No, they couldn't have. The Redskins are a team of remarkable strength and determination. Boring, perhaps, but disciplined and smart. "If the rest of Washington ran as efficiently as this football team, there wouldn't be any deficit," said Skins center Jeff Bostic, while ripping tape off his knees after the game and puffing on a big cigar.

—*Rick Telander, SI, February 3, 1992*

Mark Rypien won Super Bowl MVP after a stellar season.

PHOTOGRAPH BY JOHN BIEVER

10

1978 STEELERS

14-2 REGULAR SEASON

"Not the most dominant defensive unit Chuck Noll had, but the team with the most offensive firepower by far—with 33, 34 and 35 points scored in its three playoff games. This season, and this postseason, proved Terry Bradshaw and the Pittsburgh passing game were as formidable as the Steelers running attack ever was." —PETER KING

▸ NINE HALL OF FAME PLAYERS
▸ BRADSHAW WON NFL MVP

AT THE start of 1978, the Steelers' defense was considered over the hill. It was even suggested—perish the thought—that the Steel Curtain should be dismantled and replaced by a 3-4 defense. So the Curtain regrouped and had an intimidating year. The Steelers allowed the fewest points in the NFL (195). A year ago, for the first time in four seasons, Joe Greene didn't play in the AFC Championship Game. Instead he sat home and watched Oakland and Denver play on TV. During the telecast a camera focused on a sign in the stands in Mile High Stadium that read, JOE MUST BE GREENE WITH ENVY. Quietly, Greene got his two Super Bowl rings out and placed them on top of his television set. Now he plans to add a third ring to that collection.

—*Joe Marshall, SI, January 15, 1979*

Franco Harris scored in Super Bowl XIII (left).

PHOTOGRAPHS BY TONY TOMSIC (LEFT) AND JOHN IACONO

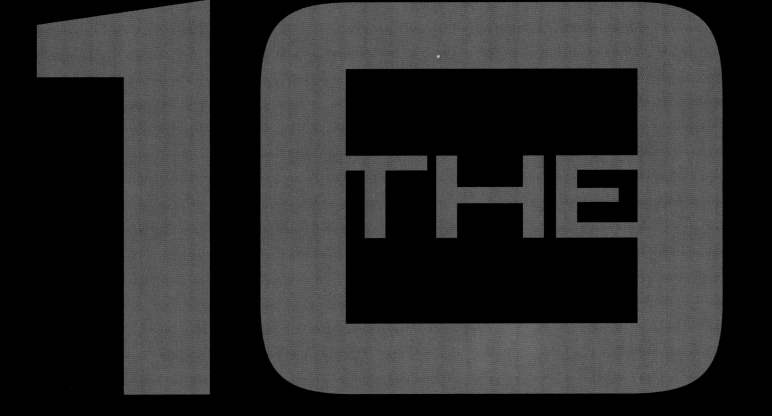

10 THE

BEST STADIUMS

THE MOST UNORTHODOX CHOICE OF ANY PANELIST IN ANY CATEGORY WAS TIM LAYDEN'S VOTE FOR THE NO.1 NFL STADIUM. IT CAME, ALMOST LITERALLY, OUT OF LEFTFIELD. THAT IS TO SAY, HE CHOSE YANKEE STADIUM. HIS EXPLANATION: "DOZENS OF THE MOST IMPORTANT GAMES IN BUILDING THE FOUNDATION OF THE LEAGUE TOOK PLACE HERE, WITH PLAYERS KICKING UP CLOUDS OF DUST ON THE BASEBALL INFIELD AND DISAPPEARING INTO DARK CORNERS OF THE BUILDING AFTER TOUCHDOWNS."

LAYDEN'S VOTE WASN'T ENOUGH TO PUT YANKEE STADIUM IN THE TOP 10. BUT THE OTHERS DID EMBRACE THE BASIC LOGIC. WHILE A COUPLE OF MODERN MARVELS MAKE THE LIST, VOTERS WERE MORE LIKELY TO EMBRACE A FLAWED BEAUTY, IF THE CHARACTER WAS RIGHT.

AND CHARACTER WAS BROADLY DEFINED. A CHAMPIONSHIP HISTORY CERTAINLY HELPED. BUT WHAT MATTERED AS MUCH, IF NOT MORE, WAS THE COLLECTIVE ENERGY OF THE FANS. FOR EXAMPLE, NO ONE HAD ANYTHING NICE TO SAY ABOUT THE PHYSICAL STRUCTURE OF OAKLAND COLISEUM ("A DUMP," SCOFFED JIM TROTTER, AND HE VOTED FOR IT), BUT IT MADE THE LIST BECAUSE NO ONE HAS ANYTHING NICE TO SAY *IN* OAKLAND COLISEUM. THE FACE-PAINTED BLACK HOLE FANS MIRROR THE HISTORIC ROGUISHNESS OF THEIR TEAM. AND WHILE THEY MAY BE 3,000 MILES AWAY FROM YANKEE STADIUM, THEY HAVE MADE A FINE ART OF GIVING THE OLD BRONX CHEER.

1

LAMBEAU FIELD

GREEN BAY

" It's the history, the intimacy and, of course, the bratwurst. " —DAMON HACK

▸ FIRST GAME HELD IN 1957
▸ CAPACITY HAS EXPANDED FROM 32,500 TO 73,142

THERE WAS a time when the Green Bay Packers' Lambeau Field wasn't the quaint anomaly it is today. Everyone played football on grass, and there were no Teflon roofs to shut out the midday sun, no domes to block the late-autumn wind. When mud-spattered linemen Forrest Gregg and Jerry Kramer hoisted coach Vince Lombardi onto their shoulders in 1961 for his first NFL title ride, only God's gray sky hung overhead. Why, the world hadn't even heard of turf toe when Lombardi stalked Lambeau's frozen sidelines in his trademark overcoat, shrieking, "Hey! Whaddaya doin' out there?" in his best Brooklynese. "With Lombardi it was never cold here," says former All-Pro Fuzzy Thurston, who played guard for Green Bay from 1959 to '67. "Before games he'd just say something like, 'Men, it's a little blustery out there today.' Blustery, see? Then he'd say, 'It's our kind of day. Now get out there and strut around like it's the middle of July.' "

—Johnette Howard, SI, January 13, 1997

At Lambeau, it's always football weather.

ARROWHEAD STADIUM

KANSAS CITY, MO.

" The sea of red displayed on game day at Arrowhead always speaks to how beloved the Chiefs remain in their home market. It's still one of the loudest outdoor venues in the NFL. " —DON BANKS

▸ OPENED IN 1972
▸ CAPACITY: 76,416

WHY YOU DON'T NEED TO REMEMBER JOE CAHN'S NAME Because he goes by Commissioner of Tailgating. WHY HIS TITLE MAKES SENSE Each football season since 1996 the Commish, 54, has logged 30,000 miles in his Monaco Signature coach, visiting about 50 of the nation's finest stadium parking lots. WHY SERIOUS 'GATERS SHOULD INVITE HIM TO HELP OUT AT THE HIBACHI Cahn founded the New Orleans School of Cooking (which he's since sold) and has prepared king salmon at a Seattle tailgate and Cuban pig in Miami. He always wears the home team's colors, and he can spin a good travel yarn—like the time John Madden invited him into the Madden Cruiser for a pregame bite of barbecue. HEAVEN IS Kansas City's Arrowhead Stadium. "They know their barbecue, know their football, and they have a lot of porta-potties out there."

— *Sports Illustrated, September 16, 2002*

Arrowhead is the NFL's fourth-largest stadium.

ARLINGTON, TEXAS

Some worried, but in-game punts have never hit the TV.

3

COWBOYS STADIUM

" Despite its excesses, Jerry Jones's vision-come-true is as close to a living room experience as you will find in a stadium. " —JIM TROTTER

▸ CAPACITY IS 80,000, PLUS ANOTHER 20,000 IN STANDING ROOM
▸ WORLD'S LARGEST HIGH-DEFINITION VIDEO BOARD

OURS IS BIGGER! proclaimed T-shirts, and this was of course true; the stadium is the largest column-free structure in the world. Moments before kickoff a series of photos appeared on the video board: the Pyramids, the Parthenon, the Great Wall, the Taj Mahal, the Colosseum and, finally, Cowboys Stadium.

— *Chris Ballard, SI, September 28, 2009*

THE KING OF TEXAS

Jerry Jones, who built his fortune by taking outsized risks, positively glowed as he oversaw—and underwrote—construction of America's largest and most expensive football palace

BY RICHARD HOFFER

His "TOLERANCE FOR AMBIGUITY"—his phrase—is high enough to register somewhere between impudence and daredevilry. Where else would you put it? When the big oil companies, who are hardly in the business of prudence, abandoned their dry holes in the late '60s, it was Jerry Jones who offered to lease their failures. He barely understood their caution anyway. Spending $14 million to drill, say, 18,000 feet and then just walking away because of something called budget—was that any way to find oil or gas? "Unthinkable," he says. "That's just unthinkable."

Jones, an independent operator and not answerable to anything like budget, kept drilling, and who knows how many times he embarrassed the big oil companies with his finds. A dry hole, after all, is simply a gusher without conviction. Jones, then as now, supplied all the conviction necessary. Maybe if he hadn't made 12 strikes in his first 13 tries—drilling between dry holes in Oklahoma's Red Fork Wells—he'd have had less of it. Then again, we're talking about a guy who, as a 23-year-old in 1966, nearly bought the San Diego Chargers from Barron Hilton with money he didn't have. (Jones had arranged for a letter of credit from a labor union.) "You sure are young," Hilton told Jones, who was born with all the conviction he'd ever require.

But let's not make him sound pathological, either, as if he lacked a mortal's ability to recognize consequence. He never actually drilled to the center of the earth for oil, and the times he came close he sweated it. When he pledged his wealth and all receivables to buy the floundering Dallas Cowboys—America's Team or not, this was a failing outfit in 1989—he needed two hands to steady a cup of coffee. Who wouldn't? In those days Dallas was the epicenter for one of the oil industry's worst depressions. Titans were being wiped out, banks closed, skyscrapers shuttered. Loans were being sold for a nickel on the dollar.

Of course his hands shook. Even beyond the economic climate, the deal was punishing, a sophisticated form of extortion, really. It was bad enough that he had to pay a $65 million for the Cowboys (quite literally America's Team, considering the federal government owned 12% of the franchise after a lending bank failed). The team was not very good, and, after three losing seasons, home sellouts were even harder to come by than victories. But—here's the extortion part—he was forced to absorb the $75 million leasing rights on Texas Stadium as well. (The total purchase price was a record for an NFL team.) In those days NFL stadiums were essentially rentals, some place you visited on Sundays. They had no income or marketing worth to NFL owners.

The deal done, Jones barely had time to count the empty suites, consider the previous season's 3–13 record, and get over the surprising fact that the Cowboys had lost $9.5 million on just $41 million in revenues the year before, when the bills began to come in. They totaled $105,000 a day. "If you want to get motivated," Jones suggests, "strap that on."

O.K., that was then, and now here's Jones in his splendid office at Valley Ranch in Irving, the three Super Bowl trophies always in his line of sight. That pitiful team he bought is valued by *Forbes* at $1.2 billion, and he has turned that albatross of a stadium into his biggest revenue producer. But what's the fun of this business, really, if your hands aren't shaking?

"Let's go see the stadium," Jones says, and we're off to 140 acres of mud. This is the latest, possibly the greatest, edifice to be constructed for the people's entertainment in this great land of ours, maybe the final frontier in sports-related architecture.

Jones, who did not answer to budget here any more than he did in the Oklahoma oil fields, did not stint on anything, even when the original cost of $650 million ballooned to $1 billion. The city of Arlington's share was capped at $325 million, meaning that Jones pays for every add-on doodad—such as two 60-yard-wide flat screens hanging over the field—out of his pocket, 100%. "And I'm an adder-oner," he says.

It turns out Jones is a bit of a stadium freak as well, going way back. Before playing Nebraska in the 1965 Cotton Bowl, his Arkansas team stayed in Houston and got a tour of the new Astrodome. "When we saw that thing—glistening—I couldn't stand it," he says. "It sucked the air right out of you." Many years later (he won't say when because it embarrasses him to admit how old he was on his first visit to New York City) Jones paid a cab driver to take him to Yankee Stadium first thing. He got out, touched it and returned to business.

When it became obvious to him that simply renovating 36-year-old Texas Stadium—"And by the way," he says, "I didn't have to do even that"—wouldn't cut it, he plunged into the new venture with his usual gusto. He got the idea for his giant screens while watching a Celine Dion show at Caesars Palace. He was visually discombobulated by the screens behind her, redundant to the Canadian songbird's performance, but mesmerized all the same. "You didn't know what you were seeing," he says, "but you knew it must have been good."

Jones actually seems to delight in the possibility of failure, however slim it really is. As he conducts a tour of his pile—"There," he points to some concrete at field level, "is where the players will come onto the field. Through a stadium club!"—you can enjoy a secondhand exhilaration. *This is what it's like to commit $1 billion!* "I'm writing a one-million-dollar check every day," Jones says, aggrandizing his risk the way any gambler would, the way he always has, the tab just higher these days. "That will keep your eye on the ball." He couldn't seem any happier. ∎

4

ORANGE BOWL

" Five of the first 13 Super Bowls took place in Flipper's home. The Dolphins went undefeated there in 1972. It stood and decayed in downtown Miami, but it represents some of the most significant moments in the history of the league. " —TIM LAYDEN

▸ STOOD FROM 1937 TO 2008
▸ DOLPHINS HOME STADIUM, 1966 TO 1986

AS THE site of 14 national championships and five Super Bowls, it served as a national proving ground. Joe Namath became a New York legend, Doug Flutie a Boston legend, Bear Bryant an Alabama legend, Kellen Winslow a San Diego legend—all because of their exploits in the neighborhood now known as Little Havana.

—*S.L. Price, SI, November 12, 2007*

Super Bowl III was but one piece of its celebrated history.

PHOTOGRAPH BY NEIL LEIFER

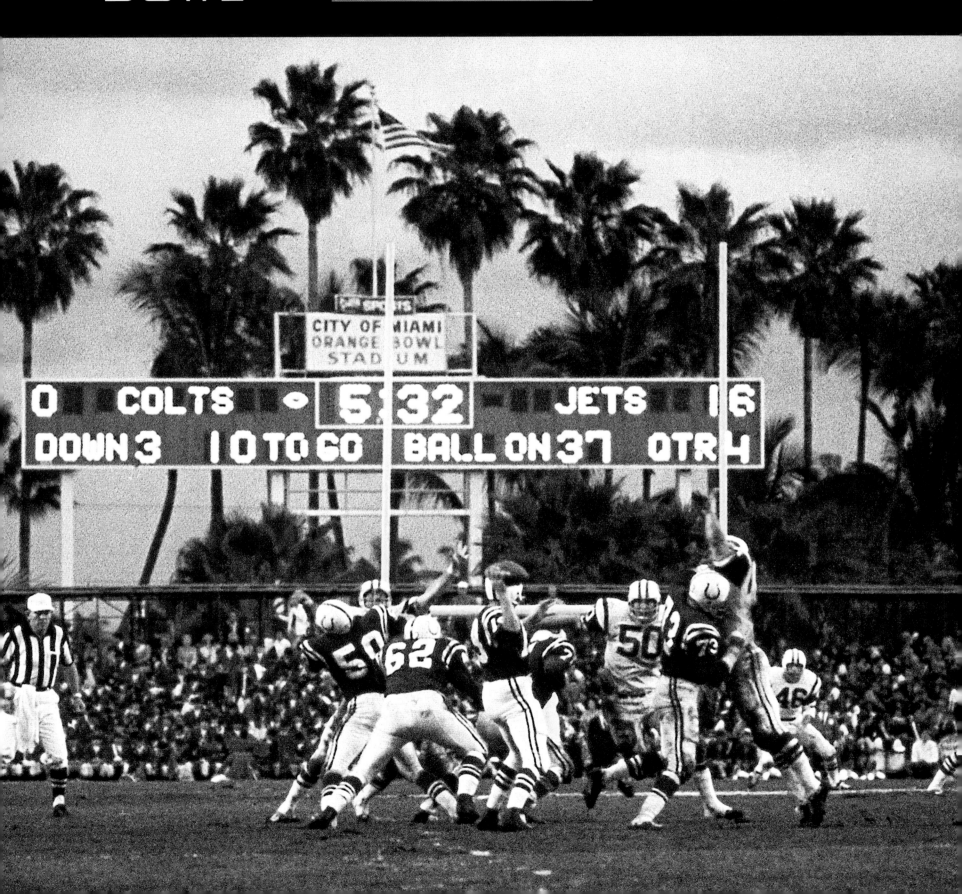

5

MILE HIGH STADIUM

DENVER

" In a Denver-Houston playoff game early in my career, John Elway was rallying the Broncos in the fourth quarter, the noise was deafening, and the ground actually started shaking. I couldn't believe it. And from the horrified look on Oilers defensive end Sean Jones's face, he couldn't believe it either. Denver won. " —PETER KING

▸ STOOD FROM 1948 TO 2002
▸ CAPACITY GREW FROM 18,000 TO 76,123

YEAH, THAT'S your seat, that little 16-inch-deep stretch of wood covered by that bleached-out skin of orange fiberglass. Yeah, it's a little small for the modern backside, especially when everybody's wearing a ski parka against the cold, but scrunch up. Everybody does. Get your breathing in sync with the rest of the folks in the row and enjoy. You're in the group now. Let me tell you about it. The south stands have room for 8,096 backsides, and 8,096 backsides have filled those spaces for 33 years. All these seats are for season tickets, most of them owned by the same people for most of that time. If you're a stranger, you stand out like a kicker's clean jersey, like Jason Elam in the fourth quarter on a rainy, muddy afternoon.

— *Leigh Montville, SI, December 25, 2000*

Mile High, as seen from a mile higher.

6

CenturyLink Field

SEATTLE

" The best of the new class of NFL stadiums, the Seahawks' new home features spectacular views of downtown Seattle to the north and Mount Ranier to the south. The 3,000-seat bleacher section called the "Hawks Nest" helps make the stadium one of the loudest in the league. " —DON BANKS

‣ DESIGNED TO BOUNCE NOISE OFF ROOF
‣ CHEERING FROM MARSHAWN LYNCH'S 2011 PLAYOFF TD AGAINST NEW ORLEANS REGISTERED AS A MEASURABLE SEISMIC EVENT

WITH THE help of smelling salts and the urgings of 67,837 fans, linebacker Lofa Tatupu played three-plus quarters with what was later diagnosed as a mild concussion and helped the Seahawks complete a declawing of the Panthers that reverberated from Grungeville all the way to Motown. . . . Sometimes Tatupu's signals weren't easy to hear, as the boisterous crowd celebrated a team it hopes can win Seattle's first major professional sports championship since the SuperSonics won the 1978–79 NBA title. "This is the craziest crowd I've ever seen in this town," said a man who should know, Pearl Jam bassist Jeff Ament.

— *Michael Silver, SI, January 30, 2006*

Seattle retired the number 12 in honor of their fans.

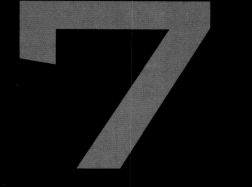

7

OAKLAND COLISEUM

" It's sparse, with no frills or particular charm, but it just seems to fit the rough-and-tumble renegade football team that has called it home in two different eras of the franchise. " —DON BANKS

‣ OPENED IN 1966
‣ RAUCOUS SOUTH END ZONE SECTIONS ARE KNOWN AS "THE BLACK HOLE"

THE DISTANCE between the visitors' bench and the barricade holding the masses at bay is approximately eight feet. To look on as the Raider fans screamed at the Cowboys in the waning minutes of the game was to understand why, in some soccer-playing nations, fans are separated from players by moats.
— *Austin Murphy, SI, November 27, 1995*

The Raiders' diehards dress the part.
PHOTOGRAPH BY V.J. LOVERO

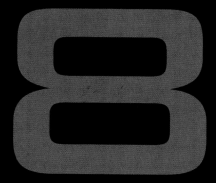

MUNICIPAL STADIUM

CLEVELAND

" Like Yankee Stadium, its seats were much too distant and much too low for football, but Jim Brown ran here. John Elway directed The Drive here. Its rusting girders and crumbling facade are a portrait of the NFL as a young man, the building blocks on which modern stadiums were built. " —TIM LAYDEN

▸ STOOD FROM 1932 TO 1996
▸ "DAWG POUND" NAME WAS COINED IN MID-1980S

HE IS home, surrounded by mementos of his career, and it emerges that the looming demise of the Cleveland Browns is more than just another incident in Lou Groza's lifetime. Of course it is. "Our first home game was against the Miami Seahawks," Groza recalls, gazing out on his backyard. "It was an exciting time, right after the war. The last time I had played football was in a freshman game at Ohio State in front of maybe 500 people. I never played in a varsity football game. So to come down that tunnel at the Stadium and to run out of the dugout and have 60,000 people cheering. . . . " He smiles at the memory. "God, it made you feel about this small." Two thick fingers are held an inch apart. "It was thrilling," says the Toe. "And the crowds have been like that for 50 years."

— *Steve Rushin, SI, December 4, 1995*

The Browns won Cleveland's last championship in 1964.

PHOTOGRAPH BY NEIL LEIFER

9

SOLDIER FIELD

CHICAGO

"The lakefront stadium has been home to more than the Bears. Some 104,000 witnessed the Tunney-Dempsey Long Count fight in 1927, and a Notre Dame–USC game later that year drew 120,000, still a record for a college football game." —MARK GODICH

‣ OPENED IN 1924
‣ BEARS BEGAN PLAY THERE IN 1971

AH, CHICAGO. It is a city built on stamina, endurance and stoicism. For more than a century waves of immigrants fleeing the poverty of European ghettos found their way to Lake Michigan's shore, there to endure the suffocating summers and savage winters, but never yielding to despair. The Bears, even when they are the recipients rather than the dispensers of violence, are a metaphor for the city itself. So for that matter is Soldier Field, its brightly painted seats and Astro Turfed surface a shining facade that distracts from but does not conceal the cracks in its ancient concrete and the 12-by-12-foot wooden beams that prop up its crumbling structure, just as the lakeshore Gold Coast stretches a thin, glamorous skin over a carcass as excruciatingly ugly as the bare-ribbed remnants of a rhinoceros.

— Richard W. Johnston, SI, December 9, 1974

After years with artificial turf, grass returned in 1988.

WASHINGTON, D.C.

RFK—the world's largest Hog pen.

PHOTOGRAPH BY LANE STEWART

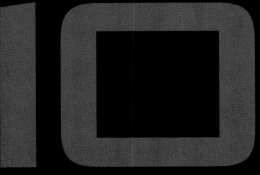

10
RFK
STADIUM

❝One of the great old barns in which I always felt honored to cover a game. It oozed football. It smelled like football. And when the Redskins were rolling, it was my favorite stadium in the league.❞ —PETER KING

‣ REDSKINS HOME, 1961 TO 1996
‣ RENAMED FROM DISTRICT OF COLUMBIA STADIUM IN 1969

IN WASHINGTON, the fans have made a federal case out of the Hogs. A pig was brought to the stadium Saturday. Hog signs were everywhere: HOGTIE THE VIKINGS. WE'RE IN HOG HEAVEN. WE'RE HOG WILD OVER THE REDSKINS. THE HOGS THAT ATE MINNESOTA. This Hog business could get to be a boar.

— Steve Wulf, SI, January 24, 1983

10 THE

BEST FRANCHISES

THE NFL BEGAN PLAY IN 1920 WITH TEAMS LIKE THE MUNCIE FLYERS AND THE COLUMBUS PANHANDLES IN ITS LINEUP. SADLY, OF THOSE 14 ULTRAORIGINALS, ONLY TWO, THE DECATUR STALEYS (WHO BECAME, IN 1922, THE CHICAGO BEARS) AND THE CHICAGO CARDINALS, WHO EVENTUALLY MIGRATED TO ARIZONA, SURVIVED LONG ENOUGH TO SEE THEIR FOOTAGE BROKEN DOWN BY RON JAWORSKI ON ESPN.

BUT WHILE MOST ORIGINALS FOLDED, NEW FRANCHISES ENTERED THE FRAY. PAGING THROUGH THIS SECTION IS LIKE READING THE ORIGINS ISSUE OF A COMIC BOOK—YOU CAN SEE THE KEY CHARACTERS COMING TOGETHER, EACH ADDING AN ESSENTIAL FACET TO THE LEAGUE.

THE MOST CURIOUS VOTE HERE WAS JIM TROTTER AWARDING 10TH PLACE TO A TRUE NEWCOMER, A TEAM YOUNGER THAN THE ELECTRONIC YELLOW FIRST-DOWN LINE ON TV BROADCASTS—THE TEXANS. TROTTER PRAISED HOUSTON OWNER BOB MCNAIR FOR RUNNING HIS TEAM WITH STABILITY: "INSTEAD OF MAKING KNEE-JERK REACTIONS AND TURNING OVER HIS COACHING STAFF AT EVERY FAILURE OR HEARTBREAK, HE LOOKS AT FACTS AND PROCEEDS IN A REASONED MANNER." THESE SAME VIRTUES LANDED THE GIANTS AND STEELERS ON THIS LIST. SO IF TROTTER'S VOTE WAS OUT OF STEP, MAYBE IT'S BECAUSE HE'S JUST A LITTLE EARLY.

1

THE
PACKERS

FOUNDED 1919

"The Packers have dominated in different eras and appear poised to continue." —DAMON HACK

▸ JOINED NFL IN 1921
▸ 13 CHAMPIONSHIPS

A MAN in his early 50s, with tattoos on his biceps and a nose that had been punched out of shape long ago, walked into the sauna in Green Bay wearing a bathing suit and looked around curiously, touching the walls and the benches and finally the stones to see if they were indeed hot. "This is the first motel I was ever in," he said. "My first vacation in 36 years. We got 11 kids, nine still home, some of 'em big full-grown kids that don't believe in work but only in stealing everything I got. So I says all right, I am going to take off a week and drive up here and see the Packer game. And my wife says she has to stay home and take care of the kids. That means I got to travel with my sister, who tells me I smoke too much and do everything wrong. But what the hell, here I am in a motel sauna bath in Green Bay, and I'm gonna see the Packers in real life. In case you don't know it, football is what made this town. Who would ever have heard of Green Bay if it wasn't for the Packers?"

—Edwin Shrake, SI, August 25, 1975

Donald Lee was one of many to take the Lambeau Leap.

PHOTOGRAPH BY JOHN BIEVER

2
THE STEELERS

FOUNDED 1933

" The Rooneys, owners since the club's founding, have done it the right way, eschewing glitz and high-priced free agents, giving back to the city and cultivating a community spirit that makes the Steelers wildly popular not just in western Pennsylvania but throughout the country. " —MARK MRAVIC

▸ SIX SUPER BOWL VICTORIES
▸ THREE COACHES SINCE 1969

THE LITTLE black notebook has been called Art Rooney's private office. It contains the most detailed information about some of his principal interests: the Steelers, the grain market, the whereabouts of his running horses. There was a time when Rooney was able to run all his business out of the black notebook—football, fight promoting, political maneuvering as Republican boss of Pittsburgh's 22nd Ward, big-time wagering on horses. But the black book does not suffice today. Rooney finds he must call upon the familiar accoutrements of modern business—lawyers and accountants, mouthpieces and peace-mouthers. Yet he clings to the little book just the same and yearns for the old days when a handshake was enough to commit a man to a business deal or put a few grand riding on the nose of a horse.

—*Gerald Holland, SI, November 23, 1964*

Art Rooney Sr.'s Steelers are a family business.

PHOTOGRAPH BY HARRY CABLUCK

THE STEEL AGE

The most important day in Steelers history may well have been the 1974 draft, when preparation—and a little luck—helped bring four future Hall of Famers to the black and gold

BY PETER KING

N MANY ORGANIZATIONS, THEN AND now, scouts write their reports, answer questions if asked and then watch as the front-office people or the coaches make the personnel decisions. That wasn't the case with the Steelers. Coach Chuck Noll had the final word on draft picks, but Art Rooney Jr. and the scouts could change his mind. "Chuck cared about what we thought," says Bill Nunn, a former football and basketball player for West Virginia State who was only the league's sixth full-time black scout when the Steelers hired him in 1969. "I remember talking to him that first year, and he told me, 'You were an athlete. I want you to go out and find me athletes.'"

Since 1950, Nunn had picked the nationally respected black-college all-star team for the Pittsburgh *Courier*, so he knew the black colleges intimately. "It was like an open market," Nunn says of the black schools. "Some teams did a little bit of scouting, but I always felt this was an untapped source, almost like Branch Rickey going into black baseball and finding all those players. The talent was sitting there." Other teams were tapping it too; the Miami Dolphins, for example, drafted 10 black-college players from '69 to '71. The Steelers just tapped it better. Pittsburgh took 11 black-college draftees in Noll's first three years; it had taken none in the previous two years. In '68, Nunn went to Arkansas AM&N in Pine Bluff and saw a tall, quick, elastic band of a pass rusher, L.C. Greenwood. The Steelers took him in Round 10 of the '69 draft. In the fall of '70, Nunn went to Texas Southern in Houston and saw one of the meanest players he'd ever seen, defensive tackle Ernie Holmes. The Steelers picked him in Round 8. In the fall of '73, Nunn went to Alabama A&M in Huntsville and saw a graceful, if slightly slow, wide receiver, John Stallworth. The Steelers got him in Round 4.

In 1974 Noll entered the draft with a large crush on Stallworth, and he wouldn't have minded spending a first-round choice to get him. The scouts wanted to take USC wide receiver Lynn Swann, despite Swann's relatively poor speed; he'd been timed at 4.65 in the 40 by BLESTO. Swann couldn't get up for races against a watch, but he seemed to find something extra when a cornerback was chasing him. Finally, in Swann's last timing by the Steelers scouts, he ran a 4.58, and Noll was convinced he was fast enough.

Four teams tied for the 20th draft choice that year, according to won-lost record. Pittsburgh lost one coin flip but won a second, versus the Dallas Cowboys, to get the 21st pick. The Cowboys later said that they would have taken Swann if they had picked 21st.

In the second round the Steelers made one of their oddest choices: Jack Lambert, a middle linebacker at Kent State. He weighed only 195 pounds. Tim Rooney, another of Art Sr.'s five sons and then a Pittsburgh

scout, recalls visiting Kent State in 1973 and listening to the coaches rave about Lambert. "When I got to see him, I was shocked," Tim says. "He was freakish for a linebacker. I was thinking how I could sell this guy as an NFL linebacker. But as I watched films, his productivity and determination kept coming through." Art Jr. went to scout Lambert himself. The Kent State team was working out in a gravel parking lot because of bad weather, and Lambert made a diving try at a tackle and came up bloody. "He's picking these cinders out, and he doesn't give a damn," Art Jr. says.

On draft day, two conflicts arose in the second round. Another prominent, and regular-sized, linebacker was available, All-America Matt Blair of Iowa State, and some of the Pittsburgh staff argued that the Steelers should take him instead of Lambert. Then there was Noll's regard for Stallworth. Pittsburgh had traded away its third-round pick, and 36 choices would be made before the Steelers would have another crack at Stallworth.

Noll turned to Nunn. "Will Stallworth be there in the fourth?"

Nunn said, "He'll be there." He was sweating because he had seen scouts from two other teams at Stallworth's last college game, in which he had caught 13 passes. Nunn sat in the draft room, thinking, "This is a huge gamble." The Steelers took Lambert. When their choice finally arrived, Stallworth was still on the board. Nunn stopped sweating. "We got lucky," he says.

On its second pick of the fourth round, Pittsburgh chose UCLA defensive back Jim Allen, who became a special-teams contributor for four years. Then, in the fifth round, the Steelers selected Wisconsin center Mike Webster, who weighed all of 225. He ran a 5.3 40. "He was what you'd call a computer reject," Art Jr. says. There were bigger and faster centers in Pittsburgh high schools. But the scouts had seen films of Webster from a postseason all-star game in which he had manhandled a top defensive line prospect. The Steelers gambled again. Webster eventually gained 30 pounds and anchored Pittsburgh's offensive line for 14 years.

Five rounds: Swann, Lambert, Stallworth, Webster. Twenty-four Pro Bowl appearances. Sixteen Super Bowl rings. Four Hall of Famers. "Maybe the best draft ever," says Bill Walsh, former coach of the 49ers.

A postscript: One of Nunn's best friends was Willie Jeffries, the coach at South Carolina State, a predominantly black school. One of Jeffries's players was an undersized linebacker, Donnie Shell, who Nunn thought would be a safety in the pros. When Shell wasn't picked in the draft, Nunn phoned Jeffries, extolling the virtues of Pittsburgh's defense and the opportunity it could provide Shell. The Denver Broncos and Houston Oilers also invited Shell to training camp. Shell asked Jeffries what he should do. Jeffries advised him to go to Pittsburgh. Shell went.

Make that 29 Pro Bowls. ∎

FOUNDED 1960

" The best expansion team in history, by far. Dallas expanded the NFL into a new frontier when the league needed it. "America's Team" is a misnomer, but it's no small task to become the team that everyone loves . . . or hates " —TIM LAYDEN

▸ FIVE SUPER BOWL VICTORIES
▸ NFL'S MOST VALUABLE FRANCHISE

3
THE
COWBOYS

The cheerleaders helped keep all eyes on Dallas.

PHOTOGRAPH BY BILL FRAKES

THE GLAMOROUS Cowboy image that G.M. Tex Schramm loves to promote is displayed nowhere so openly as it is by the Dallas cheerleaders. In their sexy, foxy way, they're a mirror image of what Cowboy football represents: entertainment dealt with as very serious business.

—*William Oscar Johnson, SI, September 1, 1982*

4

THE BEARS

Ditka consulted with Papa Bear, George Halas.
PHOTOGRAPH BY NEIL LEIFER

" The Bears won titles in the '20s, '30s, '40s, '60s and '80s. George Halas is on the Mount Rushmore of NFL architecture. I asked one G.M. candidate two years ago what team he'd most like to steward, he said, "The Bears. That's the gold standard." " —PETER KING

‣ NINE CHAMPIONSHIPS
‣ 27 HALL OF FAMERS

MIKE DITKA drafts and trades for and teaches only those players who are Bears. Ask Ditka to name his most cherished accomplishment over his football career and the answer is not the Super Bowls (two as a player, three as an assistant coach) or the All-Pro teams, but this: "I am proudest of being a Bear."

—Curry Kirkpatrick, SI, December 16, 1985

5

THE
GIANTS

FOUNDED 1925

"An old school team whose defensive roots run deep" —DAMON HACK

▸ EIGHT CHAMPIONSHIPS
▸ 18 HALL OF FAMERS

A MONTAGE of Giants history encompasses many of the classic moments in the history of the league. In the 1934 championship game it was Giants coach Steve Owen who put sneakers on his players for better footing on the iced-over turf at the Polo Grounds. In 1958 it was the Giants who lost in overtime to the Colts at Yankee Stadium in the game that launched the modern era of televised professional football. In 1960 it was Giants All-Pro Frank Gifford who was knocked unconscious by the Eagles' Chuck Bednarik, creating one of the most memorable photographs in football history. It was Giants linebacker Lawrence Taylor who not only revolutionized pass rushing but also snapped Redskins quarterback Joe Theismann's leg on *Monday Night Football* in 1985. And it was the Giants' unlikely hero David Tyree who saved Super Bowl XLII in 2008 by catching a pass against his helmet. It is the Giants' highlight reel, but it is the NFL's too.

—*Tim Layden, SI, February 16, 2012*

Phil Simms collected two Super Bowl rings in New York.

PHOTOGRAPH BY RICHARD MACKSON

6

THE
49ERS

FOUNDED 1946

"With four Super Bowl championships in the 1980s, the Niners had one of the greatest runs in NFL history." —MARK GODICH

▸ 5–0 SUPER BOWL RECORD
▸ 13 HALL OF FAMERS

THE NINERS lost the way Chicagoans voted—early and often: 5–9 the first year of Eddie DeBartolo's ownership, 2–14 in 1978. . . . On Monday, Nov. 27, 1978, San Francisco mayor George Moscone and city supervisor Harvey Milk were shot to death by Dan White, a depressed former supervisor. The Niners were playing Pittsburgh at home that night, and G.M. Joe Thomas wanted to cancel the game, but for the wrong reason. He was worried about his own safety. "I knew then that I had to make a change," says DeBartolo. He hired the anti-Thomas, Bill Walsh of Stanford, as coach and general manager. Walsh, DeBartolo, sanity and a little luck helped launch a dynasty. "What should we do with this Notre Dame kid?" Walsh teased DeBartolo, a Fighting Irish alum, when the 82nd pick came up in the third round of the '79 draft and Joe Montana was available. "What the heck," said DeBartolo. "He's a Notre Dame kid. How can you go wrong?"

—Rick Reilly, SI, September 10, 1990

Montana, Steve Young and Jerry Rice are all in Canton.

FOUNDED 1959

7

THE PATRIOTS

"Since being purchased by Robert Kraft in 1994, the franchise's fortunes improved dramatically, and the Bill Belichick–Tom Brady tandem made New England the envy of the NFL both on and off the field." —DON BANKS

▸ THREE SUPER BOWL VICTORIES ▸ NFL-RECORD 21-GAME WINNING STREAK, INCLUDING PLAYOFFS, IN 2003–04

"IN THIS GAME," Kraft said on Sunday night, after the Patriots had arrived in Indianapolis for their sixth Super Bowl under his ownership, "you better take some risks—or you'll have a nice team, and once every 10 or 20 years you'll be good. That's not what I want to be about."

—*Peter King, SI, February 6, 2012*

Kraft showed fans the bounty from Super Bowl XXXVIII.

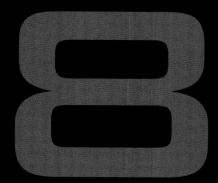

8
THE RAIDERS

FOUNDED 1960

"Al Davis was always an easy target for ridicule, especially in the last years of his life. But he protected the name of the Raiders fiercely and ensured that the silver and black always had its own persona." —TIM LAYDEN

▸ ONE AFL TITLE
▸ THREE SUPER BOWL VICTORIES

DAVIS'S RAIDERS won with a panache that fully justified their skull-and-bones fashion line: Using castoffs (Lyle Alzado, John Matuszak) and overlooked prospects (Fred Biletnikoff, Howie Long)—"He never had normal players," said Tom Keating, a defensive tackle during the glory years—Davis brought a heightened sense of physical jeopardy to the game. As he once said (when he wasn't saying, "Just win, baby"), he would rather be "feared than respected." And Davis was, although not only for the physical mayhem that players like safety Jack (the Assassin) Tatum and linebacker Ted (the Mad Stork) Hendricks visited on their opponents. Davis's dedication to winning was so exaggerated that rivals felt certain he was capable of almost anything. If he was willing to hang around celebrity golf tournaments to gauge the availability of prospects, what else might he do?

—Richard Hoffer, SI, October 17, 2011

Davis rose from coach and general manager to owner.

PHOTOGRAPH BY JOHN W. MCDONOUGH

FOUNDED 1953

Coach Weeb Ewbank ran with his Colts in 1960.

PHOTOGRAPH BY NEIL LEIFER

THE COLTS

" Rich in history, the Colts have had wildly successful eras in two different cities, with Johnny Unitas in Baltimore and Peyton Manning in Indianapolis. " —DON BANKS

IF A SIZABLE chunk of the state's population once owned Reggie Miller's Pacers jerseys, now an even greater proportion own replicas of Peyton Manning's. "I never thought I'd say it," says Bill Benner, a longtime Indianapolis sportswriter, "but Indiana has gone from a basketball state to a football state."

—*L. Jon Wertheim, SI, January 25, 2010*

▸ MOVED TO INDIANAPOLIS IN 1984
▸ FIVE CHAMPIONSHIPS

10

THE REDSKINS

FOUNDED 1932

" They've had hard times recently, but that can't obscure the Redskins' past dominance. " —DAMON HACK

▸ FIVE CHAMPIONSHIPS
▸ 19 HALL OF FAMERS

RICHARD M. NIXON, erstwhile District resident and Redskins fan: "The trouble is, Washington is a city without identity. Everybody comes from someplace else. Anywhere else people say, 'I'm from Cincinnati, I'm from New York, I'm from Topeka.' You never hear people say that about Washington. Deep down, they still think they're back home. But you take any hometown boy—well, these days I guess you have to say hometown 'person'—and they come to Washington for politics, but they need an identity with the city. And the Redskins provide that. The Redskins are the only thing in Washington that the people think of as 'ours.' Nobody in Washington gives a tinker's dam about the Kennedy Center or the Washington Symphony." . . . In 1972, the year the team reached the Super Bowl, *The Washington Post* dispatched a staff of 13 to cover the event— twice as many as covered the first moonwalk and 11 more than it took to topple a President.

—*Frank Deford, SI, July 2, 1979*

QB Joe Theismann and RB John Riggins enjoyed the '80s.

PHOTOGRAPH BY JOHN IACONO

10

THE

Best Rivalries, Uniforms, Interviews, Trades, Undrafted Players, Movies, SI Covers and the Full Results

A PANEL IS A WONDERFUL WAY TO DEVELOP A CONSENSUS, BUT IT TENDS TO TRAMPLE UNDER THE MORE PERSONAL POINTS OF VIEW. SO FOR THIS SECTION THE PANELISTS WERE INVITED TO CREATE LISTS THAT REPRESENTED THEIR OPINIONS ALONE.

SOME LISTS REFLECT PERSONAL EXPERIENCE—NO ONE BUT PETER KING, FOR EXAMPLE, CAN MAKE A LIST OF PETER KING'S FAVORITE INTERVIEW SUBJECTS. NFL EDITOR MARK MRAVIC NAMES HIS TOP 10 NFL COVERS FROM SPORTS ILLUSTRATED. GIVEN THAT THE MAGAZINE BRIDGES THE ERAS OF Y.A. TITTLE AND TIM TEBOW, THAT LEAVES MANY COVERS UNSELECTED WHICH WOULD HAVE FOUND FAVOR WITH OTHERS.

THIS SECTION CONCLUDES WITH A RUNDOWN OF EVERYONE THAT RECEIVED VOTES IN EVERY CATEGORY—AND THERE YOU'LL FIND SOME OF THE IDIOSYNCRATIC CHOICES THAT DIDN'T MAKE THE LARGER LISTS. ONE PANELIST CHOSE BO JACKSON AS A TOP RUNNING BACK, EVEN THOUGH BECAUSE OF INJURY HIS CAREER WAS LIMITED TO 38 GAMES. THE EAGLES AND THE BILLS EACH RECEIVED SOME LOVE IN THE VOTING FOR BEST FRANCHISES, DESPITE THEIR HISTORY OF FALLING SHORT, WHICH THEY DO HERE ONCE AGAIN. AS THEY SAY IN THE ENTERTAINMENT WORLD, THOUGH, IT IS AN HONOR JUST TO BE NOMINATED.

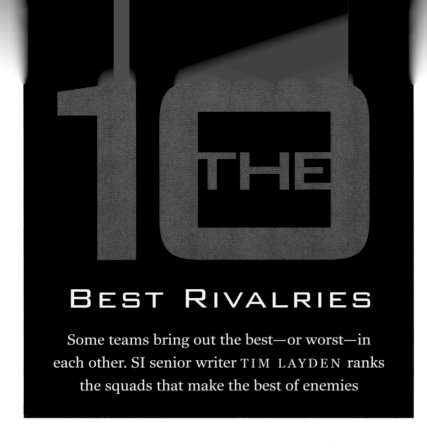

10 THE

BEST RIVALRIES

Some teams bring out the best—or worst—in each other. SI senior writer TIM LAYDEN ranks the squads that make the best of enemies

1. BEARS-PACKERS A rivalry built in the days of leather helmets and cemented when Vince Lombardi and George Halas faced off in a blood sport built on mutual respect, this one conjures up images of frozen breath, mud-splattered fields and old school warriors.

2. STEELERS-RAVENS This is almost Bears versus Packers for the new generation, with two franchises constructed for old-time physical combat and with a genuine dislike for each other to boot.

3. RAIDERS-CHIEFS The best of the old AFL rivalries now sputters along on fumes from the past. Still, the memory of those Sunday afternoon struggles between Hank Stram and John Madden endures.

4. COLTS-PATRIOTS This one was built on the Peyton Manning–Tom Brady battle, or, more pointedly, the Manning–Bill Belichick battle. For years it seemed like the Patriots had Manning's number, until his triumph in the 2006 playoffs.

5. GIANTS-COWBOYS It's splitting hairs to pick the most relevant rivalry in the hardcore NFC East, but this one gets the nod for its Big Apple versus Big D vibe that has always incited fan bases.

6. PACKERS-LIONS Another hard-knocking rivalry from the black-and-blue division, this matchup reached its peak when the Lions upset the undefeated Packers 26–14 on the Thanksgiving Day in 1962, pounding quarterback Bart Starr with 10 sacks.

7. COWBOYS-REDSKINS In the heart of the Tom Landry–Joe Gibbs era, these division foes were almost always in contention for playoff and Super Bowl spots. This felt more like a college rivalry.

8. JETS-PATRIOTS When Bill Parcells left the Patriots to coach the Jets, their twice-annual matchups were dubbed by New York media as the Tuna Bowl. In the next generation, Rex Ryan and Belichick have cranked up the enmity even further.

9. BROWNS-GIANTS Going back to the late 1950s, the Jim Brown–led Browns and Sam Huff's Giants would battle twice a year in mammoth coliseums (Yankee Stadium and Cleveland Municipal Stadium) for NFL Eastern Conference supremacy.

10. RAMS-49ERS There was a time when the only NFL franchises west of Green Bay were in San Francisco and Los Angeles, and nascent television broadcasts would beam sun-splashed late afternoon games into cold, dark Eastern homes. Twice a year, the two California rivals would tee off on each other for a special sort of bragging rights.

The Packers-Bears rivalry was intense long before QB Aaron Rodgers joined in.

10 THE

BEST UNIFORMS

SI senior writer DAMON HACK ranks the NFL's best-dressed, and finds that uniforms, like so much else, look better when you're winning

1 | ### OAKLAND RAIDERS

Is that iconic pirate smiling or smirking? Al Davis took the secret with him. *(Ken Stabler, 12, and George Blanda, above)*

2 | GREEN BAY PACKERS
The history of the game can be written in Packers green and gold. Winning never looked so good. *(Willie Davis, above)*

3 | PITTSBURGH STEELERS
Have a uniform, a city and an ethos ever been so perfectly matched? *(Jerome Bettis, above)*

4 | SAN DIEGO CHARGERS
The powder blue evokes a time, a style and a legendary receiver, Lance Alworth. *(Philip Rivers, above)*

5 | CHICAGO BEARS
A classic, timeless, no-frills uniform that evokes toughness and tradition. *(Brian Urlacher, above)*

6 | BALTIMORE/INDIANAPOLIS COLTS
Two quarterbacks, Johnny Unitas and Peyton Manning, made the horseshoe a symbol of greatness. *(Unitas, above)*

7 | DALLAS COWBOYS
The Dallas star may be loved or loathed, but it is neither ignored nor forgotten. *(Tony Dorsett, above)*

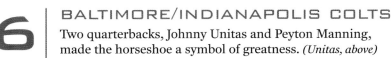

8 | TAMPA BAY BUCCANEERS
The creamsicle uniform was on the end of too many defeats to count, but it made you smile. *(Doug Williams, above)*

9 | DETROIT LIONS
I'm a sucker for blue and silver, and the Lions uniform blends them in a sleek, sharp way. *(Matthew Stafford, above)*

10 | MIAMI DOLPHINS
It's aqua, coral, white, navy, and memories of
Dan Marino and more. *(Ricky Williams, left)*

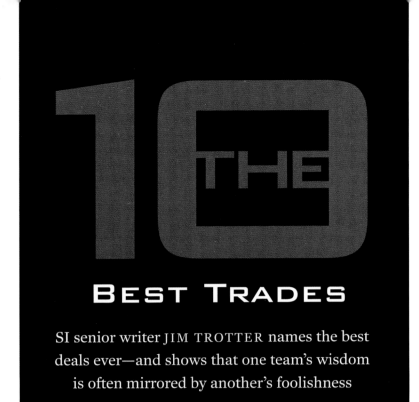

10 THE

BEST TRADES

SI senior writer JIM TROTTER names the best deals ever—and shows that one team's wisdom is often mirrored by another's foolishness

Walker certainly helped one team win a Super Bowl.

1. DALLAS ACQUIRES A DYNASTY

Minnesota believed it was a running back away from a Super Bowl in October 1989, so it sent three No. 1s, three No. 2s, a No. 3, a No. 6 and a handful of veterans to Dallas for Herschel Walker and some picks. The deal helped the Cowboys land Emmitt Smith, Darren Woodson, and Russell Maryland, among others. Seven years out Dallas had won three Super Bowl titles while Minnesota had lost four straight playoff games.

2. 49ERS MOVE UP FOR RICE

Remember Trevor Matich, Ben Thomas and Audray McMillian? No? New England chose those players with picks it acquired from San Francisco in the first, second and third round of the 1985 draft. The 49ers, moving up in the first and third rounds, chose Jerry Rice, the greatest receiver ever, at No. 16 overall.

3. RAMS FUEL THE GREATEST SHOW ON TURF

Marshall Faulk took St. Louis from agony to ecstasy after being acquired from Indianapolis for second- and fifth-round draft picks in 1999. He helped the previously woeful Rams reach the Super Bowl twice in his first three seasons, including a win in his first year. Indianapolis used the picks on linebacker Mike Peterson and defensive end Brad Scioli.

4. 49ERS GET YOUNG-ER AT QUARTERBACK

Anytime you can acquire a future Hall of Fame QB without surrendering a key player or a first-round pick, it's a lopsided deal. The 49ers did that in 1987 when they sent second- and fourth-round picks to Tampa Bay for Steve Young, successor to Joe Montana. Tampa Bay ultimately selected linebacker Winston Moss and wideout Bruce Hill.

5. FAVRE GETS A FRESH START

Atlanta drafted Brett Favre in the second round in 1991, but then gave up on him and sent him to Green Bay in '92 for a first-round pick. It was grand larceny. Atlanta used the new pick on running back Tony Smith.

6. DALLAS DEALS FOR DORSETT

Would you trade running back Tony Dorsett for Steve August, Tom Lynch, Terry Beeson and several journeymen? Of course not. Yet that's just what the Seahawks ultimately did in 1977, when they sent the second pick overall—and a shot at Dorsett—to the Cowboys for four draft picks. Dallas won the Super Bowl that year.

7. 49ERS FORTIFY THEIR RULE

In mid-season 1981, the year of its first Super Bowl win, San Francisco picked up Fred Dean from the Chargers for a future second-round pick. Dean's pass rushing was a key, and often overlooked, ingredient, in the 49ers successes.

8. THEIR KINGDOM FOR A LONGHORN

If you can get a team to give you their entire draft, that's a heist. In 1999 Saints coach Mike Ditka dealt all six of his picks, plus first- and third-round picks the next year, to Washington so he could select Texas running back Ricky Williams fifth overall. Washington's haul included cornerback Champ Bailey, tackle Jon Jansen, linebacker LaVar Arrington and cornerback Lloyd Harrison.

9. SETTING UP FOR PERFECTION IN 1972

Miami sent the third pick in the 1970 draft to Cleveland for All-Pro Paul Warfield. The Browns chose QB Mike Phipps, who threw nearly twice as many interceptions (108) as touchdown passes (55).

10. STRONG ARM, STRONGER WILL

When QB John Elway refused to play for Baltimore after being drafted No. 1 overall in 1983, Denver snagged him in exchange for QB Mark Herrmann, the rights to offensive lineman Chris Hinton and a 1984 first-round pick that was used on guard Ron Solt. All Elway did was lead the Broncos to five Super Bowls, the last two of which he won.

1. DICK (NIGHT TRAIN) LANE

After a four-year stint in the Army, he walked into the offices of the Los Angeles Rams in 1952 asking for a tryout, then finished his rookie season with an NFL-record 14 interceptions. Over a 14-year career with three teams Lane, a cornerback, picked off 68 passes.

2. KURT WARNER

From supermarket stock boy to Super Bowl–winning quarterback with the Rams, the Northern Iowa alum wrote a script that would have been too outlandish for Hollywood to buy. For good measure he was a two-time league MVP and has the three highest passing-yardage totals in Super Bowl history. Honest.

3. WILLIE WOOD

A quarterback at Southern Cal, Wood went undrafted in 1960 and then landed in Green Bay, where in 12 seasons he developed into one of the premier free safeties in football, intercepting 48 passes while playing in six NFL championship games.

4. JOHN RANDLE

With his painted face and unbridled enthusiasm, Randle was a joy to watch. He was also a terror to quarterbacks who played the Vikings and Seahawks. Out of Texas A&I, he finished his career with 137½ sacks, a remarkable number for a defensive tackle.

5. ANTONIO GATES

All his game action at Kent State came on the basketball court rather than the football field, so it's fair enough that teams passed on this unconventional tight end prospect. But since then Gates has been to eight Pro Bowls in nine seasons for the Chargers.

6. CORNELL GREEN

Another basketball star, at Utah State, Green was drafted in the fifth round by the NBA's Chicago Zephyrs, but opted to sign with the Cowboys as a defensive back. In 13 seasons he finished with 34 career interceptions and was named to the Pro Bowl five times.

7. EMLEN TUNNELL

Bypassed in the draft because teams believed he would return for a third season at Iowa after serving in the Coast Guard, Tunnell signed with the Giants in 1948. He had 79 career interceptions and was the first African-American named to the Pro Football Hall of Fame, in '67.

8. WARREN MOON

Moon headed north of the border only after NFL teams told the Washington star, who was set on playing quarterback, that they wanted him to switch to tight end. He played in the CFL for six seasons, winning five Grey Cups with the Edmonton Eskimos, and then he returned to the NFL in 1984, where he had nine 3,000-yard passing seasons in 17 years.

9. WILLIE BROWN

Undrafted out of Grambling and then cut during summer camp by the Oilers in 1963, he found a home in Denver and was starting at cornerback by the middle of his rookie season. During a 16-year career with the Broncos and Raiders, Brown finished with 54 interceptions, including an NFL-record four in a '64 game against the Jets.

10. LOU GROZA

The Toe, from Ohio State, played 21 seasons for the Browns as an offensive tackle and a kicker. The 1954 NFL Player of the Year, he became the first kicking specialist of his time, and he kicked the game-winning field in the final seconds of the 1950 NFL Championship Game. And, as happened with Lane, Wood, Randle, Tunnell, Moon and Brown, a career that began by going undrafted resulted in a more rare selection—to the Pro Football Hall of Fame.

10 THE
BEST UNDRAFTED

They weren't chosen on draft day, but these men on SI senior editor MARK GODICH'S list have since heard their name called plenty

Warner had to prove himself in Arena football and NFL Europe.

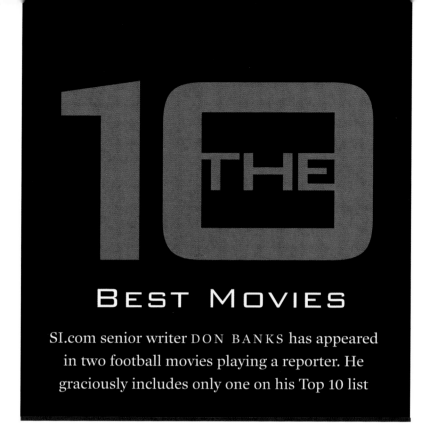

THE 10 BEST MOVIES

SI.com senior writer DON BANKS has appeared in two football movies playing a reporter. He graciously includes only one on his Top 10 list

The happy times don't last for Caan (left) and Williams in *Brian's Song*.

1. BRIAN'S SONG (1971) — For guys of my generation, just hearing a halting Billy Dee Williams (as Gale Sayers) struggle to get through that "I love Brian Piccolo" scene at the awards banquet brings a lump to the throat every time. James Caan is superb as the wisecracking Piccolo, and Jack Warden makes for a memorable George Halas, but it's the story of friendship and ultimate tragedy that grabs you and never lets you go. I can still remember almost everything about the night I first watched *Brian's Song* on ABC television in November 1971 when I was nine years old. How many movies leave that kind of mark?

2. THE LONGEST YARD (1974) — Burt Reynolds had played a little football at Florida State, and it showed in this dark, gritty and entertaining story about a group of ragtag inmates who got to stick it to the man by beating the prison guards on the gridiron. Packers great Ray Nitschke was superb as an intimidating guard–linebacker, and Eddie Albert made for one evil prison warden. The remake in 2005 starred Adam Sandler in Reynolds's quarterbacking role, with Reynolds playing a prisoner who coaches the inmates team, but it didn't begin to recapture the look and feel of the original.

3. NORTH DALLAS FORTY (1979) — The movie is based on the seminal autobiographical novel written by ex-NFL receiver Pete Gent which, much as Jim Bouton's *Ball Four* did for baseball, exposed fans to the seamy underside of the game. Nick Nolte stars as Phil Elliott, an aging and pain-pill-popping receiver for a North Dallas Bulls team that sounds more than a little bit like the Cowboys clubs that Gent played for. Former Oakland Raiders' wild man John Matuszak is memorably cast as one of Elliott's freewheelin' and fun-loving teammates.

4. EVERYBODY'S ALL-AMERICAN (1988) — This underrated Taylor Hackford film might not make everyone's top 10, but I've always loved the way the story evokes the romance and feel of big-time college football in the '50s, with Dennis Quaid starring as fictitious LSU running back Gavin Grey, "The Grey Ghost." Quaid plays the football scenes very believably and even broke his collarbone during the filming. Based on the book of the same name by longtime SPORTS ILLUSTRATED writer Frank Deford, the story follows Grey over the span of 25 years, through his heroic days at LSU and into the NFL. But in the rest of his football career and postretirement life, Grey can never quite match the magic he created on field in his glory days in college.

5. JERRY MAGUIRE (1996) — Until Kurt Warner showed up last decade, the fictitious receiver Rod Tidwell was universally regarded as the best player in Phoenix/Arizona Cardinals history. Sure, the Tom Cruise–led and Cameron Crowe–directed movie is more about the sports agent business and affairs of the heart than football, but it did add the phrase "Show me the money" to our pop culture lexicon, and I'm still partial to Jerry Maguire's plea to his client, "Help me help you."

6. PAPER LION (1968) — Does this book-inspired film look a bit creaky and dated more than four decades out? Sure. But a hopelessly young-looking Alan Alda gives a great performance as author George Plimpton, who took participatory journalism to new heights by spending a training camp with the Detroit Lions, even playing in an intrasquad scrimmage. Lions defensive tackle Alex Karras launched a nice little acting career playing himself in the film, and *Paper Lion* gives a time-capsule look at the NFL in the late '60s.

7. INVINCIBLE (2006) — If you look really quickly and really closely, I'm actually in some background shots of this Mark Wahlberg vehicle, quite credibly playing a mid-70s-era sports writer in a salmon-colored blazer and gray bell bottoms. But that's not why this movie made my list. (Well, not the entire reason, anyway). Wahlberg is a very convincing Vince Papale, the tough kid from Philly who made the 1976 Eagles roster as a long shot with no college experience, bringing his Rocky-like story to real life. Plus, the period soundtrack kicks butt.

Nolte (clockwise) pals with Mac Davis in *North Dallas Forty*; Cuba Gooding Jr. asks Cruise to show him the money in *Jerry Maguire*; Clooney huddles in *Leatherheads*.

8. LEATHERHEADS (2008) — This film has always struck me as pro football counterpart to the baseball movie *The Natural* in that this George Clooney vehicle does a superb job of recapturing the look and feel of the pro game in its struggling, formative stages, with Clooney as Jimmy (Dodge) Connelly, the captain of the almost bankrupt Duluth Bulldogs. The movie is set in 1925, and although the story is fictional, it has echoes of the George Halas-signs-Red Grange story, with a collegiate football star (Carter [The Bullet] Rutherford, played by John Krasinski) joining the Bulldogs in order to bring legitimacy to both the team and pro football itself.

9. HEAVEN CAN WAIT (1978) — Before the Rams finally made the Super Bowl in January 1980, losing to the Steelers, L.A. fans received a sneak preview of their team in the big game in this Warren Beatty comedy, in which he starred and also codirected with Buck Henry. Beatty plays Rams quarterback Joe Pendleton, who is killed (or so we think) and winds up being reincarnated into the body of a murdered millionaire industrialist, who then buys the Rams so he can play quarterback (with help getting in shape from his old trainer friend, played by—making his second appearance on this list—Jack Warden). The story ends happily, of course, with Beatty's character leading the Rams to a win in the Super Bowl (over the Steelers, no less). The premise is a little silly, but the shots of the Los Angeles Coliseum in the glory days of its Rams era make the movie eminently watchable, and cameos by Rams stars Deacon Jones and Jack Snow, as well as announcers Dick Enberg and Curt Gowdy, add to the fun.

10. THE REPLACEMENTS (2000) — Remember how the 1987 Redskins were able to win the Super Bowl in part because Washington's "scab" team built up a 3–0 record during the players' strike? Well, this is a loosely based, Hollywood version of that Redskins replacement team, with the names changed to protect the innocent. Here the Washington Sentinels are on strike, so the team's owner (played by, inevitably, Jack Warden) coaxes his former coach, Jimmy McGinty (Gene Hackman) out of retirement to lead this motley group through the final four games of the season. Quarterback Shane Falco (Keanu Reeves) is no Burt Reynolds, but this comedy has a few inspired moments along the way, and any movie that can make anything entertaining out of an NFL players strike deserves points for trying.

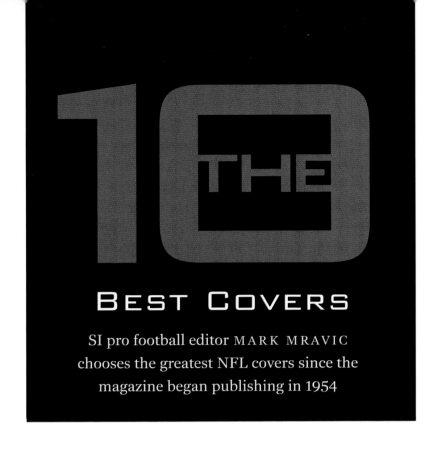

THE 10 BEST COVERS

SI pro football editor MARK MRAVIC chooses the greatest NFL covers since the magazine began publishing in 1954

Sports Illustrated

JANUARY 26, 1976 · ONE DOLLAR

PITTSBURGH DOES IT AGAIN

Lynn Swann shows the way

1 | LYNN SWANN
January 26, 1976

1. PITTSBURGH DOES IT AGAIN — Others have told me they prefer the cover with Dwight Clark making "The Catch," but I find the shot of Lynn Swann from Super Bowl X more dramatic precisely because he has not yet made the grab. The moment is pregnant with possibility, fixing for all time the tension and uncertainly that gives sports such visceral power. Will he catch it or won't he? To me this is the best pure action shot ever to appear on the magazine's cover. Also, as a Steelers fan I made a poster of it in seventh-grade art class.

2. Y.A. TITTLE — SI's first NFL cover is striking in its simplicity. There's no typography, not even to identify the subject—Y.A. Tittle, in the 49ers' old bright-red colors. I love the Lucite face guard. And how about the handle on the side of the helmet? A 49ers trainer put it there for protection after Tittle suffered a broken cheekbone, but the quarterback soon had it removed, because opponents were using the handle to yank him down.

3. DOMINATOR — Of all the great running back covers through the years, I prefer this one, which benefits from the sharpness and clarity of digital photo technology. I love Adrian Peterson's eyes, the grass kicked up behind him, the Browns linebacker helplessly sprawled in his wake. I also remember the story behind this cover. We had planned a Peterson story for Week 1 and I was a bit worried because he had done little in the first half in Cleveland. Then he broke out in the second half, capping his day with this spectacular 64-yard touchdown run. Watching in my office, I immediately e-mailed our writer at the game, Damon Hack: "COVER!"

4. THE MAN OF STEEL — Just a great portrait that conveys Jack Lambert's terrifying intensity.

5. THE SUPER CATCH — O.K., I'll give it to you. Walter Iooss Jr.'s terrific picture captures one of the great moments in NFL history, Clark hauling in The Catch at the absolute apex of his leap, sending the 49ers to their first Super Bowl. If the Swann cover was all tension, this is jubilant resolution.

6. SPORTSMAN OF THE YEAR, 1963 — A prescient cover, as Pete Rozelle was facing a huge challenge from the rival AFL in the early '60s. Here the NFL's young commissioner exudes the intelligence and confidence he would need as he laid the foundation for the league's massive successes.

7. THE SUPER CHAMPION — Neil Leifer's shot portrays Vince Lombardi's victory ride from Jerry Kramer after the Packers defeated the Raiders in Super Bowl II. It was Lombardi's last game as Packers coach.

8. TOTALLY COOL — Because of indoor stadiums, snow football is all too rare these days. The moment this shot popped up on screen in the Monday morning photo show, we knew we had one of the alltime great SI covers. Some Internet chatter speculated we'd Photoshopped the snow onto Favre's shoulders—something we'd never do. This is just a classic shot by photographer Simon Bruty.

9. "I LIED" — In this issue longtime Raiders defensive end Lyle Alzado confessed to having used steroids throughout career and blamed them for the brain tumor that would eventually kill him. I chose this cover not just for the power of the image and the headline, but also to represent SI's great tradition of investigative and enterprise work, from drug use and performance enhancers to the violence in the game.

10. JOLLY GOOD SHOW — "Hmm...Bears and Cowboys playing in London. Here's a idea: Let's get The Fridge and Too Tall Jones to pose with a Foot Guard!" This list wouldn't be complete without a nod to SI's so-bad-they're-good covers: the cheesy setups, cartoonish illustrations and straight-up head-shakers that make you look back and wonder, *What were they thinking?* Well, for one, probably, "Let's have some fun!" Can't hurt to try.

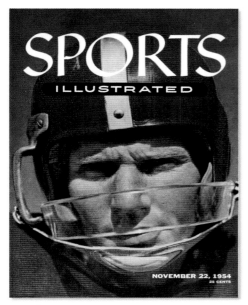

2 | Y.A. TITTLE
November 22, 1954

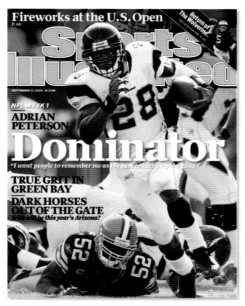

3 | ADRIAN PETERSON
September 21, 2009

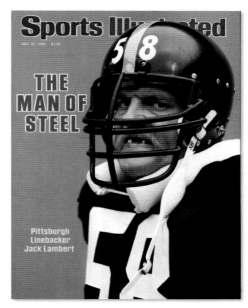

4 | JACK LAMBERT
July 30, 1984

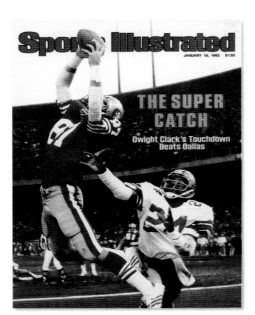

5 | DWIGHT CLARK
January 18, 1982

6 | PETE ROZELLE
January 6, 1964

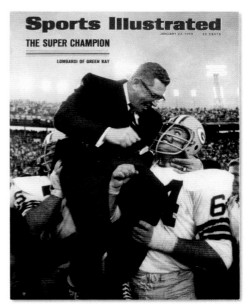

7 | VINCE LOMBARDI
January 22, 1968

8 | BRETT FAVRE
January 21, 2008

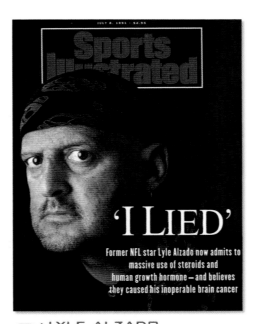

9 | LYLE ALZADO
July 8, 1991

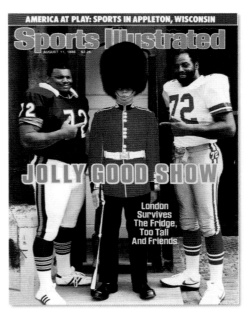

10 | THE NFL IN LONDON
August 11, 1986

The Full Results

IF THEY WERE LISTED ON A PANELIST'S BALLOT, THEY MAKE IT HERE TOO, IN THIS FULL RANKING OF EVERYONE WHO RECEIVED A VOTE IN EVERY CATEGORY

QUARTERBACKS

1. JOE MONTANA
2. JOHNNY UNITAS
3. TOM BRADY
4. OTTO GRAHAM
5. PEYTON MANNING
6. JOHN ELWAY
7. DAN MARINO
8. SAMMY BAUGH
9. BRETT FAVRE
10. TERRY BRADSHAW
11. JOE NAMATH
12. STEVE YOUNG
13. SID LUCKMAN
14. BART STARR
15. TROY AIKMAN
16. DREW BREES
17. AARON RODGERS
18. NORM VAN BROCKLIN
19. ROGER STAUBACH

RUNNING BACKS

1. JIM BROWN
2. WALTER PAYTON
3. BARRY SANDERS
4. O.J. SIMPSON
5. GALE SAYERS
6. EMMITT SMITH
7. EARL CAMPBELL
8. ERIC DICKERSON
9. MARION MOTLEY
10. MARSHALL FAULK
11. RED GRANGE
12. MARCUS ALLEN
13. LADAINIAN TOMLINSON
14. FRANCO HARRIS
15. BO JACKSON
16. BRONKO NAGURSKI
17. ADRIAN PETERSON

WIDE RECEIVERS

1. JERRY RICE
2. DON HUTSON
3. RANDY MOSS
4. LANCE ALWORTH
5. RAYMOND BERRY
6. TERRELL OWENS
7. PAUL WARFIELD
8. CRIS CARTER
9. MARVIN HARRISON
10. HINES WARD
11. LARRY FITZGERALD
12. MICHAEL IRVIN
13. CHARLEY TAYLOR
14. ELROY HIRSCH
15. TIM BROWN
16. STEVE LARGENT
17. WES WELKER
18. FRED BILETNIKOFF
19. DON MAYNARD
20. DANTE LAVELLI
21. CALVIN JOHNSON
22. LYNN SWANN

TIGHT ENDS

1. JOHN MACKEY
2. KELLEN WINSLOW
3. TONY GONZALEZ
4. MIKE DITKA
5. SHANNON SHARPE
6. OZZIE NEWSOME
7. DAVE CASPER
8. ANTONIO GATES
9. JASON WITTEN
10. TODD CHRISTENSEN
11. MARK BAVARO
12. RILEY ODOMS
13. JACKIE SMITH
14. CHARLIE SANDERS
15. BEN COATES

OFFENSIVE LINEMEN

1. ANTHONY MUÑOZ
2. JOHN HANNAH
3. FORREST GREGG
4. BRUCE MATTHEWS
5. MIKE WEBSTER
6. JONATHAN OGDEN
7. GENE UPSHAW
8. JIM PARKER
9. MEL HEIN
10. LARRY ALLEN
11. DWIGHT STEPHENSON
12. JIM OTTO
13. RANDALL MCDANIEL
14. ART SHELL
15. CLYDE TURNER
16. ROOSEVELT BROWN
17. RUSS GRIMM
18. ORLANDO PACE
19. JEFF SATURDAY
20. GARY ZIMMERMAN
21. TONY BOSELLI
22. WALTER JONES
23. JACKIE SLATER

DEFENSIVE LINEMEN

1. REGGIE WHITE
2. JOE GREENE
3. DEACON JONES
4. BRUCE SMITH
5. BOB LILLY
6. ALAN PAGE
7. GINO MARCHETTI
8. MERLIN OLSEN
9. LEE ROY SELMON
10. WARREN SAPP
11. DWIGHT FREENEY
12. BUCK BUCHANAN
13. LEO NOMELLINI
14. ANDY ROBUSTELLI
15. RANDY WHITE
16. DOUG ATKINS
17. CORTEZ KENNEDY
18. JIM MARSHALL
19. JULIUS PEPPERS

LINEBACKERS

1. LAWRENCE TAYLOR
2. DICK BUTKUS
3. RAY LEWIS
4. JACK LAMBERT
5. WILLIE LANIER
6. MIKE SINGLETARY
7. CHUCK BEDNARIK
8. RAY NITSCHKE
9. BRONKO NAGURSKI
10. JOE SCHMIDT
11. DERRICK THOMAS
12. JUNIOR SEAU
13. CHARLES HALEY
14. JACK HAM
15. TED HENDRICKS
16. BOBBY BELL
17. DERRICK BROOKS
18. DEMARCUS WARE
19. BILL GEORGE
20. ANDRE TIPPETT

DEFENSIVE BACKS

1. RONNIE LOTT
2. DEION SANDERS
3. ROD WOODSON
4. DICK LANE
5. CHARLES WOODSON
6. ED REED
7. MEL BLOUNT
8. DARRELLE REVIS
9. DARRELL GREEN
10. MIKE HAYNES
11. EMLEN TUNNELL
12. TROY POLAMALU
13. WILLIE WOOD
14. HERB ADDERLEY
15. KEN HOUSTON
16. LARRY WILSON
17. CHAMP BAILEY
18. PAUL KRAUSE
19. MEL RENFRO
20. JIMMY JOHNSON

COACHES

1. VINCE LOMBARDI
2. PAUL BROWN
3. BILL WALSH
4. CHUCK NOLL
5. GEORGE HALAS
6. DON SHULA
7. BILL BELICHICK
8. TOM LANDRY
9. JOE GIBBS
10. BILL PARCELLS
11. CURLY LAMBEAU
12. TONY DUNGY
13. JOHN MADDEN
14. DON CORYELL
15. JIMMY JOHNSON

GAMES

1. 1958 NFL TITLE GAME, COLTS-GIANTS

2. 1981 AFC PLAYOFFS, CHARGERS-DOLPHINS

3. 1967 NFL TITLE GAME, PACKERS-COWBOYS

4. SUPER BOWL III, JETS-COLTS

5. SUPER BOWL XLII, GIANTS-PATRIOTS

6. 1992 AFC WILD CARD, BILLS-OILERS

7. SUPER BOWL XLIII, STEELERS-CARDINALS

8. 1981 NFC CHAMPIONSHIP, 49ERS-COWBOYS

9. SUPER BOWL XIII, STEELERS-COWBOYS

10. 2006 AFC CHAMPIONSHIP, COLTS-PATRIOTS

11. 1943 NFL TITLE GAME, BEARS-REDSKINS

12. SB XXIII, 49ERS-BENGALS

13. 1974 AFC PLAYOFFS, RAIDERS-DOLPHINS (SEA OF HANDS)

14. JETS-DOLPHINS, OCT. 23, 2000 (MONDAY NIGHT MIRACLE)

15. 1972 AFC PLAYOFFS, STEELERS-RAIDERS (IMMACULATE RECEPTION)

16. DOLPHINS-CHIEFS, 1971 AFC PLAYOFFS (NFL'S LONGEST GAME)

17. 2011 NFC PLAYOFFS, 49ERS-SAINTS

18. 2001 AFC PLAYOFFS, PATRIOTS-RAIDERS (TUCK RULE)

19. BEARS-49ERS, DEC. 12, 1965 (SAYERS 6 TDS)

20. 1940 NFL TITLE GAME, BEARS-REDSKINS

21. 2010 PLAYOFFS, PACKERS-CARDINALS

22. SUPER BOWL XXXIV, RAMS-TITANS

23. 1932 NFL TITLE GAME, BEARS-SPARTANS

24. DOLPHINS-BEARS, DEC. 2, 1985

25. RAIDERS-JETS, NOV. 17, 1968 (HEIDI GAME)

26. 2009 NFC TITLE GAME, SAINTS-VIKINGS

PLAYS

1. IMMACULATE RECEPTION, 1972 AFC PLAYOFFS

2. MANNING-TO-TYREE, SUPER BOWL XLII

3. THE CATCH, 1981 NFC PLAYOFFS

4. THE HOLMES TD, SUPER BOWL XLIII

5. MIRACLE AT THE MEADOWLANDS, EAGLES-GIANTS, NOV. 19, 1978

6. HARRISON'S RUNBACK, SUPER BOWL XLIII

7. MUSIC CITY MIRACLE, 1999 AFC WILD CARD

8. JONES'S TACKLE, SUPER BOWL XXXIV

9. SWANN'S CATCH, SUPER BOWL X

10. HAIL MARY, 1975 NFC PLAYOFFS

11. TOM BRADY "TUCK RULE," 2001 AFC PLAYOFFS

12. "HOLY ROLLER," RAIDERS-CHARGERS, SEPT. 10, 1978

13. ALAN AMECHE TD, 1958 NFL TITLE GAME

14. TONY DORSETT 99-YARD RUN, COWBOYS-VIKINGS, JAN. 3 1983

15. SCOTT NORWOOD WIDE-RIGHT KICK, SUPER BOWL XXV

16. TOM DEMPSEY 63-YARD FG, SAINTS-LIONS, NOV. 8, 1970

17. MARSHAWN LYNCH 67-YARD TD RUN, 2010 NFC PLAYOFFS

18. CHUCK BEDNARIK HIT ON FRANK GIFFORD, EAGLES-GIANTS, NOV. 20, 1960

19. MARCUS ALLEN 74-YARD RUN, SUPER BOWL XVIII

20. NATHAN VASHER 108-YARD RETURN, BEARS-49ERS, NOV. 13, 2005

21. ADAM VINATIERI SNOW FIELD GOAL, 2001 AFC PLAYOFFS

22. SAINTS ONSIDE KICK, SUPER BOWL XLIV

23. MONTANA-TO-JOHN TAYLOR, SUPER BOWL XXIII

24. JOHN RIGGINS 43-YARD TD RUN, SUPER BOWL XVII

25. GALE SAYERS 85-YARD PUNT RETURN, DEC. 12, 1965

26. CLARENCE DAVIS'S "SEA OF HANDS" CATCH, 1974 AFC PLAYOFFS

Seattle's Steve Largent finished 16th among wide receivers.

SINGLE-SEASON TEAM

1. 1985 BEARS
2. 1972 DOLPHINS
3. 1984 49ERS
4. 1962 PACKERS
5. 1989 49ERS
6. 1992 COWBOYS
7. 2007 PATRIOTS
8. 1966 PACKERS
9. 1991 REDSKINS
10. 1978 STEELERS
11. 1975 STEELERS
12. 1979 STEELERS
13. 2004 PATRIOTS
14. 1950 BROWNS
15. 1955 BROWNS
16. 1999 RAMS
17. 1994 49ERS
18. 1968 JETS
19. 1971 COWBOYS
20. 1996 PACKERS
21. 1976 RAIDERS
22. 1940 BEARS
23. 1948 BROWNS
24. 2000 RAVENS
25. 2007 GIANTS
26. 1929 PACKERS

STADIUMS

1. LAMBEAU FIELD
2. ARROWHEAD STADIUM
3. COWBOYS STADIUM
4. ORANGE BOWL
5. MILE HIGH STADIUM
6. CENTURYLINK FIELD
7. OAKLAND COLISEUM
8. MUNICIPAL FIELD
9. SOLDIER FIELD
10. RFK STADIUM
11. HEINZ FIELD
12. RELIANT STADIUM
13. THREE RIVERS STADIUM
14. SUPERDOME
15. YANKEE STADIUM
16. RICH STADIUM
17. GIANTS STADIUM
18. M&T BANK STADIUM
19. SPORTS AUTHORITY FIELD AT MILE HIGH
20. LA COLISEUM
21. LINCOLN FINANCIAL FIELD
22. TAMPA STADIUM
23. LP FIELD
24. COTTON BOWL
25. CANDLESTICK PARK
26. KEZAR STADIUM

FRANCHISES

1. PACKERS
2. STEELERS
3. COWBOYS
4. BEARS
5. GIANTS
6. 49ERS
7. PATRIOTS
8. RAIDERS
9. COLTS
10. REDSKINS
11. DOLPHINS
12. BROWNS
13. RAVENS
14. BILLS
15. EAGLES
16. BRONCOS
17. JETS
18. LIONS
19. CHIEFS
20. TEXANS

Helmets were ready to roll at the Super Bowl VII halftime show in Los Angeles.

THIS BOOK DRAWS FROM THE EFFORTS of a legion of SPORTS ILLUSTRATED writers, reporters, editors and photographers who have covered the NFL since the magazine's inception in 1954; FOOTBALL'S GREATEST would not have been possible without them. Special thanks also goes to Richard Deitsch, Steve Fine, George Washington, Karen Carpenter, Prem Kalliat, Joe Felice, George Amores and Will Welt for their generous help; to Geoff Michaud, Dan Larkin, Bob Thompson and the rest of the SI Imaging group for their tireless work on this project; and Time Inc. Sports Group editor Terry McDonell for his support and guidance.

TIME HOME ENTERTAINMENT: Richard Fraiman, PUBLISHER; Steven Sandonato, VICE PRESIDENT, BUSINESS DEVELOPMENT & STRATEGY; Carol Pittard, EXECUTIVE DIRECTOR, MARKETING SERVICES; Tom Mifsud, EXECUTIVE DIRECTOR, RETAIL & SPECIAL SALES; Joy Butts, EXECUTIVE PUBLISHING DIRECTOR; Laura Adam, DIRECTOR, BOOKAZINE DEVELOPMENT & MARKETING; Glenn Buonocore, FINANCE DIRECTOR; Megan Pearlman, ASSOCIATE PUBLISHING DIRECTOR; Helen Wan, ASSISTANT GENERAL COUNSEL; Ilene Schreider, ASSISTANT DIRECTOR, SPECIAL SALES; Susan Chodakiewicz, SENIOR BOOK PRODUCTION MANAGER; Anne-Michelle Gallero, DESIGN & PREPRESS MANAGER; Allison Parker, BRAND MANAGER; Alex Voznesenskiy, ASSOCIATE PREPRESS MANAGER; Stephanie Braga, ASSISTANT BRAND MANAGER; Stephen Koepp, EDITORIAL DIRECTOR

PHOTO CREDITS

COVER: FRONT (left to right, from top): Walter Iooss Jr., John Iacono, Neil Leifer, Walter Iooss Jr., Damian Strohmeyer, John Biever, David E. Klutho, John Biever, Damian Strohmeyer, Simon Bruty, Heinz Kluetmeier, Neil Leifer, Tom Lynn, Walter Iooss Jr. **BACK** (left to right, from top): Damian Strohmeyer, David Bergman, Peter Read Miller, Mickey Pfleger, Heinz Kluetmeier (2), Simon Bruty, Brian Bahr/Getty Images, Jon Soohoo/Getty Images, Ronald C. Modra/Sports Imagery/Getty Images, John Biever, John W. McDonough, Neil Leifer (2). **BACK FLAP:** Fred Lyon.
SECTION OPENERS: Page 22: Bill Frakes; Page 40: Peter Read Miller; Page 58: Bill Frakes; Page 74: Reed Hoffmann/AP; Page 90: John Biever; Page 106: Ezra Shaw/Getty Images; Page 122: Heinz Kluetmeier; Page 138: Heinz Kluetmeier; Page 154: Peter Read Miller; Page 170: John Biever; Page 192: John Biever; Page 214: Bob Rosato; Page 238: Damian Strohmeyer; Page 254: David N. Berkwitz; Page 270: John Iacono.
ADDITIONAL CREDITS: Page 7: Walter Iooss Jr.; Page 8 (from top): Walter Iooss Jr., Peter Read Miller; Page 9 (from top): John Biever, Walter Iooss Jr.; Page 10 (from top): James Drake, Damian Strohmeyer; Page 272: John Biever; Page 274: Fred Kaplan; Page 275 (left to right, from top): Walter Iooss Jr., David Bergman, John W. McDonough, John Biever; Page 276 (left to right, from top): Walter Iooss Jr., John Iacono, Manny Millan, John Biever; Page 277: Tom DiPace; Page 278: John Iacono; Page 279 (left to right): Diane Johnson/Wireimage.com, Howard Smith/US Presswire, Walter Iooss Jr.; Page 280: John Biever; Page 281: John Biever; Page 282: Everett Collection; Page 283 (left to right, from top): Paramount/Everett Collection, Sony Pictures Entertainment/Photofest, The Kobal Collection, Universal/Everett Collection; Page 284: Heinz Kluetmeier; Page 285 (left to right, from top): Fred Lyon, Fred Vuich, Tony Tomsic, Walter Iooss Jr., Ben Rose, Neil Leifer, Simon Bruty, Peter Read Miller, Ken Regan/Camera 5; Page 287: Corky Charles Trewin/Wireimage.com; Page 288: NFL Photos/AP.
ENDPAPERS: Illustrations by BJ Ervick.

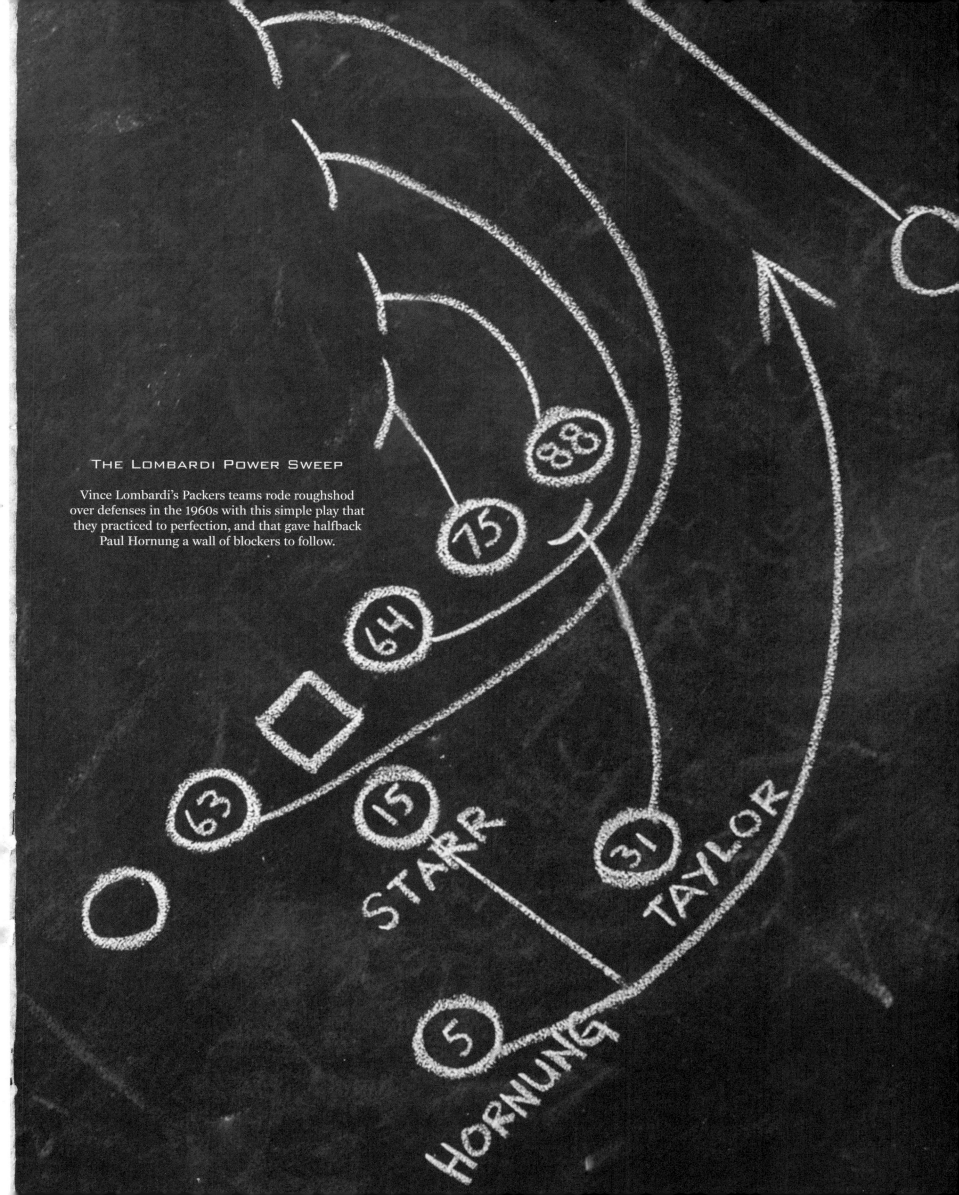

THE LOMBARDI POWER SWEEP

Vince Lombardi's Packers teams rode roughshod over defenses in the 1960s with this simple play that they practiced to perfection, and that gave halfback Paul Hornung a wall of blockers to follow.

Manning-to-Tyree

In the Giants' playbook it was called 62 Y Sail Union. The purpose of David Tyree's route was to take the top off the coverage, but it also gave Eli Manning a deep option, which he went for in the waning moments of Super Bowl XLII.

HARRISON 37

X

21

93   97

96   66   69   60

81

TOOMER

10

RESS